ENCYCLOPEDIA OF
TEXTILES

ENCYCLOPEDIA OF
TEXTILES

Judith Jerde

 Facts On File
New York • Oxford

Encyclopedia of Textiles
Copyright © 1992 by Judith Jerde

Facts On File, Inc.   Facts On File Limited
460 Park Avenue South   Collins Street
New York NY 10016   Oxford OX4 1XJ
USA   United Kingdom

Library of Congress Cataloging-in-Publication Data
Jerde, Judith
   Encyclopedia of textiles/Judith Jerde.
     p.   cm.
   Includes bibliographical references and index.
   ISBN 0-8160-2105-8
   1. Textile fabrics—Dictionaries. I. Title.
TS1309.J47 1992
677'.003—dc20   91-20756

A British CIP catalogue record for this book is available from the British Library.

Facts On File books are available at special discounts when purchased in bulk quantities for
businesses, associations, institutions or sales promotions. Please contact our Special Sales
Department in New York at 212/683-2244 (dial 800/322-8755 except in NY, AK or HI) or in
Oxford at 865/728399.

Text design by Donna Sinisgalli
Jacket design by Ellie Nigretto
Composition by Facts On File, Inc.
Manufactured by Pacific Offset LTD.
Printed in Hong Kong

10 9 8 7 6 5 4 3 2 1

This book is printed on acid-free paper.

CONTENTS

PREFACE

Textiles surround us in every aspect of our lives, in both their functional and decorative natures: in the draperies, upholstery and carpeting that furnish our homes and offices; in sheeting, towels and countless other useful articles; in the way that we express ourselves in our clothing.

The goal of this encyclopedia is to provide for the general reader information on textiles of all types, their history, and the processes of manufacture. The entries range from the basic fiber types—plant, animal and synthetic—to the very artistic processes of creating and decorating finished fabric.

They cover fabric types, methods of production and construction, technical terms and prominent individuals in the history of textiles. Readers wishing to get a general overview of the subject should consult the lengthy entries for the major textile categories, COTTON, LINEN, MANUFACTURED FIBER, SILK and WOOL, which provide information not only about the history and production of these fibers, but their care as well.

Basic information on the production of textiles can be found in the lengthy entries SPINNING, WEAVING and LOOM, while decorative processes are described in DYES, EMBROIDERY, PRINTING and FINISHING. The entries are cross-referenced for additional information.

Obsolete textiles are not included in this encyclopedia, but the reader is urged to consult additional volumes on this subject as well as to visit the many excellent historical textile collections in major museums throughout the world.

Manufacturing processes continue to be aided by new technological advances, the increasing variety of manufactured fibers, new finishing methods and innovations of computer applications to textile production. Even so, it must be remembered that technology does not render the creative artist obsolete. It gives the artist new techniques to work with, but design and innovation always have and always will begin with the creative mind. It also remains true that for all the benefits of modern technology, the basic structures of textiles remain essentially unchanged from their origins in antiquity.

The American textile industry was launched with the founding in 1792 of the first cotton mill in the United States by Samuel Slater in Pawtucket, Rhode Island. As we approach the bicentenniel of this event, we should pay tribute not only to Slater's remarkable pioneering accomplishments but also to the extraordinary accomplishments of the worldwide community of artists, engineers and craftspeople involved in the production of textiles. It is with appreciation to these many, past and present, that this book is dedicated.

Judith Jerde

ACKNOWLEDGMENTS

For their cooperation in preparing this volume for publication, the author would like to thank:

American Textile Association
Biltmore Industries
BISFA: International Bureau for the Standardization of Man-made Fibers
British Fabric Association
Burlington Mills
Ms. Elizabeth de Nesnera, Commercial Council to the French Embassy
Foreign Agricultural Services
Mr. H. Bouvier, International Sericultural Commission
International Association for Textile Care Labeling
International Fabricare Institute
International Linen Promotion Commission
Ms. Bridget Coughlin, International Linen Promotion Commission
Mr. Brian J. May, International Mohair Association, U.S.A.
International Mohair Association, London
Mr. Ronald Currie, The International Silk Association
International Textile Manufacturers Federation
Mr. Michael K. Dechamps and Mr. Albert J. Czarnecki of J. L. de Ball-Girmes of America, Inc.
Kalkstein Silk Mills, Inc.
Mr. David Herric, Knitted Textile Association
Monsanto, Inc.
Monsieur Jean-Claude Charlin and Mr. B. F. Luther, Staubli Corporation

Mr. Boris Schlomm, Amicale Industries, Inc.
Mr. Dennis Sjoberg, Department of Biological Sciences, St. Cloud State University
Mr. F. A. Rhymes, American Manufactured Fiber Association, Inc.
Mr. James A. Morrissey, American Textile Manufacturers Institute, Inc.
Mr. Ken Melling, Somet of America
Mr. Stig W. Bolgen, American Flock Association
Mrs. Alexander G. Jerde
Mrs. William Hensler
Ms. Lucille Phipps, National Cotton Council of America
Ms. Michele Adler, French Fashion and Textile Center
Elaine Swenson
National Cotton Council of America
Northern Textile Association
Pendelton Woolen Mills
Schiffli Manufacturing Promotion Fund
Silk and Art Silk Research Association
Springs Industries
Oomingmak, Inc.
Swiss Textile Association
Textile Confederation of Ireland
Mr. Tom Haas and Ms. Phyllis Grotell, the Wool Bureau, Inc.
The Zoological Society of San Diego
Mr. William Ashton, Mr. B. E. McKinnon and Mr. Thomas Hill of Valdese Weavers, Inc.
Wamsutta

ACETATE

Acetate, one of the first manufactured fibers, is created from cellulose, as are the other two early manufactured fibers, RAYON and TRIACETATE. Acetate was first produced in the United States by the Celanese Corporation in 1924. The Federal Trade Commission defines acetate as "a manufactured fiber in which the fiber-forming substance is cellulose acetate, where not less than 92% of the hydroxyl groups are acetylated."

Cellulose is the chief substance composing the cell walls of plants. When acetate was first being produced the cellulose was obtained from the fluff that adheres to the cotton seed. Today acetate is manufactured using cellulose from (high alpha) woods such as spruce and pine. The term "high alpha" refers to cellulosic substances which yield a relatively high fraction of the cellulose known as alpha-cellulose. This cellulose is insoluble when treated by a strong (approx. 18%) solution of caustic soda, and is predominant in cotton, which is used as a cellulose standard. Cellulose acetate is made through very simple chemical processes, in which cellulose reacts with acetic acid and acetic anhydride. The cellulose acetate is then dissolved in acetone. The resulting solution is extruded through a spinneret, a device employing one or more holes through which the liquid is forced. As the filaments emerge from the spinneret, the solvent is evaporated in warm air, a process which is called dry spinning. This process creates fibers of almost pure cellulose acetate that are in long strings. Both monofilament (single strand) and multifilament (multistrand) forms of acetate fibers can be formed in this manner, depending on the spinneret arrangement.

Acetate has the lustrous look of silk, is somewhat crisp to the touch, and has excellent drapability. It is resistant to moths, mildew and shrinkage. It also is color fast even when washed repeatedly or when exposed to the sun for long durations. Of interest is the fact that acetate can be spun in threads of varying size or DENIER, thus making it possible to create textiles that have the appearance of silk or shantung. Acetate is not a particularly strong fiber and has poor abrasion resistance; therefore it is seldom used for articles of clothing that will have to take hard wear.

Acetate will not receive the dyes that are used on other textiles such as cotton and rayon, so new dyes were created specifically for it. Because it is selective in the dye type that it receives it is possible to combine it with other fibers and to dye the combination in a process that is called cross dyeing, thus creating multicolored effects.

Production

The logs used in the process of making acetate are debarked and chopped into chips approximately 1 inch square. The chips are then turned into pulp stock, which is washed and bleached. The purified stock is wound into rolls and sent to fiber-producing plants.

There, the stock is mixed with acetic acid, acetic anhydride, and a catalyst. The cellulose acetate solution is poured from the acetylating mixer into storage tanks for ripening. The solution is then chilled in water, which causes it to turn into flakes that are dissolved in acetone.

Acetate (plain weave) Author's collection

That solution, either plain or with color added, is forced through the spinneret, forming a continuous filament, which, after twisting, is rewound on cones. The finished yarn may be in regular form or it may be lofted or modified by a special process, which involves the crimping or looping of the filaments so that they gain texture and bulk.

Care

Acetate is adversely affected by nail polish remover and other organic solvents, including perfumes, which can seriously stain the textile.

Always follow the manufacturer's care instructions. Many items can be washed in the washing machine but delicate ones should be washed by hand with lukewarm water and a mild soap. Do not wring or twist the garment. Proper rinsing is of great importance. The blotting of excess water with clean towels is recommended. In cases where the item cannot be laundered, acetate dry cleans beautifully.

Acetate should be ironed at a low temperature. Ironing on the wrong side while the material is still damp is recommended. The item should not be ironed to the point where it dries out, but instead hung to finish drying after all of the wrinkles have been removed. If ironing on the right side, always use a pressing cloth.

See also DYES; MANUFACTURED FIBER.

ACRYLIC

Acrylic is a generic term used to describe manufactured fibers of polyacrylonitrile. The Federal Trade Commission defines acrylic as "a manufactured fiber in which the fiber-forming substance is any long-chain synthetic polymer composed of at least 85% by weight of acrylonitrile units."

Acrylic process chart   American Fiber Manufacturers
Association, Inc.

In 1944 the acetate research division of E. I. du Pont de Nemours & Company, Inc. created the first acrylic fiber. It was not until 1946, however, that it was judged promising enough for commercialization. Subsequently many corporations, among them Chemstrand Corporation (in 1952), American Cyanamid Company (in 1958), and Eastman Chemical Products, a subsidiary of Eastman Kodak Company (in 1958), followed the lead of Du Pont, and began producing acrylic fibers under their own trade names.

Basically, acrylonitrile is derived from natural gas, air, water and petroleum. The acrylonitrile is usually combined with small amounts of other chemicals that cause the fiber to be able to absorb dyes. Acrylics come in a wide variety of colors and can by dyed at the fiber stage, the yarn stage or the fabric stage. Fibers are created by employing the EXTRUSION process, as are other manufactured fibers.

Pages 4 and 5: Acrylic   Author's collection

The acrylics are unique among the manufactured fibers because they have an uneven surface, and are lofty. The fibers are soft and woolly to the touch, and often used as a substitute for wool. Acrylic fabrics are wash and wear, and can bear repeated laundering. They are generally wrinkle-free, and resist degradation by sunlight or chemicals.

Care

Always follow the manufacturer's care instructions on the label. Most acrylics are machine washable, but it is advisable to remove the article from the washer before it spins. In order to ensure that the garment is wrinkle-free, it should be hung to dry, except in the case of sweaters. Sweaters should be dried flat on a towel. Ironing is usually not advisable, but if necessary, it should be done at a very low setting.

See MANUFACTURED FIBER.

AFTER-CHROMING

After-chroming refers to the addition of a chrome mordant to a wet, dyed fabric to increase the fastness of the dye.

See DYES.

AFTER-TREATING

After-treating is a process in which some textiles are passed through a chemical solution after the dyeing process in order to achieve a particular shade of color and to enhance the dye-fast qualities of the textile. This process is always used in conjunction with direct dyes.

See DYES.

AGNELINE

Agneline is a plain weave, coarse, heavy, black woolen fabric with a long nap. It sheds water because of a special process of FULLING that stretches the textile so that it becomes exceedingly tight, thereby resisting penetration by water.

See also NAPPED FABRICS.

Cotton all-over print Author's collection

ALBERT CLOTH

Albert cloth is a DOUBLE CLOTH of heavy wool that is reversible. It is used for outerwraps. The face and back are in different patterns, and sometimes in different colors. The construction of Albert cloth gives it added body, texture and warmth.

ALGINATE FIBERS

Alginate fibers are nonflammable fibers created by neutralizing alginic acid with caustic soda. This forms a solution that can be spun and extruded to create staple, or yarn. It is used to create very sheer wool textiles and lace by combining the alginate with other fibers and then dissolving them out by passing the textile through an acid bath. Alginate is also used in the production of some machine laces.

ALIZARIN

Alazarin is a natural dye from the madder root. This particular color, also known as "turkey red," was synthetically created in 1869 in Great Britain.
See DYES.

ALL-OVER

All-over is a term used in the design of textiles. The pattern units in design are called figures. Figures can be arranged in borders, rows, isolated groupings or all-over. In order to be classified as an all-over, the design must run from selvage to selvage.

ALPACA

Alpaca wool fabric is a lightweight plain weave material. It is stronger than ordinary sheep wool fabric, and is

Alpaca (micrograph) Dennis Sjoberg

known not only for its strength and durability but also for its soft silky beauty and luster. It is generally made with a cotton warp and an alpaca filling, although nowadays alpaca is sometimes combined with manufactured fibers, creating a blend. Alpaca is water repellent and is very warm. It is classified as a specialty fiber.

The fiber used to create the alpaca textile is from the alpaca, cousin of the llama and a member of the camel family, Camelidae. The alpaca is classified as genus *Lama,* species *L. pacos.* Though now domesticated it originally descended from the wild guanaco, native to the high Andean regions of southern Ecuador, Peru, Bolivia and northwestern Argentina. In the United States alpaca are raised in Texas. The alpaca resembles a sheep, except for an elegant long neck, which it holds erect. The adult alpaca weighs approximately 180 pounds and stands about 5 feet in height. The fleece on the alpaca are variegated in color, covering a color range that includes white, black, brown, reddish-brown and gray. The fleece hangs down from the animal in long strands that can be as much as 12 to 16 inches in length. The fiber obtained from the alpaca is 5 to 11 inches in length. Each alpaca will produce four to seven pounds of soft downy fleece each year. If fabric contains 100% of alpaca fiber it is classified as wool on the fabric label.

See WOOL.

AMAZON

Amazon fabric is woven with a fine worsted warp and a heavier weft yarn of wool. The fabric is warp faced (more warp threads are visible). The SATIN WEAVE of Amazon is not visible because the finishing process that it undergoes obscures the weave entirely. The hand, or feel, of Amazon is very soft due to the nature of the yarns and the finishing techniques that are employed in its production.

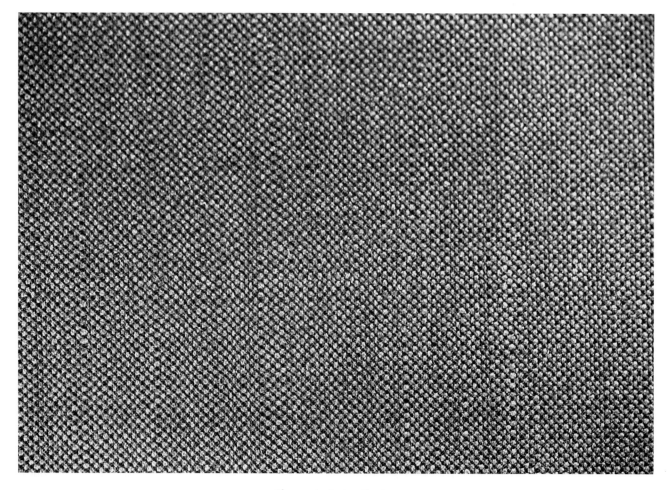

Alpaca   Author's collection

AMERICAN SYSTEM

The American system is one of three systems employed in the spinning of yarn. (The other two are the BRADFORD SYSTEM and the FRENCH SYSTEM.) Created in the 1960s in the United States, the American system employs techniques used in both the French and Bradford systems in that it spins both long and short fibers for use in the manufacture of worsted fabrics. The system uses fibers that are slightly twisted and held in place by pins during the combing process, producing yarn that is smooth, compact and lustrous. A very rapid and efficient method that has greatly improved production output, the American system has largely supplanted both the Bradford and French systems in the United States.

See also SPINNING.

Angora rabbit Boris Shlomm Amicale, Inc.

ANGORA HAIR

Angora yarn is spun from the long, pure-white hair of the angora rabbit. The Angora rabbit is a member of the rodent family. Most Angora rabbits are found in Asia Minor and Turkey. They produce the softest and finest of all the hair fibers. Angora yarn is very soft and will not felt (interlock with one another). It is widely used for knitted goods. This term should not be confused with MOHAIR, obtained from the Angora goat. Angora is not classified as wool.

APPLIED PRINTING

The term applied printing refers to any printing process that is done on white, natural or bleached fabric, or to a textile that has been previously dyed a plain color. The printing techniques that are used in today's market are very sophisticated.

Rotary screen printing is one technique for rapid and very high-quality printing of large amounts of fabric. In this process, cloth passes beneath rollers in which a pattern of tiny holes has been etched. The roller is actually a drum that holds the dye, which is forced through the holes onto the fabric. Each roller has a pattern that contributes one color toward the entire design. As many as a dozen colors can be printed as the cloth moves past the rollers. This technique has become so sophisticated that the patterns are considered to be works of art in themselves.

Roller printing is another high-speed method of applied printing. Designs for each color are engraved on rollers, and modern machines with electronic controls produce clear, high quality patterns as the fabric moves past the rollers. Roller printers can operate today at speeds up to 200 yards of fabric per minute.

In heat transfer printing, a pattern printed on paper is transferred to fabric through heat and pressure. This technique is much like ironing a transfer on a piece of fabric.

At present, computers are used to monitor dye color in all of the printing processes, ensuring that each color in a pattern is precisely the color intended. The process is used with synthetic dyes and is used on all types of fabric.

See also BLOCK PRINTING; DYES; PRINTING.

ARGYLE

Argyle is readily identified by its distinctive diamond shaped patterns of two or more colors. Argyle originated in Scotland, where it was patterned after the woolen tartans worn by the dukes of Argyl of the Campbell Clan in the Western Highlands. Today argyles are usually knit. In order to be a true knit argyle the intarsia or bobbin method, must be employed. The bobbins are used to hold small amounts of contrasting color. Each bobbin is used as a new ball of yarn. In this manner the pattern is knit into the piece, not superimposed. The designs for intarsia or bobbin knitting are created by following charts showing each stitch as a square.

See KNITTING; TARTAN.

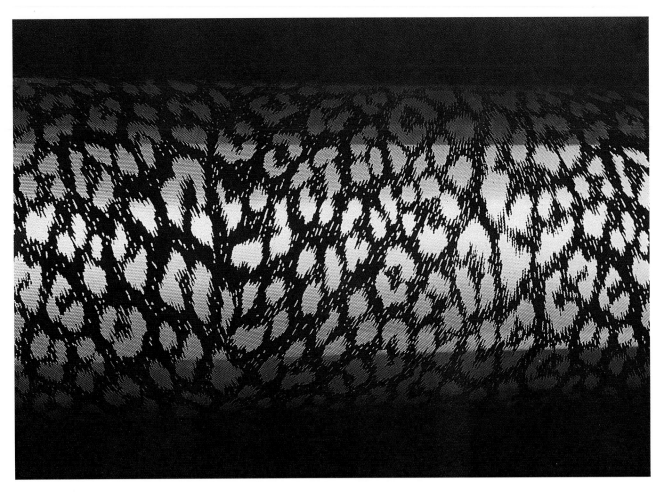

Applied printing   J. L. de Ball-Girmes of America, Inc.

ARKWRIGHT, SIR RICHARD (1732–1792)

Richard Arkwright was born of poor parents in Preston, England. As a child he spent a great deal of time around the textile factory in Preston and it became clear that he had great mechanical abilities when, at the young age of 12, he made suggestions to the factory owner that improved the machines and thus their productivity. Unfortunately, he was not apprenticed to the textile factory but was instead apprenticed to a barber. When he took up that profession, he became known for his industriousness and discovered a process to dye hair. He began to gather hair from women in the village, paying them a minimal amount for it, taking it back to his shop and dyeing it. He then sold it at great profit to wig makers, in this manner doubling his income. Nonetheless, he continued to show an interest in the textile factory and in order to expand his knowledge in

that area he moved to Nottingham, England, which was the center of the cotton hosiery industry. There, in 1769, he invented a new spinning frame that provided a superior method for the drawing of cotton. The frame used rollers that revolved at different speeds for the drawing process.

Arkwright is also credited with starting the first cotton mill in Cromford, Derbyshire, England, in 1771. He was soon recognized for his organizational skills with the factory operations and was called upon to consult with many other mills in England to help them to make improvements that would increase both efficiency and productivity. Because of his contributions, he was knighted and is remembered as "The Father of the Factory System." During his lifetime he was also granted patents for carding and roving machines in 1770 and 1771.

See SPINNING.

Argyle The Wool Bureau, Inc.

ARMURE

Armure is a French term named after the patterns of the chain mail or armor worn in the crusades. Armure was originally a rich, heavy, lustrous silk textile with a patterned or pebbled surface, created by irregular or broken weaves, that somewhat resembled chain mail. Now it is made of any fiber or blend of fibers. The pattern is made by floating warp threads over the surface, giving a raised effect. Common patterns include BIRD'S-EYE, diamond, and rib effects as well as two-color designs and stripes. Today, the textile is created in silk, cotton, wool and manufactured fiber. The term also is applied to some textiles that are constructed of metallic fibers.

ART LINEN

Art linen consists of a plain weave in which the threads have not been calendered, so that they are round, smooth, and have a soft finish. Often the fabric is linen but occasionally it is cotton. The fabric can be unbleached, bleached, or even dyed. Art linen is used extensively for needlework because of its pliability.

ASTRAKAN

Astrakan, which originated in Russia, is a thick woven or knitted pile weave fabric that is luxurious in appearance. The textile has lofty loops or curls on the surface, imitating Astrakhan lamb, Persian lamb or beaver pelt. Lesser grades use a double weft yarn that consists of one yarn that is fine and one yarn that is coarse. During the weaving process the coarse thread is given slack, allowing it to loop and curl. The loops are sometimes cut. At present these pile weaves are made of a wide variety of fibers, including manufactured fiber, silk, wool and mohair. When mohair is employed it gives the fabric added luster. The best grades of Astrakan are made of thread that has been curled before weaving.

See also PILE.

AZO DYES

Derived from the word azote, meaning nitrogen, azo dyes are fast to washing and to strong bleaching agents, but are not as fast when submitted to light. Azo dyes are used not only for natural fibers but for a wide variety of manufactured fibers as well. The shades of color, most commonly red, orange and wine, are desirable because of their brilliance. The colors may have a tendency to crock, or run, so caution must be taken in laundering of them.

See also DYES.

B

BACK-FILLED

There are two ways to back-fill fabric. By the first method, a heavy SIZING is applied to the back of a fabric in order to fill the areas between warp and filling yarns, thus making the textile firmer. This is sometimes referred to as back-sizing. Washing frequently removes this filling. By the second method, back-filling, an extra filling yarn is woven into the back of a fabric to give it added strength, texture and warmth. The first method may not be permanent, but the second method becomes an integral part of the textile and defines a certain pattern, such as piqué.

BACTRIAN CAMEL

See CAMEL HAIR.

BALANCED CRÊPE

See CRÊPE.

BALANCED FABRICS

Balanced is a term that is applied to fabrics that contain warp and weft yarns of equal size and textural likeness.
See WEAVING.

BALBRIGGAN

Hundreds of years ago, balbriggan was a cotton knit from Balbriggan, Ireland, which became famous for its production of the first bleached hosiery. It was executed in a lightweight plain stitch and was tubular in construction, used primarily for underwear. Now, the tubular material is machine-knitted and can be either cotton or a blend, frequently having a soft napped back. Originally balbriggan came only in tan or cream, but it is today found in a wide variety of colors.
See also KNITTING (HISTORY OF).

BALLOON CLOTH

Balloon cloth made of cotton was originally used for hot-air balloons. In order to trap the air needed to keep the balloon aloft, it was given a special coating on the exterior. The balloon cloth that is on the market today, used for apparel, bears little semblance to the original textile. It is a very fine lightweight cotton, usually pima, with a high thread count, in a plain weave. Balloon cloth has a high luster because it has undergone the MERCERIZATION process.

BANNOCKBURN

The term Bannockburn originally applied to a fabric named in honor of the battle of Bannockburn, where the Scottish defeated the English on June 24, 1314. The original textile was a CHEVIOT and was created with ply yarns of different colored single threads, causing a muted or speckled effect. The textile was created alternating single and ply yarn with a two up, two down twill, in which each warp yarn floats over two weft yarns and then under two weft yarns; the warp yarns then move one yarn outward and one yarn upward, creating a

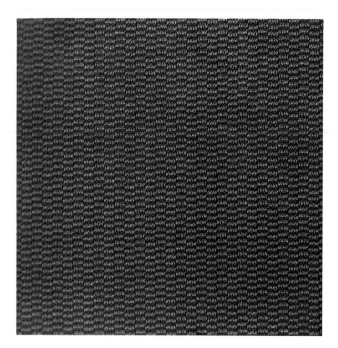

Barathea (worsted)   Author's collection

diagonal line. The term is now applied to a soft twilled wool or manufactured fiber. It no longer is always a cheviot, but retains the speckled effect through the use of various novelty weaves. It is also characterized by a slight nap.

See also TWILL.

BARATHEA

Of English origin, barathea is made of high quality wool yarns. It is often created in a broken twill weave and has the appearance of a heavily slubbed surface. Today barathea is available in a fine textured WORSTED that has the same grainy or pebbly surface that its predecessor had. Barathea is imitated in manufactured fibers, blends and silk.

BARK CLOTH

Bark cloth is not a woven or knit textile, but one that is created by beating the inner bark of certain trees and shrubs into a fabric. It can loosely be called a felted fabric. The process of manufacture consists of a combination of beating and soaking. The moisture softens the fiber, while the beating slowly causes the fibers to adhere to one another. The trees and shrubs that lend themselves to this process most readily are the

breadfruit tree and the paper mulberry. Bark cloth is still created in Vietnam and certain islands in the Pacific Ocean, but is quickly disappearing. When used for an article of clothing, it has usually been painted or dyed for ornamental effect.

BASKET WEAVE

The basket weave is a derivation of the PLAIN WEAVE that has paired warps and paired wefts. It resembles the weave used in basket making, thus its name. In England the weave is frequently called the matt weave. There are many variations of this weave, one being the "half basket," which consists of paired warps and predominant wefts.

See WEAVES.

BATIK

Batik is a method of applying colored designs to a fabric. As is the case with many art forms that have been passed down to us from ancient times, the history of batik is unclear. We do know that the process dates back 2,000 years, however, from early examples of batik found in tombs in Egypt. But exactly when and where the technique originated remains a mystery.

The best known batik comes from Indonesia, specifically Java. Batik is practiced in Java today almost exactly as it was hundreds of years ago. Although the techniques employed there are greatly admired for the intricacy of color and pattern they produce, it is generally agreed that the technique is more formalized than some of the other methods of fabric coloring being used today.

The art of batik was in vogue in the second decade of the 20th century, reaching its zenith in 1919. Unfortunately, after World War I it began to decline, which many feel was the result of the coming of a new technological age, an era less interested in individual expression and more concerned with technological advances of mass production, which could duplicate effects with a great deal of accuracy. Batik enjoyed a resurgence, however, in the 1960s and 1970s and is still practiced widely by individual artists and craftsmen the world over.

Opposite: Batik ("Joan's Garden")   Judith Goettemann

Process

Batik can be a simple process using one dye, or it can become very complex, using up to twenty dye baths and wax applications. There are several ways of achieving the batik effect. One method is to cover with wax all the areas of the fabric not to be colored. Batik is thus a form of RESIST DYEING. After the dyeing, the wax is removed by boiling the textile. This method of dyeing produces complex patterns, and often many different colors are produced by repeating the process several times. Another interesting effect occurs when color penetrates cracks in the wax.

The effects of batik can also be achieved by tying knots, stitching patterns, or stitching and tying objects into the textile. The stitches, knots and objects create patterns on the fabric when it is dyed. One particularly interesting method of applying wax to the fabric is the use of the Tjanting, a small pipelike tool that distributes the wax in intricate patterns. The use of the Tjanting allows great freedom of expression and design. Commercial manufacturers currently do not use this technique, but have been able to duplicate its results to some degree.

BATISTE

Batiste is named in honor of the French linen weaver Jean Baptiste. Jean Baptiste was well known during the 13th century for the delicate, gossamer-like textiles that he produced. It is not known whether one of the linen textiles was named batiste at that time, or whether the name originated later in his honor. Batiste is no longer made of linen. In the 19th century it was made exclusively of fine, combed cotton. Now it is copied in manufactured fiber, in a combination of cotton and dacron. Batiste is characterized by a lengthwise streak that is caused by using a two ply yarn. It is created in a plain weave, in a wide variety of colors and prints. When batiste is made of pure cotton today, it has usually undergone a MERCERIZATION process which causes its strength and luster to increase. It is known for its launderability.

BAYADÈRE

Bayadère originated in India. It is a textile that consists of straight, horizontal stripes. The stripes, which can be woven or printed, are usually of very brilliant colors, giving it startling beauty. The textile is created in both the plain and twill weaves. The fabric was originally

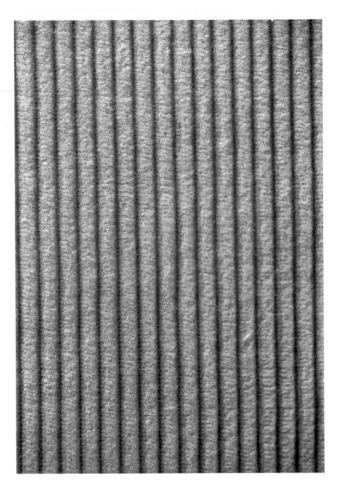

Bedford cord (cotton)   Author's collection

made of silk, but now is found in manufactured fibers as well. When the stripes have an undulating or wavy pattern, the textile is called MOIRÉ.

BEDFORD CORD

Bedford cord is distinguished by its pronounced vertical ribs, which always run in the direction of the warp. It is a heavy-duty textile, available in many weights and qualities. The heavier weights are produced by using cords with a low twist and high bulk yarn that are completely covered by the weft. The textile's name refers to the weave and not to the fiber of which it is made. It was first made of worsted and is in the PIQUÉ family. It is now produced in cotton, linen, wool and manufactured fibers,and is available in a wide range of colors. The origin of the term is unclear; it is perhaps named after Bedford, England, or New Bedford, Massachusetts, where the fabric is known to have existed as early as 1845.

BENGALINE

Bengaline was first produced in Bengal, India, and was made of blends of silk and cotton and silk and wool. Today it is created of many fibers, including manufactured fibers. It is executed in a plain or rib weave in which more threads are used in the warp than in the filling or weft. The warp threads create a cross ribbed effect that obscures the filling threads. Bengaline is a durable textile that is distinguished by its luster. ≡

BEVAN, E.J.

E. J. Bevan was an English chemist who, together with Charles F. Cross, experimented on the process of developing synthetic fibers in 1893–94. Their experiments led to the development of regenerated cellulose, leading in turn to the production of MANUFACTURED FIBER. ≡

BIRDSEYE

Birdseye is a fabric that is made of cotton or linen in a LENO WEAVE. It is a member of the PIQUÉ family. The threads are twisted, making the fabric absorbent. It is frequently called diaper cloth. The fabric has an all over design that is geometric in composition with a dot at the center, resembling the eye of a bird. Birdseye is also

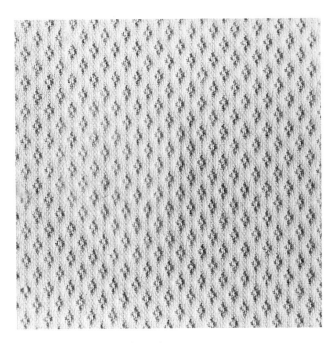

Birdseye (cotton)   Author's collection

≡

found with diamond designs that are created by floating the filling or weft yarns over warp threads in a regular formation.

When birdseye is made of linen, it is often created in a novelty twill weave and used for reversible items such as toweling. Occasionally the term birdseye is applied to worsted textiles that have been given a finish that has indentations on the face of the textile. When birdseye is used to describe knit textile it is called a twill back and is achieved by knitting every other needle on the dial and all needles on the cylinder of a knitting machine. The overall effect is one of "salt and pepper." ≡

BLEEDING

Often called crocking, bleeding refers to the loss of color from a textile during the washing or dry-cleaning process. The dyes run or fade and can stain the lighter ground of a fabric. Many advances have been made in the stabilizing of textile dyes so that this problem can often be avoided. Also, new labeling laws now require that labels with instructions for proper care be placed on a garment to help reduce this problem. Nonetheless, spot testing a fabric before dry cleaning or washing is recommended.

See also DYES. ≡

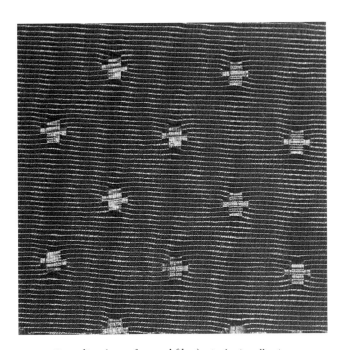

Bengaline (manufactured fiber)   Author's collection

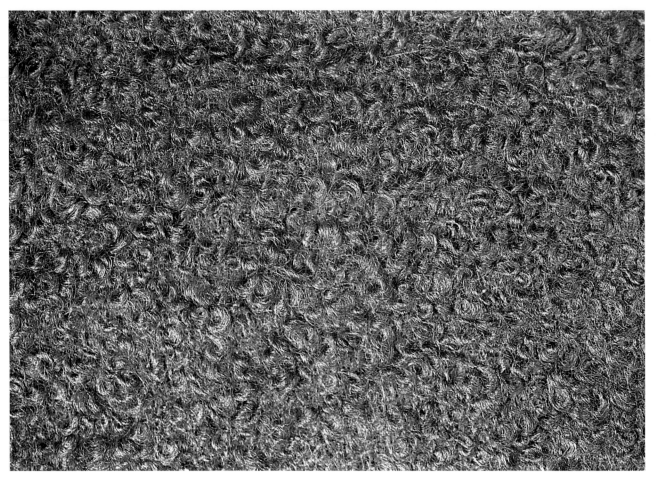

Bouclé (wool)   Author's collection

BLEND

A blend refers to a fabric in which two or more types of fibers have been combined. Frequently the filament or manufactured yarns have been divided and blended within one strand of the thread or yarn, producing a blend. There are also woolen or worsted blend fabrics made of yarns that are partially wool and partially manufactured fiber. This textile is referred to as manipulated cloth. When the WOOL PRODUCTS LABELING ACT of 1939 was passed, it required that the percentages of each fiber be included in the labeling of all blended products. Laws today require that on a garment or textile the predominant fiber in a blend be listed first, followed by each successive fiber present. The International Bureau for the Standardization of Manufactured Textiles (BISFA), based in Paris, was established so that there would be greater consistency among manufacturers for the composition of a particular blend. The bureau operates worldwide, and keeps manufacturers in touch with the newest methods and developments in the field.

BLOCK PRINTING

Block printing is a slow but highly artistic means of printing on fabric. A design is carved into a block of wood. The carved block is dipped into a dye that has a thick consistency, and then pressed on the textile. A different block is used for each color. Many intricate patterns can be created by overprinting with different designs. Block printing is not a process used by the mass production industry, but rather by those individuals or groups that produce art fabrics. The history of the evolution of block printing is unclear, but printing blocks from India exist that date from 3000 B.C. India is generally recognized for having had the greatest impact on the history of dye-decorated fabrics. It is also known that the Chinese were decorating fabrics with block print as early as 400 B.C.

See also PRINTING.

BLOTCH PRINTING

See PRINTING.

BOLT

A bolt is a length of loomed cloth that has been rolled and placed on a thick paper core. It is often referred to as a "piece," or cut. Depending on the width of the fabric, bolts are either rolled or wound flat. Fabrics 45 inches and 54 inches in width are most commonly wound flat while fabrics 60 inches in width or more are rolled. The yardage on the bolt depends upon the texture and density of the textile. By law the textile type and yardage are listed on one end of the bolt. There are no standardized widths and lengths for fabrics, although the most commonly found widths are 45 inches and 54 inches.

BOMBAZINE

The term bombazine is from the Greek word for silkworm. Originally it was a textile made entirely of silk but today can be found in a silk and worsted combination and occasionally in manufactured fibers. It is executed in a plain or twill weave and is characterized by its soft, fine quality.

BONDING

Bonding refers to the joining of two fabrics, or to the joining of a fabric to some other material, such as foam. The technique of bonding is a valuable one, for it can give body and stability to a fabric, as well as make it water repellent. The art of bonding has progressed dramatically since its inception in 1960. For example, items are being bonded through the use of ultrasonics with such subtlety that it is impossible to perceive that they were bonded with the naked eye. Most often the fabric is bonded by placing an adhesive on the wrong side of the textile over which is laid a very thin piece of foam (often polyurethane). Heated rollers then press the bonding agents to the fabric. The foam or other agents are sometimes melted into the fiber. The materials most often used for bonding are laminated foam, cotton, or acetate.

BOTANY WOOL

Botany wool is now a term that applies to any fine wool. Originally, it referred to wool exclusively from the merino sheep. Botany Bay in New South Wales, Australia, was famous for its production of extra fine wools.

See WOOL.

BOUCLÉ

Bouclé is a French word meaning curled. A bouclé fabric has a looped or curled surface, which creates great textural variety. The loops may occur on one or both sides of the fabric and may be used either as the warp or filling yarn. Sometimes the bouclé yarns are of uneven width. There are now a great variety of fibers used for bouclé they can be of wool, cotton, blends, or made entirely of manufactured fibers. Occasionally they consist of a cotton core around which another fiber has been spun. The yarn with which the textiles are created is classified as a novelty yarn, and is very popular. Bouclé yarns are also used extensively in the knitting industry, and in the process of hand knitting.

See YARNS.

BRADFORD SYSTEM

The Bradford system is one of three systems that are largely employed in the spinning of yarns; the other two are the AMERICAN SYSTEM and the FRENCH SYSTEM. The Bradford system was developed in Yorkshire, England, during the 19th century, for the handling of longer fibers. It embodies a sophisticated system of combs that separate the short from the long fibers. When spun using this system, the fibers are very compact and smooth. The Bradford system has been supplanted largely in the U.S. by the American system, which still embodies some of the Bradford characteristics.

See also SPINNING.

BROADCLOTH

Originally, fabric came only in the narrow widths achieved by early looms. When technological advances permitted the weaving of broader textiles, the fabrics were named broadcloths. Today, the term has a completely different meaning. There are now two types of textiles referred to as broadcloth: wool broadcloth and cotton broadcloth. They are different from one another in both their fiber content and in the FINISHING processes that are used in their execution.

Silk brocade (front)   Author's collection

Woolen broadcloth is executed in either a plain or twill weave. It is characterized by its luster and soft hand, making it ideal for tailoring. The textile is face-finished (finished on one side only) and undergoes a shearing (clipping) and polishing process. Woolen broadcloth is also made of a blend with wool and manufactured fibers.

Cotton broadcloth is executed in a plain, tightly woven rib weave with single or two-ply yarns. The yarn for cotton broadcloth usually undergoes a MERCERIZATION process that gives it added strength and luster. It is also pre-shrunk. Today cotton broadcloth is also frequently found in blends with manufactured fibers.

BROADCLOTH, CARDED

Carded broadcloth is a textile created by using a medium size warp yarn and a coarser filling. It consists of a plain weave with uncombed yarn, and has a ribbed effect.

BROCADE

The term brocade is taken from the French word *brocart,* meaning ornamented. Historians tell us that brocades were originally created by hand in China and Japan as early as the 12th century B.C. Occasionally, true brocades are still made by hand, usually by artists and craftsmen not producing for the mass market.

Brocade can be described technically as patterning through the use of supplemental wefts. The term brocade can often be confusing, because through the years it has to some degree ceased to be considered as a weave and is frequently used simply to refer to any fabric that is patterned. As a result there is a tendency to avoid using the term.

Brocades can be identified by raised figured patterns, created by free floating weft yarns on a plain weave. The face of brocade is easily distinguished from the back. The effect of the brocade is that of embossing, in that it creates raised patterns in the fabric. The inlaid weave can be done in a wide variety of patterns, often with silver and gold threads, and can be created on a ground of damask, twill, satin, or plain weave. Brocades are typically woven on a JACQUARD loom, though other weaving techniques may be employed. Brocades are now available in cotton, wool, silk, rayon and blends.

See also BROCATELLE; CALENDERING; EMBOSSING.   ═

BROCATELLE

Brocatelle is very similar to BROCADE, in that it also has a raised effect. Although both are now produced on a JACQUARD loom, brocatelle is made of much heavier yarns, and its figures stand out in very high, almost exaggerated, relief. Brocatelle is also done frequently in the SATIN WEAVE. The relief is created by employing extra backing threads. The warp yarns float over the backing yarns, making the design stand out. The textile is most lustrous when it is made of silk, but is also made of cotton, wool and manufactured fibers. It comes in a wide range of weights and qualities.   ═

BUCKRAM

Buckram is a very open, coarse textile of PLAIN WEAVE, mainly used as a stiffening in sewing construction. Cotton buckram is coated with a special SIZING or resin to create its stiffness.   ═

BULKING

Bulking is a texturing process that creates air spaces between the fibers of a textile. This is achieved by disrupting the fibers on high speed machines that twist and crimp the fiber, so that they are no longer parallel to one another. The technique is used both on woven and

Silk brocade (back)   Author's collection

═══

knitted fabrics. Yarn and fabrics that have undergone the bulking process are soft and fluffy. The first bulking processes were carried out with acrylic fiber.

BURLAP

Burlap is a very coarse, heavy plain-weave fabric that is made of JUTE or HEMP. Poorer grades of burlap are used for gunny sacks and certain types of upholstery wrapping. The better grades are bleached and dyed and used in the crafts market. Burlap has poor washability, and its colors often fade or crock when the fabric is moistened.

BURNT-OUT FABRIC

Burnt-out fabric refers to the intricate patterns that are created by using different yarns in the weaving process and then destroying one of the yarns with chemicals. The effect is often incorrectly referred to as voided fabric, usually when applied to velvet. This system in a way is much like a printing system in which chemicals, instead of dyes, are used in patterns. The process can be used on all kinds of textiles, including velvet in which the pile is destroyed, leaving the ground. Lace can also be created by using the same method.

See also EMBROIDERY; LACE; VOIDED; VELVET.

BUTCHER LINEN

Butcher linen is a plain weave textile, originally made of linen, but now made of cotton and manufactured fibers as well. It is also called butcher cloth and is frequently finished with a resin that imitates linen.

See also FINISHING; LINEN.

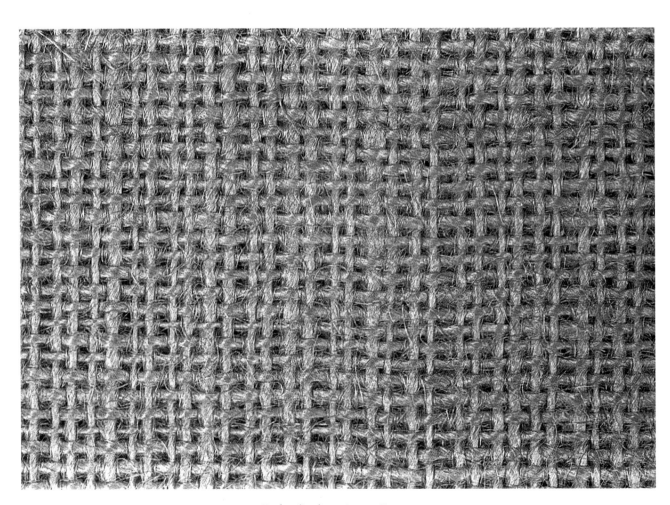

Burlap (jute)   Author's collection

C

CABLE THREAD

See YARN.

CAKE

Cake refers to a form of centrifugal spinning that is applied to viscose rayon. After the fiber has been spun it is placed in a cylinder that revolves at high speeds. When the fiber is removed, it has the appearance of a solid cake. The "cakes" are often dyed at that point in the process. The yarn is then rewound in preparation for the weaving process.

CALENDERING

Calendering is essentially an "ironing" process that produces a smooth, flat, glossy surface free of wrinkles. The results are achieved by passing the fabric, usually cotton or linen, between heated rollers under pressure. There can be up to ten rollers, depending on the effect desired. The greater the heat and pressure, the higher the resulting luster of the fabric. Calendering occurs after all other chemical finishes have been applied. The process is not always a permanent one, and sometimes it is removed by washing.

In friction calendering, the fabric passes through rollers that are rotating at different speeds. The technique produces a high luster. Another calendering technique, chasing, uses from 5 to 10 rollers. The fabric is sent though the rollers doubled, face to face. The threads of the two textiles imprint on the opposing fabric giving it a striated dull luster.

A special calendering technique called Schreinering, developed by Ludwig Schreiner at the turn of the century, uses a roller that has been etched with hundreds of parallel lines. When a wet textile is impressed by this type of roller, the finished product tends to hide all irregularities and still has a very high luster. The process is executed by having one of the rollers etched or embossed with a design, while the other rollers that are applied to the textile are padded. One of the best-known examples of this is MOIRÉ.

See also FINISHES.

CALICO

Calico is one of the oldest textiles known. Originally, calico came from Calcutta, a seaport in southwest Madras, India, from whence it derives its name. It is known that Vasco da Gama brought calico, then called *pintadores*, to Europe from India about 1497.

Calico was executed in a plain weave of carded cotton, printed by the resist method. Calico always has body and is available in many weights and qualities. The designs, motifs and colors of the fabrics were complex and refined for resist prints, and frequently the repeat went undetected. Naturalistic motifs were a favorite, and were done with polychrome effects. The designs were usually very small. The calicos were so successful in England, where they were imported as early as 1631, that English competitors soon produced them. Even though the

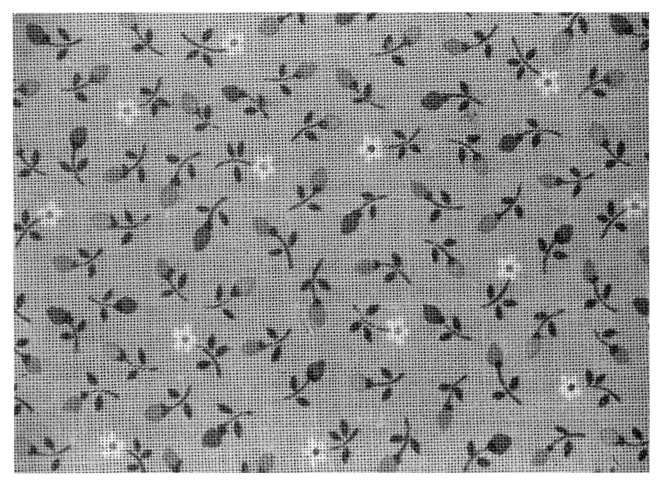

Calico (cotton) Author's collection

English textiles were not nearly as intricate or colorfast as those from India, a law was passed in 1700 to stop the importation of the Indian fabric.

Calico has been replaced by the use of percale in today's market, although the term is still used to refer to certain printed designs.

See also PRINTING.

CAMBRIC

The name cambric originated from the town of Cambrai, France, where the fabric was first created. Cambric is a lightweight fabric of cotton or linen, executed in a plain weave. The fabric is treated with a special sizing or resin and then calendered, which imparts a high gloss. There also exists a linen plain weave cloth that originated in Ireland that is called Irish cambric. It has a very high thread count.

In France, a version of cambric called demi-mousseline is produced that is very lightweight and usually created with stripes. It is made of cotton or linen. Another type of linen cambric is made in Scotland, called batiste d'ecosse. It is also distinguished for its very fine quality, and usually is a plain color.

CAMEL HAIR

Camel hair is the undercoat of the domesticated Bactrian camel. The Bactrian camel as we know it today is a cross between the dromedary, which is Arabian, and the Bactrian, which is Asian. Originally, the Bactrian probably lived in Afghanistan, which in ancient times was called Bactria. It is a two-humped camel having hair as long as 10 inches in length that it sheds once a year. The fur is tan to dark brown. The Bactrian camel is approximately 7 feet tall at the shoulders, and an adult weighs approximately 1,500 lbs. It is interesting to note that this camel, from the family of Camelidae, is the only one of that family to live in desert areas. The other four members of this family are the ALPACA, guanaco and llama.

The fiber of the camel is obtained either when the animal sheds or by shearing the animal. The WOOL PRODUCTS LABELING ACT classifies camel hair as wool. It can be either pure camel hair or, since it is very costly, camel hair blended with other wool fibers. Camel hair fabric is most often created with a twill weave. The textile can have a deep nap or a flat finish, depending on the desired effect. The textile is characterized by its luxurious soft quality and excellent draping ability.

See also TWILL.

CARDING

Carding is the mechanical process that separates the raw fibers of wool and cotton. It is sometimes applied to waste silk fiber as well. In this process, as part of the preparation for SPINNING, remaining impurities in the fibers are removed, which causes the fibers to be more nearly parallel to one another. The fibers are passed between cylinders, one of which has teeth set into it. The fibers are thus brushed or combed, causing them to become more regular. Carding is often referred to as the combing process.

Bactrian camel Boris Shlomm Amicale, Inc.

Dr. Wallace H. Corothers American Fiber Manufacturers Association, Inc.

CAROTHERS, DR. WALLACE HUME (1896–1937)

Dr. Wallace H. Carothers was head of the chemical division of E. I. du Pont de Nemours and was involved in the invention of NYLON. In 1928, the corporation launched a research program to study polymers. Knowing that the polymers could be joined together as a long chain, chemists found that by suitable chemical recombination, they could be drawn out and stretched to several times their original length. In 1931, Dr. Carothers presented a series of papers to the American Chemical Society concerning this topic and called a new fiber that had been produced this way "66," because of its molecular structure. It was not until 1938, after exhaustive research and experimentation, that Du Pont announced the creation of the first non-cellulosic textile fiber (one not made from plants), which they called nylon. Du Pont began commercial production of nylon in Delaware in 1939.

See also MANUFACTURED FIBER.

Cashmere   Author's collection

CARTWRIGHT, EDMUND (1743–1823)

As early as 1604 in Leiden, Holland, engines were used to propel shuttles, and it is recorded that by 1610 shuttles were being propelled by engines in London as well. Edmund Cartwright, an Englishman, is given credit for a further advancements using engine power, which included both an improved power loom driven by steam with a vertical warp and an engine-driven combing machine. By 1790 Cartwright was operating a mill with 400 working looms. The workers in the weaving industries were fearful that the mechanization of the loom would put them out of work, and a series of rebellions followed. During that year the mill, with all its contents, was burned to the ground. It was only a temporary setback, for inevitably technology prevailed.

See LOOM.

Cashmere goat   Boris Shlomm Amicale, Inc..

Challis (wool) Author's Collection

CASHMERE

Originally spelled Kashmir, cashmere came from the undercoat of the wild cashmere goat of India and Tibet. The wool of the cashmere goats was used to create the famous cashmere, or kashmir, shawls. In the wild, the goats would rub themselves against shrubs and bushes during the molting season. The scattered fleece would have to be gathered by hand, an arduous task. The goats were not shorn, nor are they today, although they are more domesticated than was the case in the past. The precious wool grows under a thick, coarse outer coat. The wool is obtained by stroking the goat with crude stiff combs once a year. Each goat produces about 4 ounces of wool a year. Only 4 million pounds are produced annually.

Very little cashmere comes from Kashmir anymore, although the cashmere goat still lives in the main in the high plateaus of the Himalayan ranges in inner Asia. China is now the major supplier of the world's cashmere. Attempts are being made to raise the goats in other areas of the world, such as New Zealand, Australia, and the United States. Today, because the cashmere goat lives in such inaccessible regions it is difficult to obtain the hair, limiting the annual quantity of cashmere available and raising its price.

Cashmere is classified as WOOL, and is one of the most distinguished textiles in the wool family. It is silky, soft and very fine.

The fabric created with cashmere used for coating or heavier textiles is a twill weave. The wool is also used for knitwear such as sweaters, for which the Scottish industry has become so well known. Because it is difficult to harvest, and not as plentiful as other types of wool, articles of pure cashmere are very expensive. Cashmere wool is often combined with other fibers in an effort to lower the cost of the finished product. The natural color of cashmere wool is gray, brown and, very rarely, white. It receives dye very well, and the finished product is available in a wide variety of colors.

There are many textiles made in imitation of cashmere that do not necessarily have cashmere in them. These textiles can be made of silk, rayon or manufactured fibers. They usually are twilled textiles that employ a worsted filling. Some are very soft and have high luster. The Textile Fiber Products Identification Act of 1960 requires that the content of these textiles be included on the label.

See LABELING LAW.

CELLULOSE

Cellulose is the fibrous carbohydrate substance forming the skeletal wall structure of plants. COTTON seed hairs are the purest source of cellulose, yielding approximately 90% of dry weight, whereas FLAX yields 60-85%, and so-called high alpha woods, such as spruce and pine, yield up to 50%. The latter are today the major source of the world's supply of cellulose.

There are three variants of cellulose in natural sources, defined by their chemical solubility in alkaline and acidic solutions. The cellulose predominant in cotton (called alpha-cellulose) is taken as the standard, and other celluloses are referred to it. This type of cellulose remains undissolved after treatment with a strong solution (approximately 18%) of caustic soda. Wood pulp having a high proportion of this cellulose are called high alpha woods.

When the soluble fraction from this treatment is subjected to acidification, a second type of cellulose solidifies, which is known as beta-cellulose. The type of cellulose that still remains in solution after the two treatments is referred to as gamma-cellulose.

Cellulose is widely used as the chemical raw material for the manufacture of cellulosic fibers such as RAYON and ACETATE.

See also LINEN.

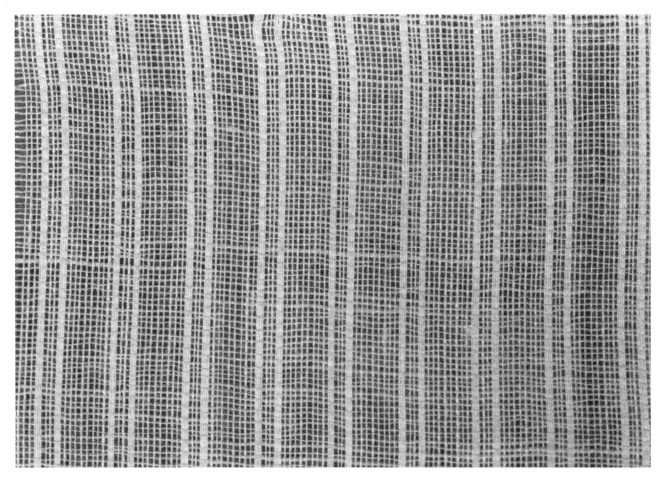

Chambray (cotton)   Author's collection

CELLULOSE ACETATE

See ACETATE.

CHALLIS

Once called "nun's veiling," challis was originally created in Norwich, England, in the 1830s of silk and worsted. The term comes from the Indian word "shalee," which means "soft to the touch." Challis is an exquisitely soft fabric in a plain weave that was originally made of silk and wool worsted, but now can be found in a high-quality, very fine pure wool. It is also currently made of a wide variety of textile fibers, including manufactured fibers. When challis is printed with advanced printing methods the design seems to acquire a depth of extraordinary beauty. Flowers are among the popular motifs of the printed wool challis.

CHAMBRAY

Chambray was first created in Cambrai, France. It is a plain weave textile that is executed with a colored warp and a white filling of either combed or carded fibers, which imparts a variegated character to the textile. It is one of the most popular fabrics. Often it is printed with very intricate designs using one of the modern processes such as roller or screen PRINTING. The textile is also found in stripes and there are also other novelty treatments such as embroidery. Though it was primarily made of cotton in previous times, today it is also made of many blends and is characteristically WASH AND WEAR.

CHAMELEON

Chameleon has a changeable appearance that is created either by combining fibers of different colors that reflect light at different angles, or through a combination of different types of fibers. Originally made of silk, chameleon now is created in many manufactured fabrics under a variety of trade names.

See also SHOT.

de CHARDONNET, COUNT HILAIRE

See RAYON.

CHARMEUSE

Charmeuse was originally a French lightweight silk, created in a SATIN WEAVE, that was known for its luster

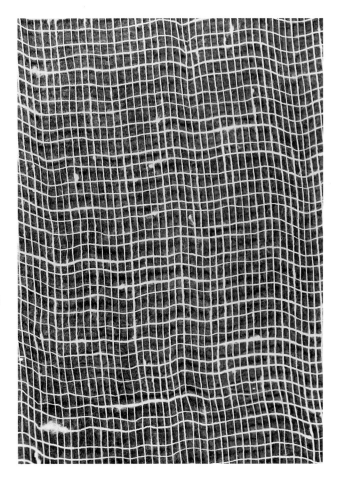

Cheesecloth (cotton) Author's collection

and its drapability. Today, it is still found with a lustrous face and dull back. It is made with a twisted yarn in the warp and a crepe yarn in the weft. It is found in both prints and solid colors in cotton, rayon and manufactured fabric.

CHARVET

Charvet is executed in a herringbone weave with a warp face. It is characterized by its very soft, silky, lustrous hand. Originally made of silk, it is now imitated in manufactured fiber.

CHASING

See CALENDERING.

Pages 30 and 31: Chameleon shot cloth Author's collection

Charmeuse (silk) Author's collection

CHEESECLOTH

Cheesecloth is a soft, lightweight, loosely woven cotton that has a low thread count. It is executed in a PLAIN WEAVE. It is also referred to as gauze or tobacco cloth. It is most frequently white in color, but receives dye well and is available in colors. Cheesecloth has many household uses, is used as a medical supply, and is frequently used in craft projects.

CHENILLE

Chenille, from the French word for caterpillar, was developed from a technique used in the United States in the 18th century called candlewicking, in which tufts of cotton were arranged on a cotton ground at intervals to form elaborate patterns. Executed by hand, candle-wicking is not widely practiced today. In chenille, developed from this technique during the 19th century and executed by machine, the tufts are not placed on the ground at intervals, however, but in long continuous lines. Originally chenille was created exclusively in silk. Today, chenille yarns are made in a LENO WEAVE of cotton, silk, wool or manufactured fibers that is cut lengthwise between the warps, thus producing strips of pile. The chenille strips are then used as the weft in a textile, which may be single or double face. Chenille is not a rugged textile, for its tufts are not fixed in place and can easily be pulled out of the textile ground. It is classified as a cut pile textile.

CHEVIOT

Cheviot originated in the hills of Scotland and was a product of the wool of the cheviot sheep. It was a rugged, uneven, heavy worsted textile. Cheviot is occasionally created in a plain weave but is most often executed in a

TWILL weave. It is no longer made exclusively with cheviot wool, but is found in many fibers, including manufactured fiber. The twill weave has a napped surface, created by a finishing process.

Cheviot also refers to shirting textile created in cotton, a blend of cotton and manufactured fiber, or purely manufactured fiber. It is a medium-weight textile that is executed in a twill weave and most often found in stripes. See also TWEED.

CHEVRON

Chevron refers to a HERRINGBONE twill.

CHIFFON

Chiffon was originally made of silk, but today it is made of rayon, silk, nylon and other manufactured fibers. It is always made with a highly twisted yarn that produces a very fine transparent textile. The fabric is created in a plain weave, with warp and weft threads of the same size. Though it is delicate and light in appearance, it is durable, although care must be taken not to allow the textile to be stretched by hanging. Sometimes chiffon fabric is given a sizing that imparts a slight stiffness. Chiffon is available in a wide variety of colors. Radiux chiffon is a chiffon that has a high luster, due to the fact that it is created with a cotton warp and a rayon filling.

CHINA SILK

China silk was originally handwoven in China, and was sought after because of its luster and soft delicate quality. Today it is reproduced by machine in silk as well as in manufactured fibers. The China silks that are produced today are heavier than their predecessors. They are executed in a PLAIN WEAVE characterized by irregularities. See SILK.

Chenille (manufactured fiber)   Mrs. Alexander G. Jerde

Chiffon (silk) Author's collection

CHINCHILLA CLOTH

Chinchilla cloth originated in Chinchilla, Spain, and is characterized by a spongy, soft, thick feel. The textile is executed in a twill weave in wool with a double or triple construction with a napped surface. Today it is imitated in manufactured textiles and is available in a wide variety of colors. It is given a special finish to obtain a curled or knotted surface on the face of the textile. There is no relationship between the textile and the animal of the same name.

CHINÉ

The silk chiné textiles of the 18th century offered many splendid examples of this warp print, still created today. The warp is printed before weaving, rendering the pattern indistinct and shadowy. The colors are also softer and less distinct than the colors usually used in textile printing. Chiné is executed in a plain weave, and is considered by many to be one of the most stunning textiles available on the market. Today, the chiné effect is sometimes achieved through a CALENDERING process.

See SILK.

CHINTZ

The word chintz means varied in nature in Hindustanee. Chintz appears to have originated in 18th-century India. Originally, the textile was hand painted with dyes in very bright motifs. It is one of the most popular textiles on the market today, not only because of the rich variety of colors and patterns, but also because of the glaze with which it is finished, which imparts a sheen and high luster to the textile.

Modern chintz is a PLAIN WEAVE cotton fabric, friction calendered, and is either printed or executed in solid

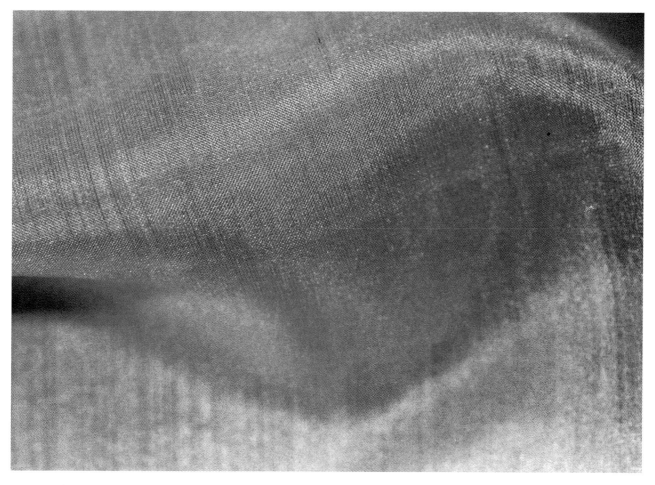

China silk Author's collection

colors. Some of the early glazes that were used to create chintz were wax, starch and various types of glue. These were not totally satisfactory, for they would crack under pressure and heat, and be destroyed if washed. Today many advances have been made with resins that are baked onto the surface of the cotton, so that in some cases the glaze is not destroyed by laundering.

See FINISHING.

CIRÉ

Ciré undergoes a special CALENDERING process that gives the fabric such a high luster that it is often referred to as a patent leather finish. The word ciré, from the French meaning waxed, refers to the lustrous quality of the fabric, not its weave. Originally it was created through the use of heat and various waxes, but those methods have been replaced by contemporary resins. Today, the ciré process is employed predominantly on silk and manufactured textiles.

See RESIN.

COMPOUND FABRICS

Compound fabrics are those that are created by weaving two or more sets of warp and/or filling threads that are interconnected or integrated in some way. These are heavy textiles, usually of wool and usually reversible, and many times the face and back of the fabric are of contrasting colors.

See DOUBLE CLOTH.

COMPOUND TWILL

A compound twill is a twill that combines two or more twill weaves, producing an overall twill effect with each weave remaining distinct.

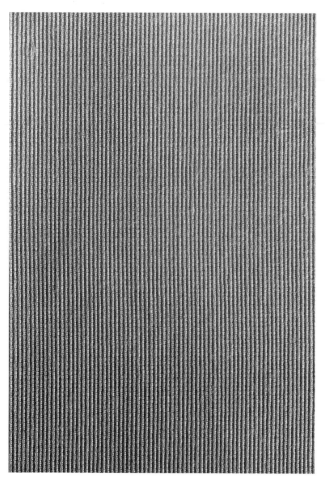

Corduroy (cotton, manufactured fiber blend)
Author's collection

CONSTRUCTION

Construction refers to the structural make-up of a textile, its weave, and to its components, fibers or filaments.

CONTINUOUS FILAMENT

Continuous filaments are manufactured fibers created in filaments, or rods, by an EXTRUSION process, in contrast to natural fibers (with the exception of raw silk), in which fibers must be spun together to form continuous yarns. All manufactured fibers are continuous filament. The filaments can be extruded in various deniers, or weights, that are determined by the fiber size and its chemical composition.

See MANUFACTURED FIBER.

CORD EFFECTS

Fabrics that have cord effects have a distinct rib on the surface. The rib can run either with the warp or the weft. Corded fabrics exist in many weaves, of which both PIQUÉ and POPLIN are examples. The cord effects can be achieved in any woven textile.

See BEDFORD CORD; CORDUROY; OTTOMAN.

CORDUROY

Corduroy is a fabric that takes its name from the French expression *cord du Roi,* which means "cord of the king." It is a ribbed, cut-pile textile and is executed in either plain or twill weave. It is created by an extra system of filling yarns in which the weft floats over three or more warp yarns. After weaving, the floats are cut on special machines and then brushed into fluffy cords, also called wales. Corduroy is now usually made of cotton or manufactured fibers and is produced in wide or narrow wale. The narrow wale is often referred to as pinwale. The textile is available in a wide range of weights, qualities and colors. It is durable and ranges from heavy to lightweight.

COTTON

Cotton is one of the world's major textile fibers. It is also one of the most versatile, being used either alone or in many blends for a seemingly infinite variety of apparel and household and industrial products.

Cotton is the fibrous matter that surrounds the seeds of various shrubs or woody herbs of the mallow family, Malvaceae. The fiber is obtained from multi-stemmed bushy plants that grow from 3 to 5 feet in height. It is composed of 87–90% cellulose, similar to the cellulose found in other natural products such as wood and linen. It does contain very small amounts of other substances, however, such as minerals, waxes and pectic products. They serve to protect the plant from the weather.

There are four main types of cotton: American Upland, Egyptian, Sea Island and Asiatic. All four types resemble one another in appearance, but bear flowers of different colors that bloom at varying times and have different fiber characteristics. American Upland is grown in almost every cotton-producing country and makes up 90% of the world crop.

American Upland is a plant with cream-colored flowers and stands 1 to 7 inches in height. It gives a large yield, with white fibers ⅞ to 1¼ inches in length. The

AREA, YIELD AND PRODUCTION; WORLD AND SELECTED COUNTRIES AND REGIONS

REGION AND COUNTRY:	1987/88	1988/89	1987/88	1988/89	1987/88	1988/89
	1,000 HECTARES		KG/HA		1,000 BALES	
WESTERN HEMISPHERE						
United States	4061	4812	791	699	14760	15445
Brazil	2312	2285	327	314	3468	3300
Mexico	230	255	956	1110	1010	1300
Argentina	515	510	547	374	1295	875
Colombia	233	215	577	628	618	620
Paraguay	400	450	438	411	804	850
Peru	137	155	739	646	465	460
Guatemala	40	34	1198	1153	220	180
Nicaragua	60	40	591	680	163	125
Venezuela	59	65	480	419	130	125
Others	65	64	442	483	132	142
TOTAL	8112	8885	619	574	23065	23422
EUROPE						
Greece	202	240	871	925	808	1020
Spain	79	132	1042	874	378	530
Others	46	46	284	284	60	60
TOTAL	327	418	830	839	1246	1610
AFRICA						
Egypt	416	420	845	752	1614	1450
Sudan	321	300	416	435	613	600
Zimbabwe	260	280	410	373	490	480
South Africa	204	210	346	363	324	350
Tanzania	470	470	175	174	378	375
Cameroon	95	105	474	518	207	250
Nigeria	320	320	94	112	138	165
Chad	160	190	299	286	220	250
Others	1538	1682	297	301	2099	2323
TOTAL	3784	3977	350	342	6083	6243
ASIA AND OCEANIA						
China	4844	5577	876	753	19500	19300
USSR	3527	3450	700	801	11345	12700
India	7400	7700	207	232	7027	8200
Pakistan	2568	2440	573	599	6764	6650
Turkey	586	707	916	924	2465	3000
Australia	232	183	1190	1338	1268	1125
Syria	128	171	835	910	491	715
Israel	40	49	1497	1511	275	340
Burma	183	180	148	151	124	125
Thailand	66	81	376	376	114	140
Afghanistan	50	50	435	435	100	100
Others	368	378	406	408	686	709
TOTAL	19992	20966	546	552	50159	53104
FOREIGN TOTAL	28154	29434	509	510	65793	68934
WORLD TOTAL	32215	24246	544	537	80553	84379

NOTE: Totals may not add because of rounding.

Harvest season beginning August 1.

Bales of 480 lb. net.

SOURCE: Prepared or estimated on the basis of official statistics of foreign governments, other foreign source materials, reports of U.S. agricultural attaches and other foreign service officers, results of office research and related information.

March 1989
FOREIGN PRODUCTION ESTIMATES DIVISION, FAS,USDA

Chiné (calendered manufactured fiber)   Author's collection

Egyptian type of cotton has lemon-colored flowers and produces long silky light tan fibers 1½ inches in length. The American variant of this strain is pima cotton, which yields fibers 1⅜ inches in length. *Sea Island* cotton is grown in the West Indies. It has yellow flowers and is a slow grower. It produces a low yield of white fibers 1¾ inches long, used for high-quality textiles. The *Asiatic* strain produces a low yield of short, coarse, harsh fibers. It is rapidly being replaced by other types.

History

Most authorities believe that cotton was first grown in India, for graves containing remnants of cotton textiles dating to the third millennium B.C. have been found there. There are also indications that cotton was used on the North American continent in Pre-Inca times, possibly dating as early as 2500 B.C.

Columbus made note to the effect that cotton yarn existed on Watling's Island, when he landed there on October 12, 1492. The conquistadores also discovered very fine cotton textiles in Peru, Mexico and in the southwestern part of what is now the United States. How the cotton plant became indigenous to the United States is still shrouded in mystery. It was not introduced by the English, a common misconception. Cotton was introduced into Europe during the crusades and there are 13th-century written references to cotton in England. It did not, however, find common usage in Europe until the 17th century.

With the invention of the spinning frame and the spinning mule in England during the industrial revolution, along with the invention of the cotton gin in the United States, cotton production and manufacturing increased dramatically. Prior to the mechanization of those efforts every process was done laboriously by hand, even the difficult ginning stage. The cotton seeds had to be separated from the cotton bolls by hand, a lengthy and sometimes costly effort with yields too small for commercial production. In 1791, after the invention of the cotton gin by Eli Whitney, cotton production increased by a factor of 75. This resulted in a greatly increased need for manual labor for picking the cotton in amounts required by the gins, and as a consequence, the importation of slaves in cotton growing states grew to over 4 million just prior to the American Civil War (1861–65). In 1769, the Scotsman James Watt patented the first steam engine; in 1785, he applied steam power for the first time in a cotton mill.

Cotton mills and factories began to emerge in the United States despite the fact that English manufacturers attempted to keep mill machinery out of the country. SAMUEL SLATER, known as the "Father of the American Cotton Textile Industry," came to the United States from England in 1789 and from memory reconstructed three textile machines of British design for the first cotton mills in New England. In 1793, he built a mill in Pawtucket, Rhode Island, which began to rival the English mills in the production of cotton textiles.

In 1822 the Merrimack Manufacturing Company started the first cotton mills at Lowell, Massachusetts, and many other mills sprang up in both northern and southern states. The one essential factor was ready access to waterways to supply water power to run the mills and to provide a means of transporting the processed cotton. By 1860, more than 2.5 million bales of cotton were exported to England. During the Civil War, there was a general breakdown of commerce and industry. This period also marked the end of essentially free slave labor for the cotton industry in the United States.

In 1881 an international cotton exposition in Atlanta encouraged better methods of planting and ginning, and mills began to spring up again, increasingly in the southern states. Around 1890 the boll weevil infiltrated from Mexico, necessitating the search for more insect-resistant types of cotton. By 1895 the South had largely recovered from the economic impact of the war and was gaining impetus in the raising of cotton and its industrialized production. By 1920, the South was producing more finished cotton cloth than New England.

Production

Cotton grows best in fertile, well-drained soil. It must have good moisture, but requires dry conditions after the cotton bolls are fully mature. Cotton seed is sown in ploughed soil or soil that has slight ridges in it. In the United States the planting is done in April or May. Today the planting process is highly mechanized, and the plants are fertilized and often treated with insecticide at the same time. When the plants have begun to grow sufficiently they are thinned to avoid overcrowding and to assure that the plants are in rows.

As the plants mature they bear numerous pink-white flowers. When the flowers fade, seed pods (bolls) remain

Pages 40 and 41: Chintz (cotton)   Author's collection

Cotton field National Cotton Council of America

that contain up to eight cotton seeds. As the seeds begin to develop they are covered with a white fluff or fiber. Before the cotton plant is fully mature, or ripe, the fiber is shaped much like a cylindrical tube throughout which a substance called lumen is found. The growing process continues until each seed becomes completely enclosed with as many as 4,000 fibers. As the fibers grow and expand, the boll bursts. When the cotton fiber is thus

Harvesting cotton National Cotton Council of America

Sorting cotton National Cotton Council of America

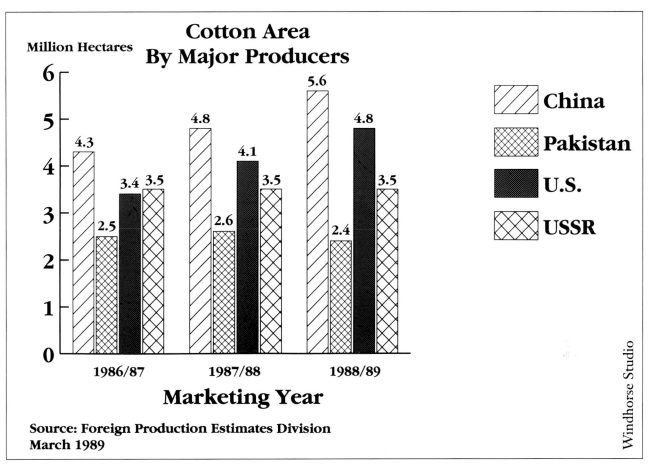

Cotton area by major producers   United States Department of Agriculture

exposed to the sun, the lumen dries up, causing the fiber to flatten and twist. During this period in its development it is essential that there not be heavy rainfall.

Ginning   National Cotton Council of America

The cotton is collected by large harvesting machines. Before the advent of this important piece of equipment all of the cotton was painstakingly picked by hand. The harvesting machine collects the bolls but does not separate the seeds from the fiber. Originally the seeds had to be removed by hand, but the process was made more efficient by the invention of the cotton gin. During the ginning process the cotton is fed into the gin, where the fibers are removed from the seeds. The process also separates the more desirable long (½ to 2 inch) fibers from the short fibers.

The short fibers, referred to as lint, are not used for yarn or thread but are an important raw material as a convenient and cheap source of the cellulose, which is the basis of many rayons. The separated seeds are then used for other by-products such as cottonseed oil. After ginning the cotton still contains a certain amount of dust and twigs and is referred to as raw cotton. It is at this point that the cotton is compressed into huge bales that are distributed to the mills that will manufacture it into yarn and fabric.

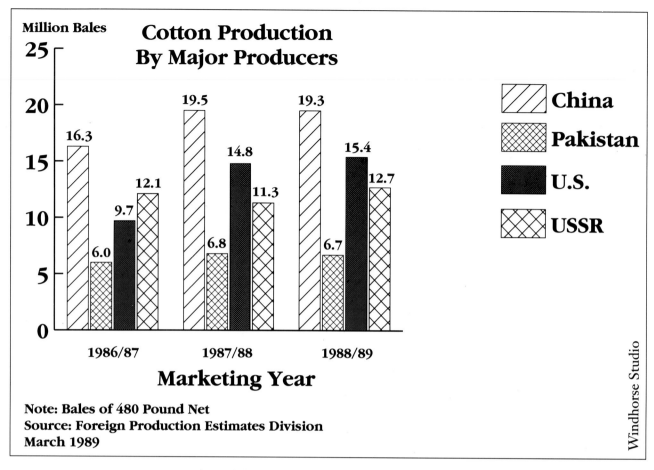

Cotton production by major producers   United States Department of Agriculture

Cotton is produced in many countries around the world, with the largest producers being China, the United States, the Soviet Union, India and Pakistan.

Qualities

Cotton is valued partly because it is the most elastic of all the vegetable fibers (although not as elastic as the animal fibers). Cotton is able to withstand high temperatures, which allows it to be laundered repeatedly. It also readily accepts dyes. Because the center of the cotton fiber is hollow, air can freely circulate through the fiber, allowing it to "breathe," which enhances its properties as an apparel textile. (As noted, cotton also provides the basic cellulosic material for some manufactured fibers such as rayon.) Nowadays cotton is combined with other fibers in blends such as cotton/wool, cotton/linen, and cotton/manufactured fibers, thus combining the best qualities of each fiber.

With the advances in finishing techniques during the last 10 years many ways have been discovered to treat cottons chemically to enhance its qualities. Certain chemicals make it crisp to the hand or touch, as well as chemicals make it wrinkle-free, flame-retardant, and waterproof. Treating cotton can also make it resistant to mildew, and enhance its strength and luster.

The Care of Cotton

Always consult the care label and follow the manufacturer's instructions before washing cotton. Because of the many blends that now exist on the market and because of trims or linings that have been placed on a garment, washing may sometimes be inadvisable. If washing is recommended, follow these guidelines:

THE CARE OF COTTON

COTTON TYPE	WASHING	DRYING
Pure White	Hot water and detergent. (White cotton can be sterilized.) Bleach can be used, but excessive or prolonged bleaching may weaken the fabric.	Tumble dry at moderate heat. Can be ironed safely at temperature of 400 degrees (F).
Pure Colored	Moderately hot water and detergent. Bleach is generally not recommended.	Tumble dry at moderate heat. If necessary, iron at moderate temperature.
Cottons with Finishes (except chintz: dry clean only)	Follow manufacturer's washing instructions. Often the use of chlorine bleach will yellow the textile due to resins in the finish.	Tumble dry, usually wrinkle free.
Cotton Knits	Wash with detergent by hand or on delicate machine cycle. Do not wring or stretch. Rinse thoroughly.	Dry flat on absorbent towels, carefully shaping. Press on wrong side with warm iron.

COTTON GIN

See COTTON.

COTTONADE

Cottonade is a heavy cotton fabric done in a TWILL WEAVE with a warp face. It is a very firm textile that can take heavy wear, due to its durable finish. Its most common form is blue-and-white stripes, but it is found as well in a wide variety of other colors.

COUNT

Count refers to the number of warp and filling yarns per inch in a fabric. It is also called the thread count. When count is included on a fabric label, warp count is indicated by the first number on the label, followed by the filling count. For example, 68 x 52 would mean there are 68 ends in warp and 52 picks in filling, per inch. There are now advertising and labeling regulations in regard to count.

COVERT

Covert cloth is a speckled twill cloth that was frequently worn for hunting, primarily in England. (Covert is a thicket or hiding place of game.) Today, the fabric closely resembles the original covert textiles in that it is executed with two-ply warp threads, one of dark yarn and one of a light yarn, which creates the pebbled or flecked appearance. It is further characterized by its durability and firm finish. It is closely woven, and created in both wool and cotton. Covert cloth comes in a variety of weights and qualities.

CREASE RESISTANT

A textile with crease resistance has durable finishes that prevent the fabric from wrinkling. Today this is done mainly by the addition of a resin applied with heat.

See also DURABLE PRESS; FINISHING; WASH AND WEAR.

CRÊPE

Crêpe is created by using yarn that has been twisted to an extreme degree under tension. After weaving, it partially relaxes, forming a fabric with an irregular wavy appearance. It is executed in many weights using a plain weave. Crêpe is made of many fabrics, including wool, cotton, silk and manufactured fibers. Balanced crêpe refers to a crêpe that has alternating yarns of S and Z crêpe twists in both the warp and weft. Balanced crêpe textiles are rarely produced today.

Crêpes are also created by using various chemicals and embossing techniques. One of the chemical treatments is the application of a solution of caustic soda (sodium hydroxide). It is usually done by using a resist

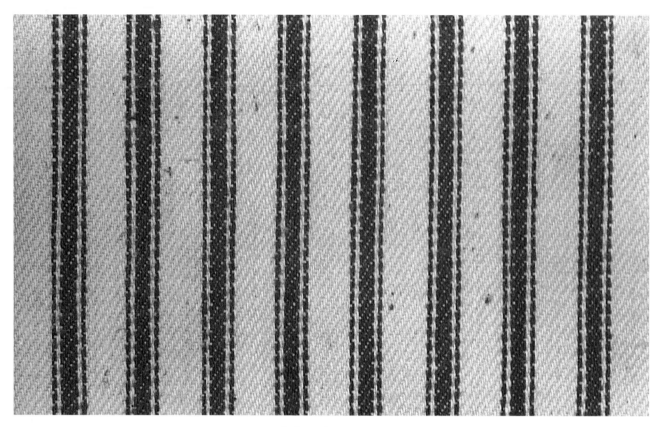

Cottonade (cotton)   Author's collection

method in which areas of the fabric that are not to be affected are coated to protect them from the action of the caustic soda. The uncoated areas shrink, creating a puckered effect that is called plissé if it is done in vertical lines, or blister crêpe if produced by an area resist. This fabric should not be confused with the crêpe weave.

CRÊPE DE CHINE

Crêpe de chine is a very fine, silky, high-luster, lightweight fabric. It is executed in a plain weave, with very tightly twisted S and Z twist yarns of silk, manufactured fabric and rayon that alternate in groups of two, creating a crêpe-like effect. Today crêpe de chine is made of both silk and manufactured fibers.

See S TWIST and Z TWIST.

CREPON

Crepon is a very heavy CRÊPE textile. The crêpe effect is executed in the direction of the warp and employs highly twisted threads. Today, it is available in silk, wool or manufactured fiber.

CRETONNE

Cretonne was first produced in Creton, a village in Normandy. The fabric is made in either twill or plain weave and is distinguished by its large floral patterns, usually on a plain ground and a dull surface, due to the FINISHING process. It is often described as CHINTZ without the glaze. Today, it is made of cotton, linen and manufactured fiber as well as blends.

CRINOLINE

Crinoline is a very rigid, loosely woven plain weave cotton fabric that is used as stiffening. It is stiffened today by the use of resins as well as starches.

CROCKING

Crocking occurs when improper DYES or dye methods are used. Some dye remains on the surface of the fabric and may rub off, which is referred to as crocking. If such a fabric is washed, it crocks or runs, which can be ruinous to the surrounding fabric and other garments.

Crêpe (silk) Author's collection

CROMMELIN, LOUIS

Louis Crommelin is credited with furthering the linen industry in Ireland in the 17th century. When the Edict of Nantes was revoked in 1685, instituting religious persecution once again, Crommelin migrated from his native France to Ireland, taking with him a vast knowledge of the art of linen weaving. Although Irish linen weaving started as early as the 11th century, Crommelin is thought to have given it impetus due to his expertise in the field and his ability to attract others to him who were equally qualified.

See LINEN.

Pages 48 and 49: Cretonne (cotton) Author's collection

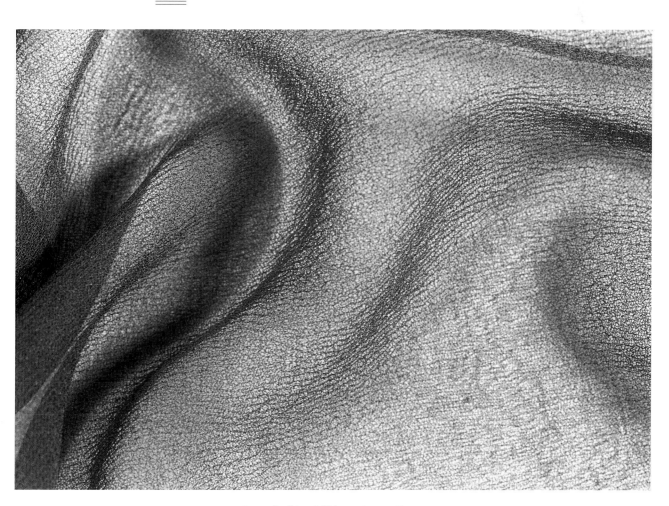

Crêpe de chine (silk) Author's collection

CROMPTON, SAMUEL (1753–1827)

Born in Firwald, near Bolton in Lancashire, England, Samuel Crompton invented the mule spinning frame in 1779. His device is said to have been given that name because it was a cross between two techniques previously invented by James HARGREAVES and Richard ARKWRIGHT, the spinning jenny and spinning frame. Crompton's spinning frame draws fibers through the use of carriages and rollers. Until recently, modern machines still employed Crompton's principles, but with the advent of more rapid methods it has largely fallen into disuse.

See SPINNING.

CROSS, CHARLES F.

Charles F. Cross was an English chemist who, together with E. J. Bevan, experimented with a process of developing synthetic fibers in 1893–94. Their experiments led to the development of regenerated cellulose, leading in turn to the production of MANUFACTURED FIBERS.

CUT VELVET

Cut velvet is produced on a JACQUARD loom with a brocaded pattern of velvet on a ground of chiffon or another light fabric.

See also VELVET.

Cretonne (cotton)   Author's collection

DAMASK

Damasks originally came from China and there are written references to them as early as the 13th century A.D. The term was first applied to any elaborate textile. Later, damasks came to be associated with the ancient city of Damascus, a center of trade between East and West, hence the name damask. The textiles were laboriously created by hand in China, but are now created exclusively on the JACQUARD loom in a SATIN WEAVE.

Damask is characterized by area patterning, which is caused by reversing the structure of the weave. The pattern becomes visible because of a contrast in luster between the warp and weft yarns. Damasks can be single or double; the double damasks are reversible. The textiles are now available in silk, cotton, linen, and combinations of rayon and natural fibers as well as manufactured fibers.

DEGUMMED SILK

Degummed silk is made by a process in which the gum, or sericin, is removed from silk yarn or fabric in order to bring out the luster of silk. This is achieved by boiling the silk in hot water, which can be done before or after the silk has gone through the weaving process. When the sericin has been removed the silk is much lighter in weight. In some cases, all of the gum is not removed in order to maintain a degree of dullness and to retain greater strength.

See also SILK.

DELUSTERING

Delustering is a process by which MANUFACTURED FIBER is made less shiny. RAYON is delustered by placing a colorless pigment in the solution during its spinning process. Similarly, titanium dioxide is added to ACETATE, and barium sulphate or zinc oxide is added to NYLON. The chemicals change the nature of the textile solutions prior to extrusion, dulling them.

DENIER

The term denier derives from the name of an ancient Roman coin, the denarius, known from the time of Julius Caesar (100 ? – 44 B.C.). Louis XI of France reinstituted the use of the term during his revival of the silk industry in 15th-century France, where it became a unit of measurement of the fineness of silk fibers. The term is now applied to yarns and many other fiber types, including MANUFACTURED FIBER.

Damask (linen) International Linen Promotion Commission

The denier is defined as the weight of a standard strand of fibers 450 meters in length. One denier weighs 50 milligrams (.05 grams). For fibers of the same type, having the same specific gravity or density, this definition translates directly into an indicator of fiber diameter, with finer fibers having lower denier, thick fibers having higher denier.

DENIM

Denim originated in Nimes, France, as a textile used for work clothes. Denim is a heavy cotton fabric that is completely washable. Sometimes it is referred to as jean. Originally, denim was executed in a twill, but today it is done in many different weaves. While it was first woven with blue warp threads with a white filling, today it is executed in all colors, as well as prints and plaids. The term "blue jeans" is derived from the textile jean, which was a cotton twill executed of carded yarns and dyed blue. Today, denim is also made of cotton and manufactured fiber blends.

The evolution of the use of denim is an interesting one in that it progressed from a textile used exclusively for highly functional clothes to a high-fashion statement in the late 1960s and throughout the '70s. In the '70s, it became popular to wear blue denims or jeans with applique, embodying elaborate hand and screen prints. Many museums have collections of these articles of clothing, as social "documents."

DERIVATION WEAVES

Derivation weaves are often called novelty weaves, and in the textile trade are called fancies, although the term fancies is not accepted as a technical term. The weaves are variations of the three accepted basic weave structures, plain, satin and twill weaves.

See NOVELTY WEAVE; WEAVING.

DESIGN FLOCKING

See FLOCK PRINTING.

DEVELOPED DYES

A developed dye is one in which an added chemical or developer is added to the dye bath, causing the textile color to be fixed to a greater degree. The use of developed dyes is expensive, because they require added steps in the dye process, but the dyes can then withstand repeated washings. These dyes are used on most fabrics, with the exception of silk.

See also DYES.

DIMITY

The term dimity is taken from the Greek word *dimitos*, which means double thread. Dimity is made of cotton that has been combed, usually mercerized, and given a finish. In its plain form dimity is executed in a plain weave that is characterized by lengthwise spaced cords, or ribs. The ribs are created with single, double or triple

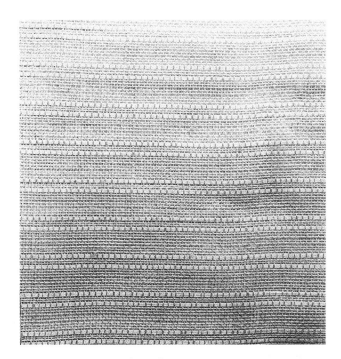

Dimity (cotton) Author's collection

threads, and thus dimity can display great variety. Dimity is also produced with checks. Though most commonly found in white, dimities are also dyed and printed.

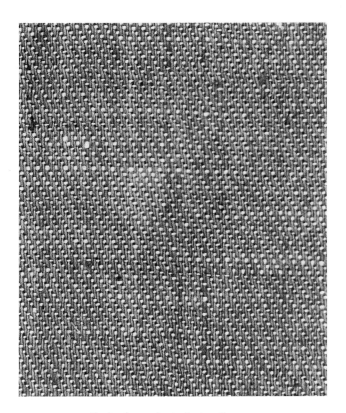

Denim (cotton) Author's collection

DIRECT DYES

Direct dyes are frequently called salt dyes. They render very bright colors. Direct dyes are used on textiles that are cellulosic (rayon, cotton, linen, etc.). This process is preferred, where possible, because it does not require the article or fabric to be pretreated; the fabric can simply be immersed in the dye bath. The salt helps aid the dye's absorption into the textile.

See also DIRECT PRINTING; DYES; PRINTING.

DISCHARGE PRINTING

Discharge printing is often referred to as extract printing because color is discharged or extracted from areas on a textile, creating a white pattern on a colored ground. This process is carried out by passing the textile through rollers that discharge a bleaching agent through the fabric according to a set pattern. This technique is used most often on cottons.

See also PRINTING.

DISPERSE DYES

Disperse dyes are a class of dyes that were used originally on cellulose acetate, but are now used on a wide range of fibers that do not absorb water, including nylon, acetate, polyester etc. The dyes are adsorbed by the fibers in a very hot solution.

See DYES.

DOBBY LOOM

See LOOM.

DOESKIN

Doeskin is a compact, nap finished cotton or wool, in which the fibers have been drawn to the surface and straightened in one direction. It is executed in either the satin or twill weave. The surface is face-finished (finished on one side only), creating a surface that obscures the weave. The fabric is smooth and soft to the touch.

DONEGAL TWEED

Donegal tweed is named after the county where it was first produced, Donegal, Ireland. Originally, it was woven entirely by hand, but today power looms are used in its manufacture. There are many imitations of Donegal tweed on the market today, executed in a wide variety of qualities and weaves. A true Donegal tweed, however, is characterized by slubs of many colors that are woven into the fabric. Made of wool, it has a speckled or flecked appearance and can be of either medium or heavy weight. A true Donegal will specify by label, "Donegal Tweed, Made in Ireland."

See TWEED.

DOTTED SWISS

The term dotted swiss refers to the origin of the textile, Switzerland, as well as its pattern. There are examples of dotted fabrics embroidered in the 18th-century, but the

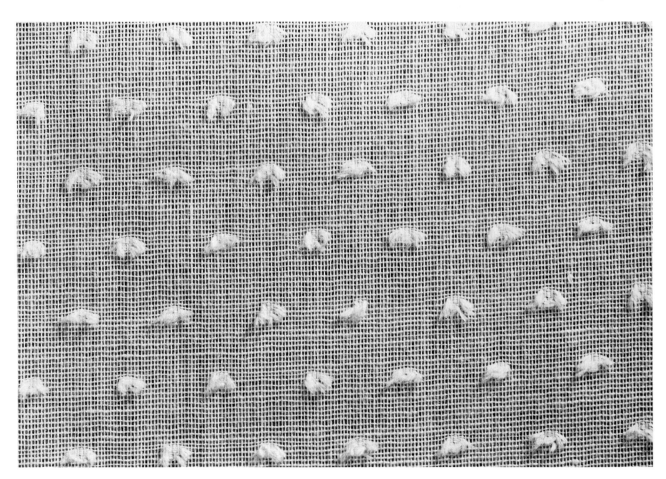

Dotted swiss (cotton) Author's collection

Donegal tweed (wool) Author's collection

first machine-made dotted swiss textiles were created in Switzerland during the 19th century, on a swivel loom that required that the dots be hand tied after the creation of the textile.

Originally, the Swiss used a stiff finish that they had perfected for textiles that came to be called swissing. The technique was used on many types of cotton, particularly ORGANDY, but is now obsolete.

Dots no longer require hand tying. On some types of dotted swiss, the dots are now applied using a FLOCKING technique that does not require weaving the dots into the textile. In modern dotted swiss the dots are always spaced at very regular intervals on a lightweight ground, usually LAWN. Today, most dotted swiss textiles are also treated with a permanent resin finish.

DOUBLE CLOTH

Also referred to as lined cloth, double cloth is executed so that different colors or patterns are visible on the face and back of the textile. (It is considered a generic term.)

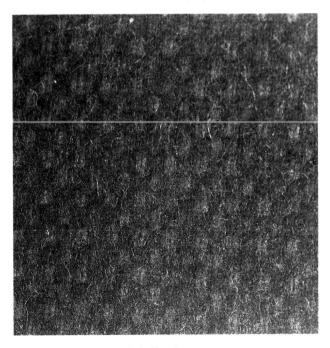

Wool double cloth (front) Author's collection

Wool double cloth (back) Author's collection

It is made by weaving two cloths one upon the other, with special threads that attach the two together. The textiles always have two sets of warps and two sets of filling or weft threads. Double cloths are characterized by their heavy weight, warmth and reversibility. They are created in both wool and manufactured fibers.

Today, the effect can also be created by BONDING two textiles together, but the bonded imitations are not true double cloths for they do not contain the threads that weave the two textiles together.

DOUBLE KNIT

A double knit is a knitted fabric that is done on a circular knitting machine containing a double set of needles, causing both sides to be identical, in contrast to single knit, which is different on the face and back. It is often reversible and has the appearance of having been knit

Double knit (wool/manufactured fiber blend) Author's collection

twice. The fabric is firmer and has more body than a single knit.

See KNITTING.   ≡

DOUPION

Doupion is created when two silk worms are spinning close to one another and the silk becomes united. When this occurs it is necessary to reel both cocoons at the same time, giving rise to an irregular slubbed silk. Today it is a much desired silk for apparel because of the textured character.

See SILK.   ≡

DRAPER, GEORGE OTIS (1867–1923)

George Draper was an American inventor credited with a dozen variations on the spindle between the years 1876 and 1887. All of his inventions were also patented

between those years. His son Ira DRAPER also contributed to the textile industry.

See LOOM; SPINNING.   ≡

DRAPER, IRA

The son of George DRAPER, Ira Draper was an American credited with having improved the fly-shuttle hand loom in 1816. He also invented the loom temple, a moving device that allowed the weaver to handle two looms at a time, in 1818. He continued to make improvements to his devices throughout his career and is the founder of the Draper Co, in Hopedale, Massachusetts.

See LOOM.   ≡

DRAWING

The purpose of drawing is to bring a mass of fiber to a size or fineness that is appropriate for the fabric that will

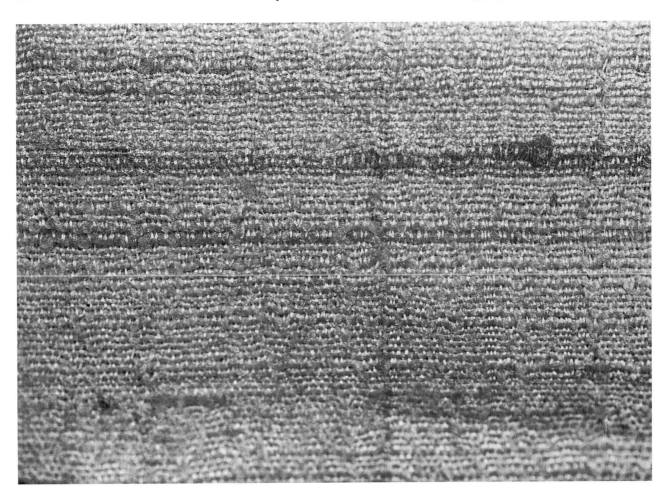

Doupion silk   author's collection

Duvetyn   Author's collection

be produced from it. This process also causes the fibers to be more parallel to one another. The process is executed by running the fibers through a multiple series of paired rollers, each successive set rotating at a greater velocity than the previous one. Drawing is done only to WORSTED yarns. See also WOOL.

DRILL

Drills are very durable fabrics that are much like DENIM, or jean, but differ in that they are of much heavier weight. They are a warp-faced twill, and occasionally embody herringbone effects. Drills are made of cotton or blends and are washable.

DUCHESSE

Duchesse is a SATIN, revered for its high luster. It is executed in a satin weave with a very high count of warp

threads. Originally made exclusively from silk in France, it is now imitated in manufactured man-made fibers. Today the term has become confusing for it is often applied to textiles that do not have a high thread count and vary in weave structure. Care must be taken in the purchase of the textile.

DUCK

Duck originated in Denmark, and is taken from the Danish word *doek,* meaning cloth. Originally, it was used exclusively for uniforms for sailors or for summer wear. Today, duck is a heavy plain weave cotton fabric. The term encompasses many fabric types, but is usually used to refer to those of the canvas family, although duck is much lighter than canvas. Duck is found in a wide variety of colors, including khaki, and is also printed. It is also available in a broad range of qualities.

DUPLEX PRINTING

Duplex printing is a technique that imparts a pattern to both sides of a fabric. With modern technology, registration of a pattern is so perfect that it is almost necessary to view the textile through a microscope to detect that it is a print and not a weave. The process is executed by sending the textile through a special duplex printing machine with rollers that print the textile. The technique is much like roller printing, but in duplicate.

See PRINTING.

DURABLE PRESS

Durable press is a technique that puts a finish on a garment, or on the fabric before the garment's manufacture, which causes the garment or textile to retain its shape and, most importantly, to shed wrinkles. This invention can perhaps be regarded as one of the most significant achievements in the modern textile industry, for it eliminated much of the drudgery of sprinkling and ironing.

See also FINISHES.

DUVETYN

Duvetyn is a fabric that was originally created in Paris, France, and is taken from the French word *duvet*, which means down. It is constructed in a twill weave and has a soft, napped, velvety surface that obscures the weave, particularly if it is created of wool. It is face finished, using a system of emery rollers that raise the surface fibers. The textile is then sheared so that the fibers are of equal length and it is then brushed. Today, duvetyn is created of many fibers including cotton, wool, silk and manufactured fibers. Although duvetyn is heavier, it is sometimes called SUEDE CLOTH.

DYES

Dyes are natural or manufactured substances used as coloring agents to impart color and decoration to fibers, yarns, textiles, fabric and many other materials. The coloring effect lies in a property possessed by only a relatively few types of organic molecules, that of selective absorption of only a portion of the spectrum of wavelengths of visible light. As a result of this property, the light that we see reflected from a dyed fabric contains only the part of the spectrum that was not absorbed by the dye, and hence the fabric appears colored.

Another important property of a dye is its permanence, that is, its ability to retain its coloring effect through a substantial amount of wear and cleaning. This property is known as the fastness of the dye. Fastness is determined by many factors, including the mechanism by which the dye attaches itself to the fiber, which in turn depends on the type of fiber and dye being used.

The materials from which dyes are made are called dyestuffs, which for most of history were various naturally occurring materials such as roots, bark, berries etc. Since the middle of the 19th century a great number of synthetic dyes has been created in laboratories around the world.

Natural Dyes

The use of natural dyes is probably as old as the use of cloth and clothing itself. When we attempt to look back to the origins of dyes and the dyeing process, however, we find the record is obscured by the lack of surviving ancient artifacts. Unlike many other forms of artistic expression, textiles, and thus the dyes they contain, deteriorate very rapidly when they are exposed to light, high humidity and moisture, and temperature changes. Those few textiles that have remained intact for many centuries have been found largely in dry, warm climates, limiting the scope of our understanding of the history of textiles and dyes.

Thus for the earliest record of this subject we must turn to secondary sources, such as, for example, sculptures showing highly decorated clothing, of the Babylonians and Assyrians, that imply that those peoples must have employed dyes of some kind. There are records of early peoples of India referring to dyed textiles in religious ceremonies dating to 2500 B.C. Interestingly, a fragment of textile showing dye was found in India around Mohenjo-Daro that is dated approximately 5,000 years ago. The fragment, dyed with madder and also showing evidence of a mordant, or fixative, demonstrates a sophisticated attempt to create permanent dyes at a very early date. The Phoenicians, who were great traders, dealt not only in textiles that were dyed but in the dyes themselves. There is evidence that their dyes and fabrics were of high quality. They perfected a reddish purple dye from the shellfish *Murex* known as Tyrian purple, which became famous throughout the ancient world.

Perhaps the most tangible early evidence that we have of dyes and even the techniques used in dyeing in ancient times comes from the Egyptians, who, it is generally felt, brought dyes to Egypt from Persia. It is well established that by 2500 B.C. the Egyptians were using red and yellow shades in their dyeing. By 1450 B.C., the Egyptians were weaving intricate and delicate textiles and dyeing them in a wide variety of colors. Early and unrefined mordants were also being used to set the dyes at that time. One can conclude that the dyes were being used long before that time because of the sophisticated level of development that is evident in the textiles.

Thousands of examples of dyed textiles have been unearthed from Egyptian tombs dating back to the fifth century B.C. Dyed textile fragments of Greek origin also exist from the fifth to the first century B.C., having been unearthed in Crimea, and there are accounts of the dyes indigo, cochineal and saffron being used by 134 B.C.–5 A.D. Thus, it appears that wherever textiles have been found, we also find the universal urge to color and decorate them.

As one studies dyes worldwide, it is also possible to conclude that the knowledge of the art of dyeing and the materials themselves were disseminated among societies, at least in part, due to the constant wars in ancient times. As people fled the ravages of war and moved or were taken to new lands, they took their knowledge and dyeing materials with them.

One may speculate that the earliest forms of dye and dyeing techniques consisted merely of rubbing leaves or berries on a cloth for decorative purposes. As the interest in coloration grew, the dyes used began to be derived from those berries, plants and woods that rendered particular colors. Since most such natural colors fade or disappear rapidly with use, the attempt to make the dyes somewhat more permanent resulted in the use of a mordant. One of the earliest mordants was urine, and we know the Egyptians made great use of it in their advanced dyeing processes. At best, even with the developed Egyptian dyes, the color was unpredictable, but greatly favored were purple and a deep blackish red.

By the 14th century the dye industry was growing in importance in England and France, but the dyers themselves did not enjoy a prestigious place in society. Dyeing was seen as secondary to textile production itself. Only when books started to be printed during the 15th century was increased attention paid to pigments and the art of dyeing. During this time laws and regulations were enacted for the control of dyeing, one of the world's first attempts at quality control. It was during the 15th century in England that guilds for dyers arose, greatly improving the prestige of the profession.

In the 17th century very carefully controlled scientific experiments on dye formulas were conducted in Paris at the Academy of Science. The Academy published a series of books that classified dyes and described exact dyeing processes. These books remained influential for several hundred years. It was during the 18th century, however, that France led the world in the development of natural dyes that many feel will never be equaled. The dyes had a clarity of color, accompanied by a complexity of textile design, that was extraordinary.

Process

The process for refining natural dyes can be very complex, but remains much unchanged from its early introduction. The first step is collecting materials and the second is preparing the dye. The raw materials—berries, stems, bark, blossoms, etc.—are first crushed. Then they are simmered in a porcelain container in a small amount of water for several hours, depending upon the density of the material. Porcelain is used to prevent the leaching of metal or other substances into the dye, which would alter the color of the dye. The solution is then strained.

After these processes it is necessary to add a mordant to the natural dye. The study of mordants is an art in itself, for the type of mordant that is added to the dye causes it to render a certain color. Therefore, each "recipe" for a certain type of natural dye differs. Even following the same recipe on successive days may render a different color because the dyestuff material will have dried more.

The following list represents some of the more well-known natural dyes, including those used in ancient times.

A CHART OF COMMONLY KNOWN NATURAL DYES

*represents known ancient dye

* alkanet roots	red-purple-brown
* annatto	oranges
* barberry plant	copper, tan, green
* black walnut hulls	brown, tan
* black walnut leaves	gold
* bloodroot	orange, red, pink
chrysanthemum blossoms	yellow
* cochineal	purple-reds
* chamomile	yellow, gold
* cutch	brown
cockleburrs	brass, brown
coffee	tan
congo red	brilliant red
crab apples	pinks
dahlia blossoms	yellow
dandelion blossoms	lt. yellow

day lily blossoms	yellow
elderberries	green-grays
floribunda rose plant	tan
* fustic	yellow
goldenrod blossoms	yellow
goldenrod stems	gray-green
* henna	rust, red-brown
hickory	tan
hemlock bark	brown
hollyhock blossoms	orange, rust
* indigo	blues, greens
* kermes	scarlet
lavender	pinks
lily of the valley	yellow-green
* logwood	blue, black
* madder root	reds
marigold blossoms	yellow
mullberries	gray-lavender
multiflora rose plant	tan
* orchil lichens	purple
pecan hulls	golden brown
* pokeberry	reds
Queen Anne's lace	pale yellow
red cedar	red-brown
red oak bark	tan
white oak bark	gray
red onion skin	gold
* safflower	yellow, tan
* saffron	yellow, red
* sandal wood	red
sassafras	red, tan
seaweed	tan
sedge	yellow-green
sumac	tan, gray
tea	tan
tomato vine	red-brown
turkey red	brilliant red
tumeric	crimson
* turmeric	yellows
tyrian purple	deep purple
* weld	yellow
*woad	bright blue
yellow onion skin	yellow
zinnia blossoms	yellow

Synthetic Dyes

The year 1856 marks the beginning of a totally new era in the history of dyes, with the development of the first of what was to become a long list of synthetic dyes which gradually replaced natural dyes commercially because of their lower costs and superior fastness. Although natural dyes are no longer used in mass-reproduction dyeing, they are still used by artists and craftsmen the world over.

WILLIAM PERKIN, a young English chemist, created the first synthetic dye in 1856 while trying to make synthetic quinine. Called mauvine, it was a mauve dye produced from the coal tar distillate aniline. Perkin's work initiated a worldwide industry of research and production of synthetic dyes, which currently number in the thousands. Most of these are derived from coal tar distillates, including benzene, toluene, napthalene and anthracene, in addition to aniline.

No synthetic dyes are effective on all textile fibers. There are four major categories of dyes, based on the mechanism by which they become fixed to a fiber: by surface adsorption, ionic bonding, adhesion and covalent bonding. Each major category has one or more dye classes.

Physical Surface Adsorption. The two classes of dyes that attach to a fiber by surface adsorption are the direct dyes and disperse dyes.

Direct dyes are most effective on cellulosic fibers such as cotton and linen, which possess a strong affinity for adsorbing them directly from the dye solution. They are not particularly fast against washing. Certain direct dyes can be further developed to their final shade after they are fixed in the cotton by chemical reaction with azo or naphthol compounds. These are referred to as *developed dyes.*

Disperse dyes are used on fibers that do not absorb water (hydrophobic fibers), such as nylon, acetates, polyesters and other synthetics. They are aqueous suspensions of very fine and slightly water-soluble organic compounds, adsorbed by the fibers from a very hot solution. The water and light fastness of disperse dyes are quite good.

Ionic Bonding. The classes of dyes that attach to the fiber by forming ionic bonds with the fiber structure are mordant dyes, acid dyes and basic dyes.

Mordant dyes have an affinity for a metallic oxide that is applied to the fiber, rather than for the fiber itself. Various metals, such as tin, copper, iron, aluminum, and especially chrome, have been used for this purpose. The choice of mordant can affect the specific color produced by a given dye. Many of the ancient natural dyes, such as alazarin, madder and logwood, are mordant dyes as well as anthracene-derived synthetic dyes. A more recent development has been to combine the dye with the metallic compound in a water-soluble substance called a *pre-metallized dye*. This avoids the necessity for a two-step dyeing process, but requires a strong acid bath for fixing to the fiber. Mordant dyes and the pre-metallized form are used on protein fibers such as wool and silk, and occasionally on nylon. They achieve very good wash fastness and fair to good light fastness. The colors produced are rather dull.

Acid dyes are commonly used for dying wool and the other protein fibers. They require an acidic agent in the dyebath, which bonds to the positively charged ions on the fiber. A leveling agent such as Glauber's salt is used to promote even distribution of the dye throughout the fabric being dyed. Acid dyes are known for their brilliant colors with fair to good wash fastness and very good light fastness.

Basic dyes react similarly to the acid dyes, except that they bond to the negatively charged ions on the fiber rather than the positive sites. Acetic acid is used as a leveling agent. They can be used on protein fibers with a mordant such as tannic acid, where they produce exceptionally brilliant colors. However, their fastness on these fibers, particularly to light, is quite poor, which limits their usefulness. The main application of basic dyes now is in dying the acrylics, where their fastness is very good.

Pigmentation or Mechanical Adhesion. These dyes are characterized by very fine suspensions of water-insoluble pigments, which are made to adhere to the fibers by the action of resin binders in the case of printing dyes, or by undergoing an intermediate chemical state in which they

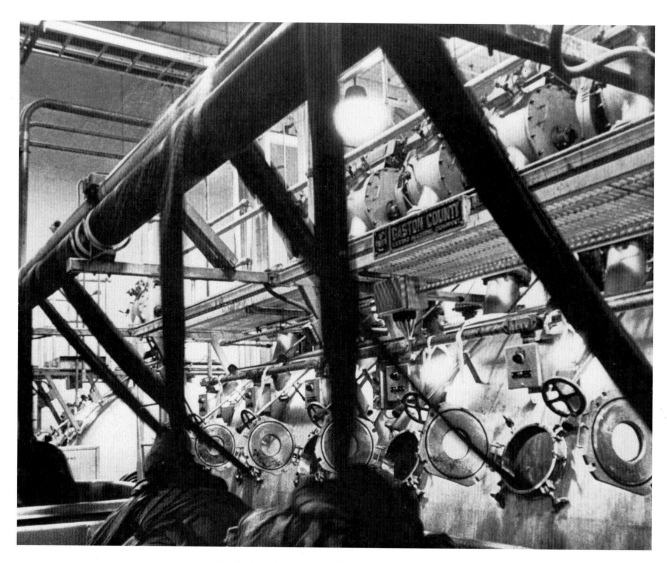

Vat dyeing   American Textile Manufacturers Institute

Spool used for yarn or warp threads in beam dyeing
Valdese Weavers, Inc.

become water soluble and have a great affinity for the fiber.

Vat dyes are among the oldest of known dyes and display the greatest fastness for washing or light exposure. Ancient examples are indigo and Tyrian purple. Modern vat dyes are synthetic. Vat dyes are all insoluble in water and must be changed chemically in order that they may enter into solution and be taken up by the fiber. The term "vat" refers to the original process whereby the dyestuffs were fermented in large vats to remove oxygen, a process known as chemical reduction. Today reduction to a colorless or "leuco" form is accomplished by combining the dyes with a reducing agent such as sodium hydrosulphite. These reduced dyes are soluble in an alkaline solution and have strong affinity for cellulosic fibers, and somewhat less for protein fibers. After this process, the dye is converted to its final color through oxidation by exposure to the air.

Vat dyes are most successfully used on cotton, rayon and silk.

Sulfur dyes resemble vat dyes in that they must be reduced to a soluble state for the dyeing process. They are a fairly inexpensive way to dye cotton with better fastness properties than the direct dyes.

Azo dyes are perhaps most noted for the brilliant reds attainable on cotton, with very good fastness. The fiber is first immersed in a colorless alkaline solution of naphthol, called the coupling component. The second stage is to add a diazoic salt, which reacts with the naphthol to produce a colored dye within the fiber structure.

Covalent Bonding. The inability to achieve acceptable color fastness in cellulosic fibers except through the difficult and expensive vat process led to research for a dye that could attach to cellulose via a strong covalent (molecular) chemical bond. This resulted in the

Spool emerging from the dye vat after dyeing process
Valdese Weavers, Inc.

development in 1956 of fiber-reactive dyes by Imperial Chemical Industries in England.

Reactive dyes can be used to dye rayon and silk, as well as all the cellulosic fibers. When salt is added to the solution containing the reactive dye, it reduces the solubility of the dye, so that its likelihood to be adsorbed by the surface of the fiber is enhanced. This is called the *exhaust* stage of the process. Leveling, or the even spreading of the dye, can occur in this stage, because no chemical bonding or fixing to the fiber has occured. Such bonding takes place in the second stage, when an alkali such as sodium carbonate is added to the solution. Repeated rinsing and soaping remove the unfixed dye.

Synthetic dyes have become increasingly important because they are not only easier to use, but the color can be standardized. With present technology, colors are tested and monitored by computer for color accuracy during the dyeing process.

There are special dyes for manufactured textiles that are applied either before or after extrusion. If they are applied before extrusion it is done in a process called solution or melt dyeing. If applied after extrusion it is called cross-dyeing. The new dyes and their techniques have allowed wide and varied changes to occur in the dyeing and printing of textiles.

Methods of Dyeing

Many different processes are used in dyeing fabrics.Some of the most common methods are listed below.

Jig Dyeing. A dyeing process during which a roll of fabric passes through a dye bath in a continuous motion while being held at full width until the desired color is achieved. The fabric may be sent through the dye bath many times until the desired hue and chroma are achieved.

Piece Dyeing. A dyeing process during which a fabric is twisted like a rope and continuously passed through the bath until the desired color is achieved.

Beam Dyeing. A special method of dyeing yarn that is to be made into textiles. The process involves the winding of the yarns or warp threads around spools or packages. The spools are placed in a special vat and the dyes are spread through the fiber from the center out. The process is then reversed and the dyes are sent from the outside to the inside. Cotton yarns and beamed warp yarns are most often dyed in this manner.

Bale Dyeing. In bale dyeing, the warp yarns in the textile are sized to make them more crisp, but no other finishing technique is employed. The fabric is then run through a cold water dye bath. The sized yarns readily accept dye, whereas the filling threads do not. This results in a two-tone effect in the fabric. CHAMBRAY is imitated in this manner.

Pressure Dyeing. Pressure dyeing refers to any of a number of dye processes in which the dye and the material to be dyed are enclosed in a pressure vessel, which allows the dyeing to be done at temperatures above the normal boiling point of water.

Solution Dyeing. When a coloring agent is introduced into the polymer solution of a manufactured fiber before extrusion, the process is called solution dyeing or melt coloring. The color thus becomes part of the fiber itself, and textiles made from solution dyed fibers are extremely colorfast.

Chain Dyeing. Chain dyeing refers to a special dye process for delicate fabrics that prevents stretching. In preparation for the process, fabric pieces are connected like links in a chain, forming a continuous loop. They are then placed on a reel and run in a continuous manner through a dye bath. Chain dyeing is sometimes called continuous dyeing.

Fall-on Prints. Fall-on prints refers to a technique by which dyes are applied to a fabric by printing, and are caused to overlap one another, creating different colors or tones.

See also AZO DYES; DEVELOPED DYES; DIRECT DYES; PRINTING.

Interior of beam dyeing vat   Valdese Weavers, Inc.

E

ELASTOMER

An elastomer is a synthetic rubber product that has the capability of being stretched to many times its original length and to return to its original length. Specifically, the American Society for the Testing of Materials (ASTM) requires that, to qualify as an elastomer, a substance should be capable of being stretched repeatedly to at least three times its original length, and upon release of the applied stress, to return with force to its approximate original length. As with natural rubber, elastomers derive their elastic properties from their molecular structure, and should not be confused with so-called "stretch yarns," which derive a limited amount of stretch from some mechanical modification of the yarn or weave structure.

Elastomeric textile yarns can be extruded or cut from a sheet of rubber. The primary examples are those based on SPANDEX and neoprene.

ELECTROSTATIC PRINTING

Electrostatic printing is a process by which wet fabric is drawn under a patterned stencil, over which powdered dyes are suspended. The fabric is given an electrostatic charge that attracts the powdered dye. It dissolves upon contact with the wet textile, creating a pattern. The textile is then heat dried.

See also PRINTING.

EMBOSSING

Embossing is the treatment of fabric with engraved heated rollers that impart a raised design to the textile or that flatten certain sections of it. Early on in the development of this technique the embossing was not permanent, but now resins have been developed that will resist water and dry cleaning solutions, giving the embossing a lasting quality. Embossing is executed on cotton, linen and manufactured fiber and on both flat-faced and napped textiles.

See also CALENDERING; FINISHING; VELVET.

EMBROIDERY

Embroidery is an art and a craft that has been practiced for centuries as a means of ornamenting clothing and textiles. One may define any type of embroidery by saying that it is ornamental needlework.

Embroidery is found not only on simple clothing, but also on extravagant evening wear, as well as lingerie.

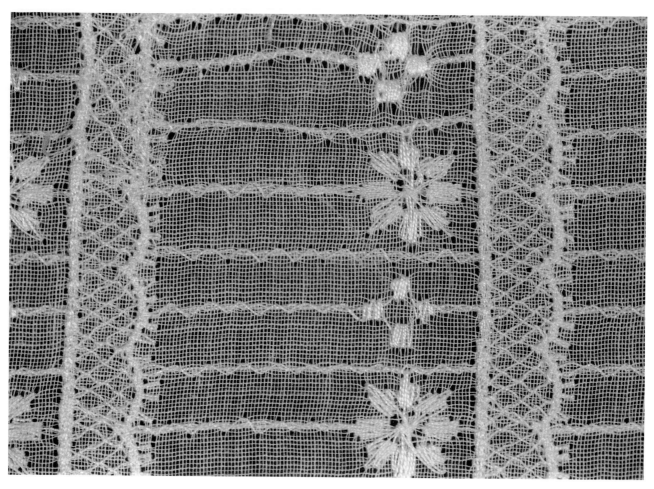

Schiffli embroidery (cotton)   Author's collection

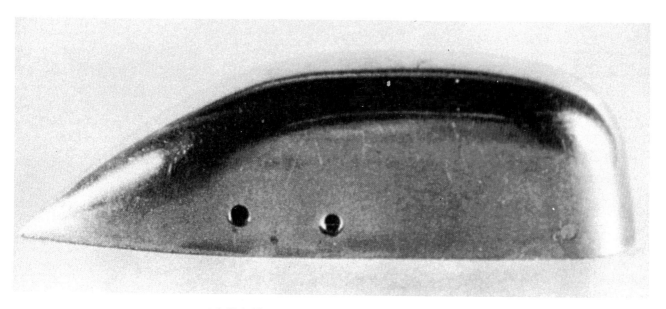

Schiffli bobbin   Schiffli Manufacturers Promotion Fund

Schiffli machine   Schiffli Manufacturers Promotion Fund

Programmed design with punched paper   Schiffli Manufacturers Promotion Fund

Various types of embroidery can often be identified by the region in a country where it is produced, and the techniques and colors used tell us much about the materials that are available as well as the character and social customs of the people of those regions. From sequined embroidery to needlework samplers, embroidery is very much a part of our history.

Embroidery dates to such early times that its origin is not recorded. We do, however, have evidence of its existence in China and India, as well as in Egypt centuries ago. There are references to gold thread embroidery from as early as the 12th century. As the craft grew, different countries developed different techniques, and when the practice was still executed by hand in Europe, thousands were employed. Embroidery was at this stage so costly that only the wealthy could afford it.

In the 1800s a very small and somewhat limited step was taken to create a small hand-powered embroidery machine. Limited as it was, the process allowed embroidery to become more affordable. In the 1860s a machine with 24 needles was invented that could be powered by hand or electricity. It was this step that truly allowed embroidery to be within the grasp of the common man. As the machine was further refined, it came to be called the "schiffli," which in German means small boat. This name refered to the machine's bobbin, which was shaped like a boat. Improvements have been made continually, and today most machine embroidery in the world is done by the schiffli machine. The modern schiffli machine is 65 feet long and 16 feet high, contains

Embroidered cotton   Author's collection

1,026 needles and weighs 10 tons. In the United States alone, 365 companies are involved in making a wide variety of schiffli embroidery. Most of them are centered in an area in New Jersey that produces 85% of the embroidery of the entire United States.

Today, many of the huge embroidery machines are run by computers. However, though the machines may be doing the meticulous work that was once done by hand, it is still the artist and craftsman, creating the designs for the finished product, that cause embroidery to retain its very high standard of quality and artistry. After a design is created, it is recorded by computer on long rolls of paper. These programs control the movements of the needles as fabric is passed through the machine. The output is continuously monitored by computer.

LACES and eyelet are also created on schiffli machines. However, lace is produced on a backing that is later dissolved, in a process called aetzing, leaving delicate lace patterns in the fabric.

END

End is a term that refers to the weaving process. The warp of a textile is created by numerous threads or yarns that run vertically in the textile. Each thread or yarn is called an end.

See also WARP; WEAVING.

ÉOLIENNE

Éolienne is a textile whose name is derived from Eolus, the Greek god of the winds. Éolienne is executed in a plain weave and is distinguished by its airy and delicate hand, which is created by a low thread count. Often silk is used, but éolienne is also found in a blend of silk with cotton and manufactured fiber. Ocassionally, cotton of a heavier nature is used in the weft, which causes it to have a slight ribbed character. A finishing process is used on the fabric that imparts a high luster.

ÉPINGLÉ

The term épinglé is taken from the French verb to pin. The textile has existed for four centuries, and was first created of silk. Today it is created in acetate, rayon or worsted and is characterized by alternating large and small ribs, causing a pebbled effect. Contrasting threads are often used, which enhance the pattern in the textile. Épinglé is executed on the JACQUARD loom.

ESKIMO CLOTH

Eskimo cloth is an overcoating fabric with a thick nap, generally made with a five-harness satin weave on the face and back, or with a twill weave showing three-quarters of the warp on the face. It is dyed in the piece or made with wide, bold stripes, which generally run in the direction of the filling in the finished garment.

ÉTAMINE

Étamine comes from the French word that means sieve, and was originally used for sifting. It was made of cotton, linen or wool. Today étamine is a worsted fabric executed in a two up, two down twill, and is finished with a very short nap. A finer version of étamine is étamine glacée.

EVEN SIDED TWILL

See TWILL.

EXTRUSION

Extrusion is a step in the process by which all MANUFACTURED FIBER is made. A solution of the raw fiber material, similar in consistency to thick syrup, is forced through a device containing from one to many holes, called a spinneret. The liquid solidifies after it passes

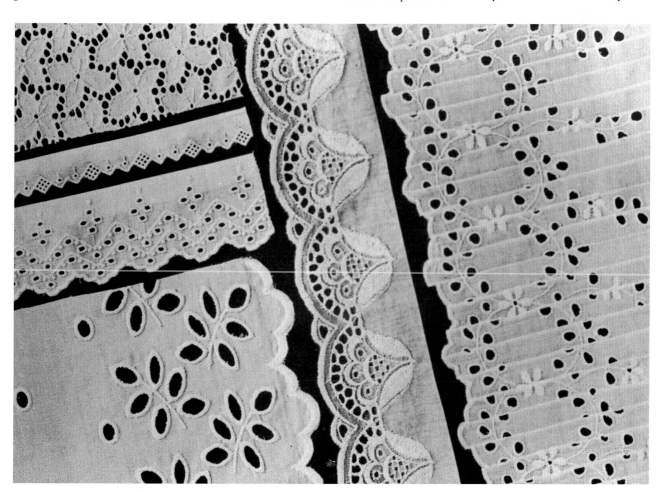

Eyelet and embroidered fabric produced by schiffli machine   Schiffli Manufacturers Promotion Fund

Spinneret   American Fiber Manufacturers Association, Inc.

through the spinneret, forming fibers. (The process is called spinning, although it bears no resemblance to the term SPINNING as applied to the making of natural yarn.)

Extrusion can produce fibers in many different cross-sectional shapes, depending on the configuration of the holes in the spinneret. Dye can be added to the fibers either before or after extrusion.

The process by which the silkworm makes silk fiber is also called extrusion.

EYELET

Eyelet can be found in a variety of patterns and colors. Eyelet is often done in an all-over pattern that covers the entire fabric surface from selvage to selvage, and can be applied to a wide range of fabrics, such as lawn and organdy. Eyelet is achieved by sets of knives, or "bohrers," that puncture the fabric. As the knives retract, needles stitch around the holes to prevent fraying and to create the see-through look. Eyelet is also used for a wide variety of exquisite edgings and trims.

See also EMBROIDERY.

FABRIC

Fabric is any cloth that is woven, knitted, felted or knotted with fiber.

The fibers used to create textiles fall into several categories:

Animal Fiber. Fiber from an animal can be either internal, such as sinew, external, such as WOOL, hair and fur, or secreted, as in the case with SILK.

Plant Fiber. Fiber that can be used in construction is found in many plants and within the plant in various areas. Two examples of plant fiber are COTTON and LINEN. Cotton is an example of fibrous hair surrounding seeds. Linen is taken from the stem of the flax plant. In past centuries bark was also processed and used in the creation of clothing but is rarely employed today.

Manufactured Fiber. Manufactured fiber is extruded through the use of a spinneret and consists of materials that are mineral based, protein based, cellulose based or are synthesized.

The fiber is constructed in one of four ways:

Woven. A loom is used to create a woven textile. Horizontal and vertical yarns are stretched on the loom. The vertical yarns are called warp. The warp yarns are interlaced horizontally with yarns called weft. Weaving can be done by machine or by hand. See WEAVING.

Knitted. Knitted textiles are created through the use of a continuous yarn and can be executed either by hand or machine. When machines are employed, single, double or multiple needles may be used, creating interlocking loops forming the fabric. See KNITTING.

Felted. Felted fabric is created by using pressure, heat and moisture to cause a matt of conglomerate fiber to interlock with itself, forming a textile. Felted fabrics are most often created by machine.

Knotting. Knotting is used to create very open textiles such as net and is executed through the use of a series of knots that are intersected by threads.

The three main weaves employed in the construction of fabric are PLAIN, SATIN, and TWILL WEAVES. Any variation upon the three main weaves is called either a novelty or a specialty weave.

For types of fabric described in this volume, see COTTON; LINEN; MANUFACTURED FIBER; SILK; WOOL; and the Subject Index. For information about the production of fabric, see DYES; FINISHING; PRINTING; SPINNING; WEAVING.

FABROGRAPHY

Fabrography is the art of printing designs on textiles by use of screens, stencils, rollers or by heat transfer methods.

See PRINTING.

FACE

Face refers to the "right side" of a fabric. Face-finished fabrics are those in which a printed design or pattern is seen only on the right side of the textile, or those which have an obvious nap or one-sided finish. Most textiles have a rather obvious face. Some important fabrics in this category are melton, chinchilla, camel hair and broadcloth. Some fabrics are created with both sides so identical it is difficult to differentiate between the two sides.

FAILLE

Faille is a plain weave textile executed by using heavier yarns in the weft than in the warp, creating crosswise ribs. The textile is distinguished by its deep luster, excellent drapability and very flat ribs. Faille is made using a wide variety of fibers, including silk, rayon and acetate, as well as other manufactured fibers. Faille is considered to be a member of the GROSGRAIN family.

FEDERAL TRADE COMMISSION

The United States Congress created the Federal Trade Commission, or F.T.C., in 1914 to administer all statutes

and rules enacted by that body, among them the TEXTILE FIBER PRODUCTS IDENTIFICATION ACT and the WOOL PRODUCTS LABELING ACT.

FELT

Felt refers to a non-woven fabric that has a conglomerate, or indiscriminate surface. A true felted fiber does not use any bonding agents. Instead, wool, fur, plant, or manufactured fibers are matted and caused to interlock through the use of heat and pressure. Felting is one of the most inexpensive ways to create fabric. Felted fabric is not elastic and is not as strong as woven textiles, usually making it less desirable as an apparel textile, with the exception of wool felt, which is extremely strong but is rarely produced today.

The felting process has a long and very rich history. It is clear that it existed in ancient times and may have

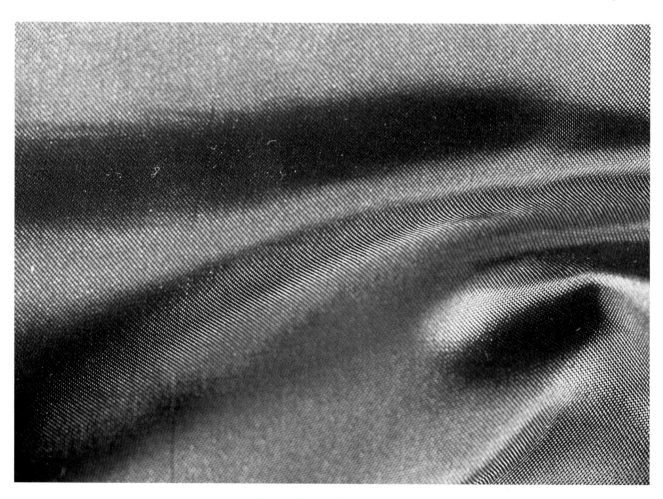

Faille (silk)   Author's collection

Felt (manufactured fiber) Author's collection

sprung up in Central Asia. It is believed that wool was found in this form long before weaving techniques had been developed. The early felting processes were quite simple. The fiber was spread in an even layer and moistened. It was then pounded as it was rolled. The process was applied repeatedly until very gradually the fibers begin to adhere to one another, creating a usable fabric.

Today the felting process is very sophisticated and is accomplished in one action involving the application of heat, pressure and chemicals. The process is so highly developed that the felt is finally set in width very accurately through the use of a machine called a finishing range. Felt now comes in various widths, and those felts that are produced from manufactured fibers are stronger than those of natural fibers. They also tend to have far greater clarity of color than felts of previous times.

The term felt refers to the ability of the fibers to interlock with one another.

See also NON-WOVEN FABRICS.

FIBER

Textile fibers are those materials, either natural or manufactured, that can be spun, felted or extruded to produce fabric. They must have a number of physical properties, such as strength and elasticity, durability, softness, good color and an affinity for dyes.

Natural fibers include those obtained from the coats of animals, like sheep, goats, camels, rabbits, llamas and alpaca, usually classified as wools. Silk is produced in a thread-like filament secreted by the silk caterpillar, or silkworm as it is commonly called. Natural fibers are also taken from the seeds, leaves and, most often, from the bast fiber of plants. The most common bast fibers are flax, jute, ramie and hemp. Bark is also used infrequently to create a felted fiber. Rarely, minerals, such as asbestos, are used for fabrics. Metals like gold and silver are also used in the form of flat threads that can embellish or be woven into a textile, although this practice is now becoming rare.

Singeing America Textile Manufacturers Institute

Manufactured fibers consist of those organic polymers that can be mechanically extruded into filaments usually referred to as synthetic fibers. Important examples of synthesized fibers are nylon, acetate and polyesters.

See COTTON; LINEN; MANUFACTURED FIBER; SILK; WOOL.

FILLED CLOTH

A filled cloth is one that has had special treatments in which a starch or other filling substance is added to close the spaces between the threads. The process also increases the weight of the fabric and can be used to create patterned effects. Filled cloth should not be confused with filling (weft) yarns. It is important to know if a garment or yardage has been filled, for many of the substances used in the filling process are removed with washing or dry-cleaning. Further, if a textile such as silk has been weighted with metallic salts, it will cause the textile to degrade over a period of time.

FILLING

Filling is an important technical term that is often confusing. Very simply, it is another name for weft. Weft and filling are also called woof, though fortunately the term is now less common. Each weft or filling thread is called a pick. In WEAVING, the weft or filling threads always run crosswise of the textile, against the warp grain, while the WARP threads run lengthwise.

FINISHING

The finishing of a fabric comes at the end of the manufacturing process. It is the stage at which a relatively plain and even ordinary cloth can take on a new character. Even those fabrics that have been dyed previously are finished. There are many hundreds of techniques used to finish fabrics. Some of the finishing processes add crease- and wrinkle-resistance to the fabric; sometimes the finishing processes add strength to the cloth through chemical and mechanical treatment. Finishes like calendering can also totally alter the complexion of the fabric's surface. Finishing can also help reduce the problem of shrinkage.

One of the first processes that is carried out in most finishing is singeing, or the burning off of fibers that extend from the surface of the fabric. The fabric itself is not damaged because it passes through the machine quickly. With modern technology the operation of most finishing machines are computerized.

Most wools go through several finishing processes. They are finished by brushing to raise the ends of the wool fibers, forming a soft, fuzzy nap. Called face finishing, this creates a wool that is softer to the touch. The nap may be cropped and brushed in one direction, as is the case with wool broadcloth, or it can be processed to have a glossy surface, as with zibeline. On occasion it is sheared to take on a velvety smoothness and is called wool plush.

Worsteds go through less radical changes in finishing. Instead of brushing, the fabric is usually cut close to the surface to give the textile a somewhat crisp feel. If the worsteds are brushed so that the weave is not seen they are called "unfinished" worsteds.

The machines used in the finishing processes vary widely. One common device used for a wide variety of finishes is the open range, in which various finishes are applied to the fabric, which is then wound around heated cylinders on top of the ranges and dried.

COMMON FINISHES

AFTER-TREATING	After-treating is a process in which a textile is passed through a chemical solution in order to achieve a particular shade of color and to enhance its dye-fast qualities.
BACK-FILLED	Adds strength and firmness to a fabric through either the application of a heavy sizing to the back of the material, which may not be permanent, or the addition of extra filling yarn woven into the back.
BEETLING	The process of pounding or flattening a textile during the finishing process, taken from the old English word "beetle," which was a heavy wooden mallet. The

process compacts the warp and weft yarns. Beetling is executed to produce greater luster.

BONDING
The joining of two fabrics, or the joining of a fabric to some other material, such as foam, to add body and stability to a fabric. In some cases, it makes the fabric water repellent.

CALENDERING
A number of finishing processes that produce a smooth, flat, glossy surface free of wrinkles. The results are achieved by passing the fabric, usually cotton or linen, between heated rollers under pressure. The calendering is not always permanent and may disappear with washing. Some textiles are now sprayed with resins that cause the process to be more permanent.

DECATING
A finishing process executed by forcing steam through layers of cloth. The process causes an expansion of the fibers, creating a smoother, more lustrous surface. Principally used on wool, it is also occasionally applied to manufactured fibers.

DELUSTERING
A chemical process by which the surface of manufactured fiber is dulled.

DURABLE PRESS
A finishing technique that causes a garment or textile to retain its shape and shed wrinkles.

EMBOSSING
A treatment that imparts a raised design to a textile or flattens sections of it through the use of heated engraved rollers.

FLAT CURING
A finishing process that imparts to the fabric the property known as durable press, or permanent press. It is done by spraying the fabric with a resin, followed by a pressing process that uses far higher temperature and pressure than usual. This process is also applied to garments after they have been constructed.

Finishing range American Textile Manufacturers Institute

Drying American Textile Manufacturers Institute

FULLING — Used exclusively on wool, this process adds body and strength to the fabric by tightening the weave through controlled shrinkage. The fabric is wetted, passed between rollers, and washed.

GLAZE — A process similar to that of friction calendering, only with the addition of a starch or resin to the surface of the fabric, often making it somewhat spot resistant. The process is permanent if modern synthetic resins have been used.

HARD FINISH — Refers to a tightly woven fabric, such as woolen or worsted, that has not been brushed during the finishing process. The result is a hard surface with no nap.

MERCERIZING — The process of immersing cotton in caustic soda (sodium hydroxide), which causes a permanent swelling of the fiber, imparting to the cotton a greater luster. This also results in increased textile strength and affinity for dyes.

PALMERING — A process through which textiles are compressed causing the face of the textile to become smooth and hard.

SIZING — Any chemical or compound that is added to a textile to change its innate qualities, causing it, for example, to become more rigid or crisp. Most often it is done by the addition of Kaolin, Fuller's earth or Chinese clay (all forms of hydrated aluminum silicate).

SWISSING — A roller process by which some cotton textiles are compressed giving them a smooth surface.

WEIGHTING — Weighting is a finishing process that employs the addition of materials to the textile to produce greater body. This is done by adding sizing agents (see sizing) synthetic resins or metallic salts to the textile.

FLANNEL

Flannel originated in Wales and is taken from the Welsh term *gwlamen*, meaning "akin to wool." Over a period of time the term was contracted to flannel. Flannel does not refer to a particular fiber type—flannels are created in cotton, wool and manufactured fibers—but rather to the weave used, which is in the majority of cases a plain weave and to a lesser degree a twill weave. Both have a slightly napped surface. The textile is created in both heavy and medium weights. It is characterized by a dull finish that obscures the weave. Wool flannel has excellent draping qualities and is used extensively in the tailoring of mens' and womens' suits.

The term outing flannel refers to a cotton textile that is executed in a twilled or plain weave and napped on one or both sides. It is generally of a much lighter weight than flannel and also comes in a wide variety of colors and qualities.

Flannelette is another type of flannel that is always made of cotton. It is executed in a plain weave, is light of weight, is napped on one side only and is often used for infant clothes and sleepwear.

FLAX

Flax is a multicellular vegetable fiber that is extracted from the fibrous bark of a plant belonging to the order Linaceae, species *Linum usitatissimum*. It is the plant from which LINEN is created.

FLOAT

Floats appear when a warp or filling yarn covers two or more adjacent threads. This type of interlacing causes long yarns to be exposed, or float, on the surface. Because the floats lie in a regular manner, light reflecting

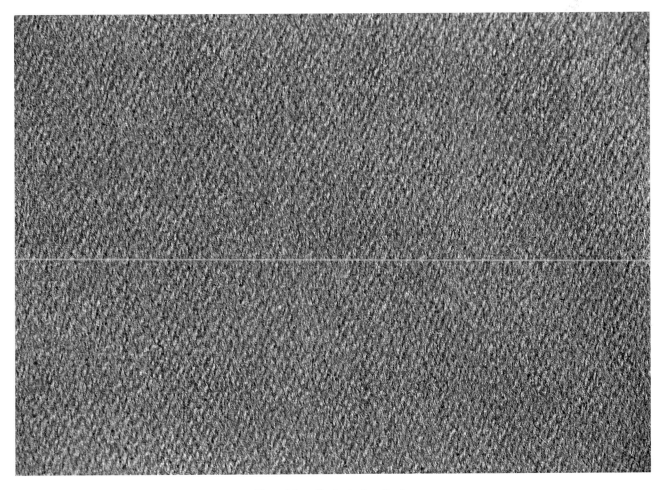

Flannel (wool)   Author's collection

on the fabric gives it a highly lustrous surface. SATIN is an example of a textile with a float structure. The longer the float, the higher the luster, but the easier it is to snag or catch the surface of the textile. Textiles with float structures must be treated as napped fabrics, i.e., pressure should not be applied to the face of the textile.

See also WEAVING.

FLOCK PRINTING

Flocking refers to the application of fine particles of natural or synthetic fiber, often in a regular pattern, to an adhesive-coated textile surface.

The process of flocking is thought to have existed as long ago as 1000 B.C. At that time the Chinese were using resin glue to bond natural fibers to fabrics. Fiber dust was strewn onto adhesive-coated surfaces to produce flocked wall coverings in Germany during the Middle Ages. In France, flocked wall coverings became popular during the reign of Louis XIV. Today the art of flocking incorporates established principles of physics and chemistry with modern technologies of synthetic fibers, high-voltage electrostatics and polymeric adhesives to produce increasingly sophisticated and unique products.

Flocked fibers are usually applied to adhesive-coated surfaces either mechanically, electrostatically or by a combination of both techniques. Mechanical flocking can be further classified by windblown or beater-bar techniques. Electrostatic flocking uses a pneumatic process to propel fibers toward a surface in a windstream.

Regardless of which technique is used, flocking involves the following steps:

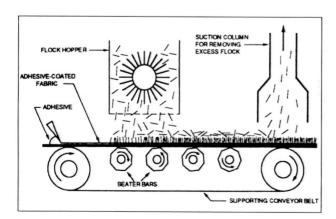

Beater bar method   American Flock Association

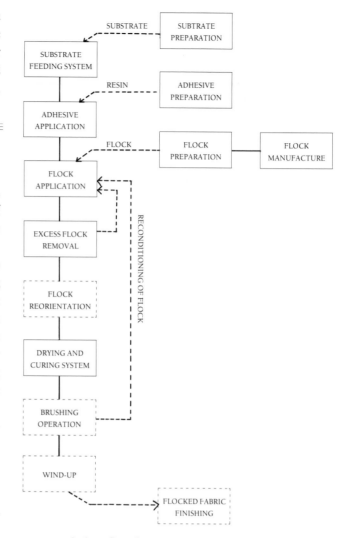

Flocking flow chart   American Flock Association

1. Application of the adhesive, sometimes in figures or patterns.
2. The flocking process, or distributing the flocking material on the surface.
3. Cleaning, which ensures the removal of excess flocking material from the surface.
4. Drying and curing of the adhesive.
5. Final cleaning, which can entail the use of suction or brushing and beating.

The beater bar method of flocking involves the passage of an adhesive-coated substrate over a series of polygonal rollers that rapidly rotate to vibrate the substrate. The vibration is used to drive the fiber into the

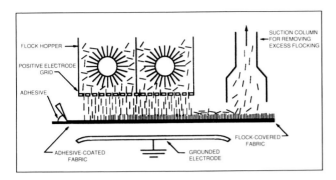

Electrostatic method American Flock Association

Electrostatic flocking is a modern technique that uses a field of static electricity to orient fibers and promote their alignment perpendicularly to the fabric. This technique is particularly effective with longer fibers. The adhesive-coated substrate passes through a high-voltage region between the grounded bed of the machine and a positive electrode grid through which the flocking fibers can pass. As they do so, they are given an electrical charge that aligns them with the electric field and causes them to be attracted to the adhesive where they become embedded. Most fibers adhering to the adhesive-coated surface are perpendicular to it, giving a dense pile finish.

adhesive. Fibers are fed to the substrate through a flock hopper.

Windblown mechanical flocking uses an airstream to deliver the fibers to the adhesive-coated surface.

Fabrics that are most often used for flocking are knits, drills, sateens, and twills, in rayon, cotton and polyester/cotton blends. Many of the adhesives that are being used now have very high resistance to solvents and thus are dry cleanable. They also are washable and possess flame retardancy in many cases. The flock itself is

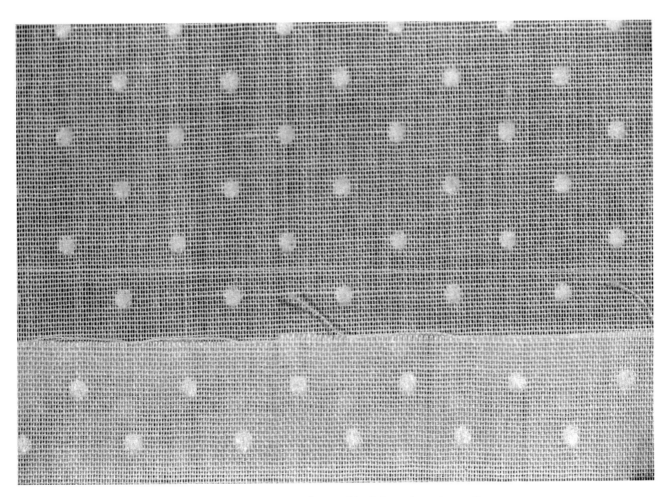

Flocked dotted swiss showing front and back (cotton) Author's collection

usually cut from fabric cuttings such as cotton, nylon, rayon and polyester. Each type has its own unique qualities.

Once a fabric is flocked it can be subjected to many finishing processes. For example, it can be embossed, so that patterns appear in the flocking. The flocked surfaces can also be printed, usually by transfer printing methods, or they can be printed by screen.

Flocking is a very large manufacturing business. More than 200 American companies are involved in the flocking industry, as are many more in Europe. In the United States the industry is supported and promoted by the American Flock Association.

See also APPLIED PRINTING; DESIGN FLOCKING; DOTTED SWISS.

FOULARD

Foulard textiles were originally created as handkerchief fabrics. They are delicate, and have a distinctive luster and a soft hand. They are most often executed using a twill weave that is dyed or printed, often with medallions, paisleys or other small, regular patterns. Originally they were created in silk but today they are found in acetate, silk and manufactured fibers.

FRENCH SYSTEM

The French system is one of three systems employed in the spinning of yarn. (The other two are the BRADFORD SYSTEM and the AMERICAN SYSTEM.) The French System was created during the 19th century and varies greatly from the Bradford System in that it spins fibers that are shorter in length ($1\frac{1}{2}$"–$2\frac{1}{2}$"). The French System does not twist or oil the fibers prior to spinning but holds them in place through a series of pins through which combs move. The yarns that are produced using this method are not as smooth as those produced by using the American or Bradford Systems.

See also SPINNING.

FUGITIVE DYES

Used to describe dyes that are not altogether fast to washing or to dry cleaning. Dyes may also deteriorate when exposed to sunlight or variations in humidity and temperature. Deterioration can also result from using a faulty mordant or by not mordanting properly.

See DYES.

FULLING

The process of fulling, exclusively used on wool, gives these fabrics body and strength by tightening up the weave through controlled shrinkage. The fabric is wetted, then passed between rollers, and washed. The greater the shrinkage, the stronger the fabric. Wool meltons and doeskins are tightened by fulling to the extent that the weave structure is completely obscured.

G

GABARDINE

Gabardine fabric is Spanish in origin, and dates back to the Middle Ages, when it was called *gabardina,* meaning protection. It was originally a wool fabric used exclusively for capes.

Today, gabardine is a very durable, firmly woven TWILL worsted with a hard, clear finish that shows single diagonal lines running from bottom left to top right on the face of the fabric, which is caused by using a greater number of warp threads than weft thread. When the fabric is to be made into men's suiting, the angle degrees of the twill is 63 degrees. The angle is frequently 45 degrees when it is to be used for women's suiting. Although wool is still the primary textile used, gabardine is now made with manufactured fibers as well. It comes in light, medium and heavy weights.

There also exists a cotton gabardine is which the threads have been pre-shrunk and mercerized. The mercerization process imparts a luster to the textile. On some occasions it is also given a napped finish on the back.

GATTAR

Gattar is a satin weave fabric made with a silk warp and cotton filling. It is known for its elegant luster and drapability. It is executed in a plain weave using 2-ply yarns in both warp and weft. The cotton filling or weft yarn gives the textile a slight texture. It is found in solid colors only. Gattar is used for elegant evening wraps.

GAUGE

Gauge is a measure of the number of needles per inch of width in knitting and hosiery. The greater the number, the closer and the finer the knit. In full-fashioned hosiery the gauge represents the number of needles per 1.5 inches. In circular hosiery knitting it represents the needles per inch.

See KNITTING.

Gabardine (wool) Author's collection

Georgette (silk) Author's collection

GAUZE

Gauze originated in Gaza, and was used as a veil or netting. The gauze weave is characterized by warps that are shifted out of parallel positions and then back again. Each one of the positions is held in place by a weft thread. Gauze can be open and lacey, or of very tight weave construction. Today gauze is created in silk, cotton, rayon and manufactured fibers. Gauze fabrics should not be confused with those produced by the LENO WEAVE, which is also a loose, open weave. The term is sometimes used erroneously in referring to any delicate, sheer fabric.

GEORGETTE

Georgette is a sheer but durable plain weave fabric, finished with a dull surface. The textile is characterized by crispness and body. Occasionally georgette is made with a crêpe-like texture. It is executed by alternating S and Z twist yarns in the weaving process. Georgette is usually done in silk, but now is found in manufactured fiber as well.

See S TWIST and Z TWIST.

GINGHAM

Gingham derives its name from the Malaysian word *gin-gan,* which means variegated. Gingham is created in a plain weave of lightweight or medium weight carded or combed cotton. It seldom comes in solid colors and is largely associated with checks and plaids in many colors. The yarn is dyed prior to the weaving process.

A variety of gingham, called tissue gingham, is made of much finer yarn, imparting a thinner, more delicate quality to the textile. Tissue ginghams also come in a wide variety of patterns and colors.

Cotton ginghams have a very high thread count. Today, a very fine worsted wool gingham is also constructed, as well as a gingham that is made of manufactured fiber.

GLAZE

Glaze refers to a finish applied to some textiles to impart a high luster. The textile undergoes the CALENDERING process, with the addition of a starch or resin to the surface of the fabric. The glazes often help to make the fabric somewhat spot resistant. Today many of the glazes can be washed repeatedly without losing their luster, for the finish has been baked into the fabric.

See also CHINTZ; FINISHING.

GLEN URQUHART PLAID

The Glen Urquhart plaid is a pattern of small woven checks alternating with squares of large checks, named after the distinctive wool tartan worn by the Scottish clan. Often called Glen plaid, it is usually created in very muted tones. The textile is often referred to as an overplaid, but it is a true double plaid in which lines cross one another at right angles. It is executed in a two up, two down twill weave. Glen plaids can be either woolen or worsted.

See also TARTAN.

GRADING

Grading refers to the classification of cotton, wool and other fibers in accordance with their evenness, length and strength. The methods of classification differ with each type of fiber, but the standards are set worldwide.

Gingham (cotton) Loven Fabrics

GRAIN

Grain refers to the direction and texture of the fiber in a given textile. Technically, there exists both a warp (vertical threads) and weft (horizontal threads) grain. The two grains should lie at right angles to one another. If they do not the textile is called off-grain. Straightness of grain is crucial to the art of sewing. If a textile is off-grain, it must be straightened before being used, which is accomplished by a wetting and stretching process. Unfortunately, some of the new resin finishes are sprayed onto the textiles; if that is done when the grain is not straight, the textiles are in a fixed off-grain state. This is found most commonly with cotton textiles. It is advisable to check the grain on a textile before purchasing it.

Straight of grain   Elaine Swenson

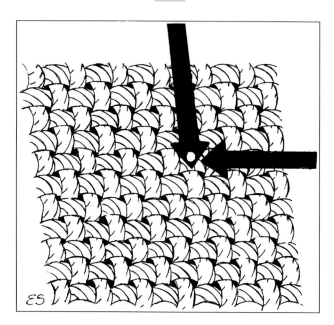

Off-grain   Elaine Swenson

GRANADA

Granada, taken from the Latin word *granum*, refers to the grainy quality of the textile. Granada is a fine face-finished worsted fabric made with a broken TWILL WEAVE that imparts a granular quality to the textile. It is woven with a cotton warp, with alpaca or mohair filling, imparting additional luster and softness to the textile.

GRANITE CLOTH

Granite cloth is a very hard-finished woolen fabric, which has an irregular pebbled surface. The surface is achieved by a special twist in the yarn. Granite cloth is often executed on a dobby loom, so that the pattern can be altered.

See LOOM.

GRAY GOODS

Greige, taken from the French word meaning natural, is considered the proper term to use for textiles that are in their natural state, that is, unfinished, undyed, or treated in any way. In the United States, greige is sometimes replaced with the term gray goods, which describes the same state. The term is an important one, for throughout the world there are mills that specialize in producing textiles and selling the yardage in its unfinished state, just as it comes off the loom. Other industries then specialize in finishing, printing, dyeing and bleaching the textile.

GRENADINE

Grenadine originated in Italy. It is created in many fibers, including SILK, WOOL, WORSTED, COTTON and MANUFACTURED FIBER. It is executed in a LENO WEAVE that is very open and light, in patterns of stripes, checks and patterns. It is given a finish that imparts a stiffness to the textile.

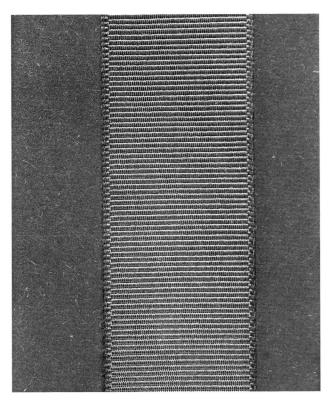

Grosgrain (silk) Author's collection

When grenadine is made with a silk warp and worsted or mercerized cotton weft, it is called satin grenadine. Executed in a SATIN WEAVE and often constructed on the Jacquard loom, satin grenadine is given a high luster during the finishing process.

GROSGRAIN

Thought to have originated during the Middle Ages, grosgrain is characterized by crosswise, or crossgrain, ribs. It is executed in a PLAIN WEAVE that employs larger threads in the weft than the warp. It is a tightly woven textile that bears a resemblance to FAILLE, but the ribs are much larger due to the larger size of the weft threads. The textile is available in both silk and manufactured fibers and occasionally cotton.

GROUND

The term ground refers to the background of a woven fabric, or that area that fills in between the designs, usually done in PLAIN WEAVE. If a design is printed onto the fabric, the original fabric is also called a ground.

HAND

Hand is a term referring to the physical properties of a fabric that give it a characteristic feel when held and manipulated in the hand. Such properties include varying degrees of roughness, smoothness, heaviness, lightness, crispness, elasticity, etc.

HANDSPUN

Handspun refers to the SPINNING of yarn or thread that is done entirely by hand. Yarns that are spun in this manner vary in thickness, lending an unmistakable rough character to the material. Although hand spinning is not employed in the mass market it is enjoying a resurgence among artists and craftsmen today.

HANDWOVEN

Handwoven refers to fabric that is entirely woven by hand. Handwoven fabrics have less precision and consistency of weave than machine-made fabrics and are considered by many to have more character. Handwoven fabrics are currently quite popular and many contemporary craftsmen use methods of dyeing and processing that are centuries old. Today, many fabrics are still being handwoven in India for the mass market in the form of brightly colored cottons. Handwoven woolen fabrics are also created in the Outer islands of the Hebrides primarily on the Isle of Harris.

See also HARRIS TWEED; MADRAS; WEAVING.

HARGREAVES, JAMES (1720–1778)

James Hargreaves, an English carpenter and weaver, is credited with perfecting methods of yarn spinning in the years 1754–1768. His most famous invention, the "spinning Jenny," named after his wife, was the first practical frame for the spinning of cotton. It operated by drawing the fiber using a carriage that could accommodate eight spindles at a time. By 1766 he had improved the frame so that it could accommodate 100 spindles. His invention not only speeded up the spinning process but was less costly. Hargreaves himself was beset by disgruntled workers who felt that his inventions threatened their livelihood. His home was burned in 1768 and he was forced to flee to Nottingham. But as in many other instances, technological innovation prevailed, and made possible a far larger enterprise, employing many more workers than would otherwise have been possible by continuing to employ the old methods.

See SPINNING.

Handwoven (wool) Author's collection

HARRIS TWEED

Harris tweed is the best-known Scottish TWEED. It is woven in the Outer Hebrides Islands, where it has been made for at least 300 years. Created in either a PLAIN or TWILL WEAVE, Harris tweed is characterized by its rugged durability and warmth. Natural dyes made from lichen and heather were used as colorants, which caused the fabrics to have very subtle tones. In the 1840s the fabric was adopted in fashionable circles for use in hunting and fishing garments.

Originally, all the steps in the processing and production of Harris tweed were done by hand, but today some of the processes are executed by machine. For example, fulling, which was done by pounding and jerking of the textile and gave rise to a very durable fabric, is now done by machine.

In 1909 the Harris Tweed Association was formed. It created its own orb trademark, which cannot be placed on a garment unless it is from the Hebrides Islands. The fabric is today considered desirable and exclusive.

HENRIETTA

Named after the consort of Charles I (1625–1649), Henrietta is executed in a twill weave meant to imitate CASHMERE. It originally consisted of a silk warp and worsted filling, but is now created in many blends. Henrietta is a very soft textile with a lustrous sheen when executed in silk and wool. Its drapability is excellent regardless of the fiber from which it is created. The textile is available in a wide range of weights and qualities.

Herringbone twill Author's collection

HERRINGBONE TWILL

Herringbone is executed in a broken TWILL WEAVE in a balanced chevron pattern that resembles the skeleton of the herring, for which it is named. It is also sometimes called arrowhead. Most often created in wool, it is found in many weights and qualities.

HICKORY CLOTH

Hickory cloth is a TWILL WEAVE fabric known for its durability. It is usually executed in a twilled cotton with colored yarns in the warp and white yarns in the filling, thus creating warp stripes. It comes in many colors, and today blends are used in this weave as well.

HOMESPUN

A PLAIN WEAVE of wool, homespun originated in the British Isles, where it was executed entirely by hand,
often at home. It was undyed and was characterized by its uneven quality and character, which was due to the hand weaving and spinning. Today, it is produced mainly by machine and is characterized by its strength and durability. It is available in a wide variety of weights and qualities.

HONEYCOMB

Honeycomb derives its name from the French Nid d'abilles, which means a "bird's nest." Honeycomb is a type of FLOAT weave fabric, often referred to as diamond weave, with an open, regular pattern caused by floating both the warp and the filling threads during weaving. Honeycomb is created in many fabrics. When executed in cotton it is made of very fine yarn and is often called waffle fabric.

HONG KONG

Hong Kong is a PLAIN WEAVE, ribbed fabric. The ribs are created by using a fine warp thread and a heavier weft thread. Hong Kong is found in a wide variety of qualities, the most superior being pure silk. It is usually found in plain colors.

Honeycomb (cotton) Author's collection

HOOKE, ROBERT (1635–1703)

Robert Hooke was an English naturalist that prophesied in 1664, in a book called *Micrographia* (1665), that it would be possible to chemically create a fiber that resembled silk. One hundred and sixty years later the prophecy came true when Count Hilaire de Chardonnet created the first synthetic textile fiber, which later came to be known as RAYON. ≡

HOPSACKING

Hopsacking was originally made exclusively of jute or hemp and was used for bagging. However, today the textile comes in a variety of weights and qualities and is created in many fibers, including cotton and manufactured fibers. Though the textile still retains its rough texture, it can be very refined and is found both in yard goods and apparel. Though commonly called BURLAP, true burlap is a coarser textile of jute or hemp. ≡

HOUND'S-TOOTH CHECK

Originally unique to a region of Scotland, hound's-tooth check is widely copied today. The fabric is executed in a broken twill with an irregular, four-point check. Though made of a wide variety of fibers, including MANUFACTURED FIBER, WOOL is still the most commonly used. ≡

HOWE, ELIAS (1819–1867)

Elias Howe was the American inventor of the sewing machine. He later stated that the fear that tailors and dressmakers had of losing their jobs to the machine was a greater obstacle than any technical obstacle he encountered. Born in Spencer, Massachusetts, Elias journeyed to Boston when he was quite young to learn the machinist's trade. It is unclear what events led up to his developing the sewing machine, but it is known that in 1845, at the age of 26, he had created a machine that could sew 250 lock stitches a minute. He could arouse

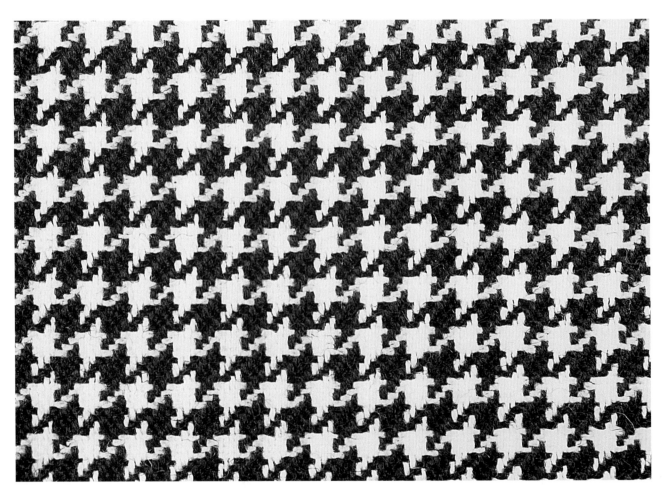

Hound's-tooth check (wool)   Author's collection

≡

Huckaback (cotton)   Author's collection

no interest in his invention, but nevertheless he patented the machine a year later. It is said that an enormous desire for wealth saw him through many years of abject poverty, and he continued his efforts to sell his machine, finally selling the rights to it to the English. However, in 1849 ISAAC SINGER started manufacturing his own sewing machines in the United States. Elias Howe went to court and fought a lengthy battle to establish his right to collect royalties on all of the sewing machines Singer manufactured. In 1854 he won his case. His dream of fame and fortune did indeed come true.

HUCKABACK

The term huckaback may be from the German word *hukkabak,* which refers to a peddler's wares, or from the toweling that was peddled by "hucksters" in England. Also frequently called huck, huckaback is a very firm fabric and is a variation of the PLAIN WEAVE, characterized by floats that create patterns on the surface of the textile and cause it to be more absorbent. Today, huck, or toweling is made both with cotton and linen.

I

IKAT

The word ikat is derived from a Malaysian word *mengikat*, which means to tie, knot, bind or wind. Ikat is one of the earliest types of textile printing. It is known that wools were being decorated using the ikat technique near the Caspian Sea as early as 500 B.C. The technique was also highly developed in India, Indonesia, Java and Peru. It is a resist form of textile decoration or embellishment, and is considered a planned method of tie dyeing. The ikat technique is achieved when the warp or weft yarns, or both, are tied for dyeing prior to the weaving process. When the yarns are woven, the ikat designs have a blurred effect, caused when the color areas do not coincide perfectly on the loom.

See also DYES.

ILLUSION

Illusion is a type of very fine net. It is executed by hand or machine using a knotting technique that creates a hexagonal pattern. It can be made of cotton, silk or manufactured fiber.

INTERLINING

Interlining is a fabric used as a support or stiffening to give a garment shape, particularly in tailoring. Sometimes an interlining is used to give added warmth as well. Interlinings are placed between the lining and the

Illusion silk Author's collection

garment fabric and are attached with special padding stitches that do not show through to the outside fabric layer. Today, some interlining materials can be bonded to a fabric through the use of heat. Interlining comes in a wide variety of predominantly manufactured fibers, as well as horsehair, canvas, crinoline and buckram, and batting of various kinds, including lambswool.

INDIGO

Indigo is a natural blue dye extracted from the stems and leaves of the *Indigofera tinctoria*, and *Indigofera anil* plants whose use dates back to ancient times. Until the

93

creation of synthetic dyes, from tar products it was used on cotton, wool and silk. Although indigo is no longer used for commercial dyeing, it is still used by individual artists and craftsmen.

See also DYES.

INTARSIA

A true intarsia knit fabric refers to one that has an inlaid design. The word comes directly from the Italian, meaning "inlaid."

See KNITTING.

JACQUARD

Jacquard refers to a complex and intricate weaving process executed on a type of power loom invented by Joseph Marie JACQUARD in 1801. The term also refers to fabrics or textiles woven by this process.

Prior to the development of the Jacquard loom, the complexity of design that could be woven into a textile on a loom was limited by the number of harness arrangements that could be used to create various shed configurations and the mechanisms that controlled the harnesses. The unique feature of the Jacquard mechanism lies in its control of individual warp thread in forming the shed for each weft thread or pick. Hundreds of these threads may be used to form the intricate patterns on the loom. The sequence in the configuration of the warp threads for each pick is pre-programmed and fed into the harness mechanism by a series of punched cards, very similar to the punch cards used in early versions of modern computers. (In this sense, Jacquard can be said to be the father of binary computer encoding.)

In the basic Jacquard mechanism, each warp thread passes through its heddle, which in turn is connected by a vertical cord with a weighted needle at one end. Punched cards are prepared with a pattern of holes through which individual needles can pass, thereby lifting the end connected to that needle. Each pattern of holes thus corresponds to a particular configuration of raised and lowered warp ends, forming the shed through which one weft pick passes. When the entire sequence of punched cards has been read, the pattern cycle is repeated, forming a regular pattern in the textile.

Jacquard power loom   Valdese Weavers, Inc.

Compared to the sophistication of other versions of the power loom, this control of each individual end in the Jacquard mechanism allows a virtually limitless complexity and size to patterns that can be created in the weave. The dobby loom, for example, is limited to approximately 24–30 harnesses, restricting it to small, relatively simple patterns of limited size in the weave.

It is difficult to overstate the impact of Jacquard's accomplishment on the textile industry. The original Jacquard loom has often been referred to as one of the most perfect machines ever made. Except for advances in speed of operation, as for example with the modern rapier shuttle, the basic operating principles have until recently remained essentially unchanged. In the last few years, however, two major advances have been made as a result of applying computer technology to the Jacquard loom.

The first of these advances is in the use of computers to aid in the design of the pattern to be woven. Traditionally, the pattern of holes that would create the Jacquard pattern had to be drawn by the designer pick by pick. Then the pattern had to be mechanically punched out on the cards, again pick by pick. Now it is possible, once the basic desired weave pattern has been drawn by the artist, for optical scanners to import the design to a computer that can color code areas of the design to the colors of yarns available at the loom, make variations of color combinations, and automatically produce the punched card sequence necessary to enable the loom to make that design.

The second advance, possibly the most important in the history of the Jacquard loom's development, is in computerizing the readout of the design pattern electronically rather than by the use of mechanical punch cards. In the latest version of Jacquard looms, the pattern codes are stored on hard disks, and actuate electromechanical lifting devices that are hooked directly to the heddles. As a result, the same loom can switch from one complex pattern to another with the push of a button, without the delay of having to physically change the entire stack of punched cards. The loom can even continue running as the pattern is changed by the computer. The accompanying photographs illustrate the capability of the Jacquard loom to produce highly complex patterns.

Pages 96 and 97: Jacquard textile   Valdese Weavers, Inc.

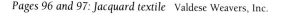

Tying warp threads   Valdese Weavers, Inc.

This scene was done by computerized Jacquard loom in silk measuring 8 ½" x 11"   SOMET of America, Inc.

A closeup shows the detail of the weave in an area measuring 1 ¾" x 2 ¾"   SOMET of America, Inc.

Other advantages of the computerized Jacquard lie in the absolutely play-free motion of the lifting mechanisms, allowing continuous loads at higher operating speeds than previously attainable. Prior to the development of these mechanisms, the limitation on speed of the Jacquard loom was in the "hook and knife" mechanism for lifting the harnesses. The mass and movement stroke of these mechanisms limited the machines to about 380 picks per minute with a fabric width of 190 centimeters. The capability of the machines with the new lifting mechanisms and computer readout of pattern has nearly doubled this speed. Thread tensions are maintained even when the loom is stopped, allowing weaving to resume with no wasted segments. The storage capacity of the program allows for pattern repeat sizes as large as over 50,000 picks, and weaving speed on a rapier loom can exceed 500 picks per minute.

Computer panel—electronically controlled jacquard loom
SOMET of America, Inc.

Jacquard punched cards Valdese Weavers, Inc.

JACQUARD, JOSEPH MARIE (1752–1834)

A Frenchman, Joseph Marie Jacquard is credited with the invention of the head motion for the JACQUARD loom, although many experiments had been carried out previously in attempts to create such a device. The Jacquard loom was first shown at the Paris Industrial Exposition in 1801. Many difficulties later beset the inventor. The French weavers saw the new loom as a threat to their livelihood and on several occasions Jacquard was mobbed and barely escaped with his life. Ultimately, his original loom was destroyed and Jacquard died in total poverty in 1834.

The short-sightedness of the weavers was overcome by the dramatic technical feats that Jacquard's loom achieved. Ironically, the Jacquard loom revived the flagging French textile industry and again brought

Above and left: Jacquard textiles   Valdese Weavers, Inc.

Jacquard computerized loom   SOMET of America, Inc.

prosperity to the city of Lyons. The basic principles developed almost two centuries ago by Jacquard, adapted to modern technology, still represent the epitome of the power loom.

See also LOOM.

JASPÉ

The term jaspé, or jasper, is taken from the Greek word *iaspis*, which means variegated. In ancient Greece it applied particularly to the color green. The fabric called jaspé is most often created of cotton and executed in a plain or twill weave. A variegated or shadowy effect is created in the textile by using two differently colored yarns that have been twisted together in the weaving process. Novelty jaspé has stripes and occasionally small dots. It is a very durable textile with variations in both weight and quality.

JERSEY

Jersey was first created on the Isle of Jersey, the largest of the Channel Islands between England and France. Originally, it was made of wool and was used for fishermen's clothing. The actress Lillie Langtry made the fabric somewhat famous for she was from Jersey and often wore garments made of the textile.

Today jersey has become a generic term for a knit or woven textile done in a PLAIN WEAVE or plain knit stitch without the distinct rib that many knit textiles have. It can be executed on circular, flat or warp KNITTING machines. Variations include a silk jersey, sometimes

Jersey Author's collection

called Milanese or tricot cloth, and a jersey flannel that is made of wool with a nap on one side. Jersey is also made of MANUFACTURED FIBERs, worsted and cotton.

JET LOOM

The jet loom is a modern high-speed loom in which a powerful jet of water or air propels the weft yarns through the shed. The loom, therefore, does not require a shuttle.

See LOOM.

JIG DYEING

Jig dyeing employs a roll of fabric that is suspended and held by the jig or dyeing machine. The fabric is slowly pulled through a dye bath. The process differs from other dye techniques in that the fabric may be sent through the dye bath many times in order to achieve the desired color. See DYES.

Jacquard showing computer versatility in changing patterns   SOMET of America, Inc.

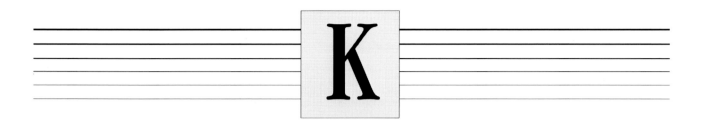

KASHA

Frequently spelled casha, kasha was originally made of vicuna, considered to be among the softest and most luxurious of textiles. The vicuna, not a domesticated animal, lives in the high elevations of Peru. It is now on the endangered species list and therefore its hair is not available on the commercial market. While most countries have laws that protect endangered species, ultimately the consumer must be aware of their endangered status and avoid purchasing articles created from their products no matter how tempting.

As textiles are no longer made from the vicuna, today kasha is made of a very fine wool or of a blend of CASHMERE and wool. It is executed in a twill weave. ═

KASHMIR

See CASHMERE. ═

KAY, JOHN (1704–1764)

John Kay is credited with having made some of the most revolutionary contributions to the textile industry through his improvements to the LOOM. Prior to his inventions, along with those of his contemporaries, Lewis PAUL, John Wyatt, James HARGREAVES, Richard ARKWRIGHT, Samuel CROMPTON, and Edmund CARTWRIGHT, textiles were woven essentially as they had been in antiquity.

John Kay's father owned and operated a woolen mill in Colchester, England. At a young age, John became an excellent machinist and engineer, and was put in charge of running the mill, where he made improvements in the carding machinery. He also improved the performance of the reed in beating the picks by making the reed of metal, including metal dents, which keep the warp ends separated. The metal dents provided a much faster and stronger beating than the traditional simple notches in the reed, resulting in finer, more durable textiles.

John Kay received his first patent in 1730, at the age of 26, for a machine that had the capacity to twist and card MOHAIR and worsted. He was also given a patent for what appears to be perhaps his greatest contribution, the fly shuttle, on May 26, 1733. (Some historians dispute this date, attributing the invention to the year 1738, because of the sudden appearance of the fly shuttle at that time.) In the old method of weaving, the shuttle was passed by hand back and forth. Kay affixed a race board beneath the warp of the loom and placed what he called a shuttle box at each end, with a spindle and picker (the mechanism that strikes the shuttle) on each box. A cord passed from each picker to a lever in the weaver's hand. As the weaver pulled the lever, the pick or shuttle would race through the warp threads.

Kay's was the first major modern improvement to the ancient hand loom, and weavers feared the improved productivity would mean the loss of their jobs. This led to a great deal of agitation and violence in Colchester. John Kay's home was burned and he fled to Leeds, where trouble followed him and he was nearly killed by a mob. He then fled to France, where he lived in poverty. His invention was capitalized on in his absence, and brought great prosperity to the mills. John tried in vain to persuade the English to honor his patent and pay him a small amount for his contributions, but he failed in the attempt and died in France in total obscurity and need. His son, Robert KAY, however, inherited his father's engineering genius.

See also LOOM.

KAY, ROBERT

Robert Kay, the son of John KAY, inherited his father's engineering genius and his contributions to the textile industry were so far sighted that some of the principles that he discovered or invented are still being used today in modern textile machinery.

Circular knitting machine
American Textile Manufacturers Institute

The most innovative of his inventions was the drop-box, which he invented in 1760. This device allowed one weaver to operate several shuttles at the same time on the same loom. These looms came to be called box-looms. Further, it was possible for many different kinds or colors of weft to be worked into the same fabric, thereby creating figures.

Robert Kay, in contrast to his father, enjoyed success and reward during his lifetime. He never recovered from the bitterness that he felt over the demise of his father and remained in France throughout his lifetime.

See also LOOM.

KERATIN

Keratin is the material that wool fiber, hair and horn are made of, and is chemically classified as a protein.

See WOOL.

KERMES

From the Persian word for "little worm," kermes is actually an insect that lives in oak trees. The famous and ancient dyestuff scarlet was created from the dried bodies of these insects. It is one of the oldest natural dyes known to man, most probably originating in Asia Minor.

See DYES.

KERSEY

Also called corsey, kersey takes its name from the village where it originated, Kersey, Suffolk, England, a woolen textile center. The earliest written records of kersey date to 1262. Kersey is a woolen fabric with a short nap that has been fulled so that it is very lustrous. There are many weights and qualities of this textile. Kersey is either ribbed or executed in a twill weave.

KNITTING

The word knit is from the Anglo-Saxon word *cynttan*, which means to create fabric by use of the hands. Early examples of knitting have been found in Egyptian tombs that date to the 5th century B.C. Knitting is known to have existed in England and Scotland as early as the 14th century. The first knitting machine was invented by the Reverend William Lee, an Englishman in 1589. The first power knitting machine was introduced in 1832, in Cohoe, New York by Egbert, Egberts and American. The

Stockinette The Wool Bureau, Inc.

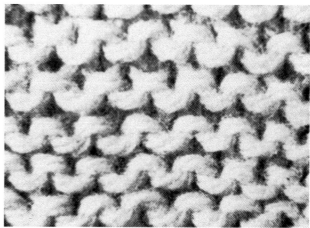

Purl knitting The Wool Bureau, Inc.

power knitting machine was not used in England until 1851.

Knitting is the construction of fabric by interlocking loops of one or more yarns. The loop is the basic structural unit in a knitted fabric. The bending of the yarn creates the loop. Originally done by hand, the fabric is created by slipping stitches from one needle to the other, making a new stitch with each change. Hand knitting is still popular the world over.

Today, there are many types of modern knitting machines, which have reached a state of great sophistication in weave and texture. The circular knitting machine produces jersey and double knits, as well as ribs and fancy jacquards. It has needles arranged in circles on a rotating cylinder and produces fabric in a continuous tube, from which garments are cut and sewn.

Hand-Knitting. From a purely technical standpoint there is only one stitch in knitting, the flat knit or stockinette stitch. For clarity however, the reverse flat or reverse stockinette stitch, is also referred to as a second stitch called purl. All other patterns in knitting are created by various combinations of these two stitches.

The stockinette stitch is smooth on the face, whereas the purl stitch has a pebbled surface. The complexity of any knitted garment lies in the hands of the creative artist and craftsperson who create it and the manner in

Weft knitting The Wool Bureau, Inc.

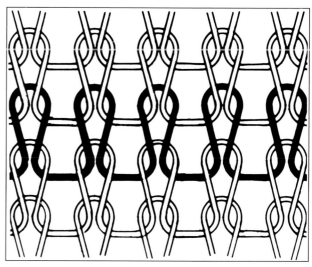

Warp knitting The Wool Bureau, Inc.

which they combine the possible variations on the simple stockinette stitch.

Machines. There are two types of knitting that are employed by machines, namely warp knitting and weft knitting. In weft knitting, loops are formed by a single yarn passing horizontally across the fabric.

In warp knitting, a parallel series of threads are wrapped simultaneously around the knitting needles forming loops in a vertical direction. Weft knitting is the more commonly used of the two types.

The three types of needles used in knitting machines: latch, bearded and compound needles. When the latched needle is used, yarn is fed into the needle hook (A). As the needle moves down a groove, a previously formed loop on the body or 'shank' of the needle causes the latch to close, trapping a new yarn in the needle hook (B). As the needle moves further down, a new loop is formed and pulled through the old loop, which is then cast off, (C) and (D). The needle then rises, allowing the loop held in the hook to move down the shank, opening the latch ready to receive new yarn (E).

Bearded needles operate in much the same way, except that a "beard" seen at the top of the shank (A), serves as both needle hook and latch. The latch on a bearded needle is not self-closing, but is closed by a presser bar. When the needle is at its highest point (A) it holds a previously formed loop on the needle shank. The new yarn is fed in below the needle beard. The needle then drops (B), bringing the new yarn under the beard,

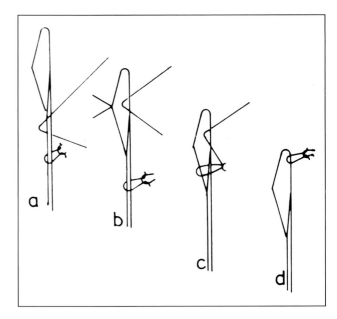

Bearded needle process   The Wool Bureau, Inc.

which has been closed by the presser bar. It remains closed until the new loop is pulled through the old one (C) which is later cast off (D). The needle then rises to receive a new yarn.

Compound needles work on the same principle as latch needles but the "latch" part is a separate piece and moves independently of the main needle. Machines that employ compound needles are capable of working at very great speeds.

Weft Knitting Machines. These machines have changed little since the days of William Lee's invention in 1859, apart from an increased degree of mechanization. Bearded needles are set into a bar and all move simultaneously, producing a complete course in one action.

Because there is only one row of needles, only plain, not rib, fabric is produced. Stitch transfer, where a loop is removed from one needle and transferred to another, causing the fabric to be wider or narrower, can be facilitated as well as tucking. The transfer principle is used for shaping the garment panels, producing "fully fashioned" or shaped knitwear.

Straight bar rib machines which contain two rows of bearded needles, set at right angles to each other, can produce shaped rib panels. Straight bar machines are generally used for better fabric produced from natural fiber yarns, for the shaping technique avoids yarn wastage and produces a garment of excellent quality.

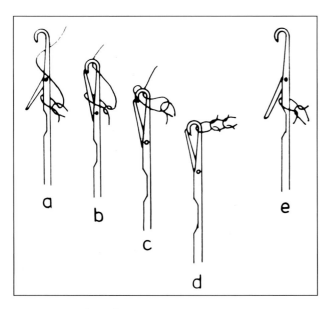

Latch needle process   The Wool Bureau, Inc.

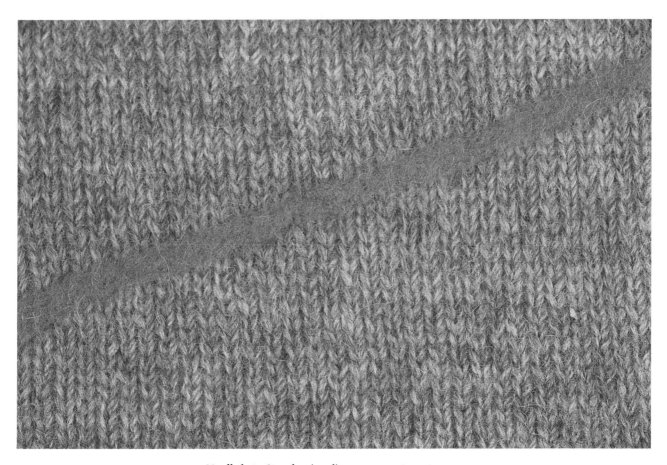

Needle knit. Singular (wool) International Wool Bureau

Circular Machines. Circular knitting machines have a circular cylinder containing the needles. They are also a weft knitting machine. The cylinders on the machines vary in size from 12 cm to 1 meter, depending upon the desired result (large or small knit). Some circular machines produce continuous length fabric and others are capable of producing body lengths for cutting into garment pieces. There have been great technological advances in circular knitting and today the patterning is largely controlled by electronics. The machines are capable of knitting continuously, thus attaining very high production rates.

Flat Bed Machines. These machines use latch needles set in grooves so they are able to slide up and down independently. They are either single bed (with one row of needles) or double bed (with two rows opposite each other). They can be used to knit rib, plain, Jacquard, pattern, lace and other novelty stitches. Generally they are used to knit rectangular panels from which garments are cut, but recent machines also have shaping capabilities.

Flat-bed machines are very versatile with regard to design, although their production speed is lower than that of circular machinery. Most modern models are electronically controlled and can be changed easily from one design to another.

Knitting machines for domestic use are basically the same as single bed industrial machines, but the needle bed is usually horizontal and the machine is of much lighter construction. A second needle bed, or "rib attachment," is usually available, hanging at right angles to the main bed. Patterning is set by manual selection or mechanical selection controlled by a punched plastic card.

Purl Machines. These can be either flat-bed or circular and are designed to produce fabrics with purl stitch effects. The latch needles are double ended and the grooves in the two needle beds (or cylinders) lie in the same plane, allowing the needles to slide from one to the other, thus reversing the loop.

Straight bar machine showing needle
The Wool Bureau, Inc.

Circular purl machine showing needle
The Wool Bureau, Inc.

Warp Knitting. Warp knitting machines are fed by a parallel series of yarns or warp and use bearded latch or compound needles. The yarn is wrapped around the needles by guide bars and the loop-forming action is similar to that used in weft machines. The structure of the knit depends on the amount and direction of the movement of the guide bar. For more complete patterns, more than one guide bar is required.

Other Machine Types. Raschel machines use latch needles set in a vertical plane and produce a wide variety of fabrics, particularly the heavier and more complex structures.

Crochet machines work on the same principle as the raschel machines but are narrower and the needles are generally horizontal. They are used for producing braids, trims, scarves and hats.

Circular single jersey machine showing needle
The Wool Bureau, Inc.

Flat bed machine showing needle
The Wool Bureau, Inc.

Cable stitch   The Wool Bureau, Inc.

Tricot machines are bearded needle machines and are usually used for the production of fabric for lingerie, lightweight furnishings fabrics and plush fabrics. They operate at very high speeds.

Modern machines are highly specialized and operate with great speed. A machine operator can knit 1 million loops in a minute. Needles of various sizes can be spaced at varying intervals and use many varieties of yarns. Thus

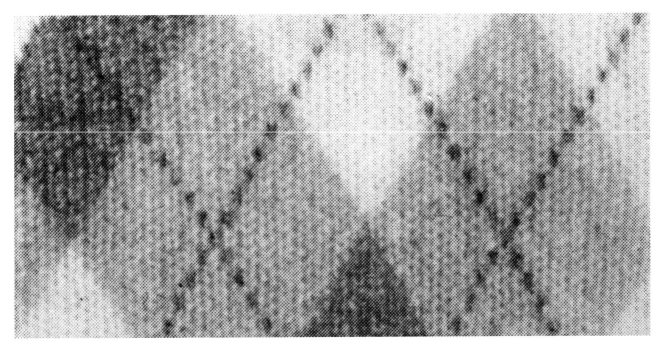

Argyle/Intarsia   The Wool Bureau, Inc.

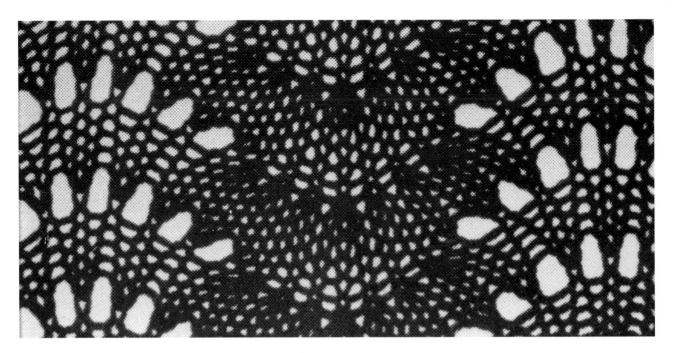

Lace stitch   The Wool Bureau, Inc.

the machines are able to create an amazing diversity of stitches as well as various qualities and weights, ranging from delicate hosiery to heavy outerwear.

Common Knit Stitches

Some of the most common stitches for both hand and machine knitting are described below:

CABLE STITCH	A stitch in which small groups of plain wales are plaited or braided with one another.
PLAIN STITCH	Produces a series of wales or ribs on the face of the fabric and cross-wise loops on the back. All loops are drawn through on the same side of the fabric.
PURL	A back-looping stitch that causes horizontal ridges. It is the inversion of the plain stitch.
GARTER STITCH	Every row is knit back and forth on two needles.
STOCKINETTE STITCH	Knitting the first and alternate rows and purling the second and alternate rows.
INTARSIA	An area of design in color that gives the appearance that it has been inlaid in the textile. The design areas are separated from each other by complete loops.

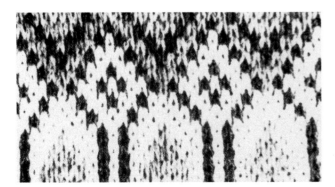

Knit Jacquard cloth   The Wool Bureau, Inc.

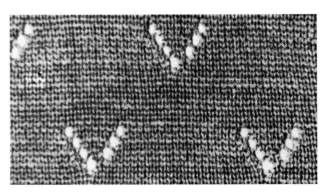

Pointelle   The Wool Bureau, Inc.

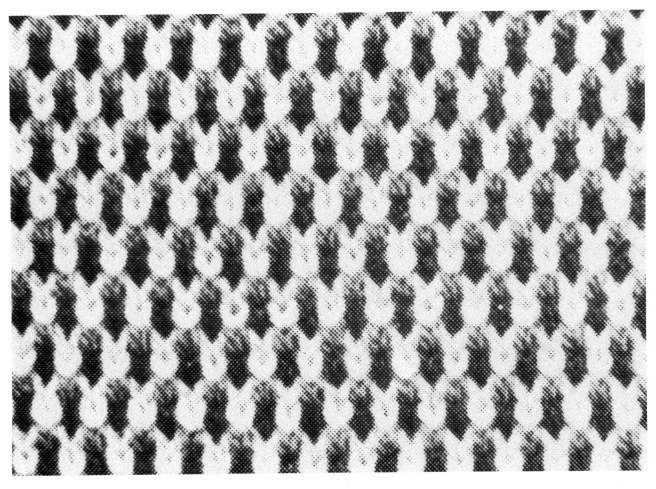

Birdseye knit   The Wool Bureau, Inc.

INTERLOCK

Created by two interknitted 1x1 rib fabrics. This double rib formation is produced by knitting alternate needles at alternate feeds.

LACE STITCH

Has a raised or open effect. It is created by the transfer of loops from the needles on which they are made to adjacent needles.

BIRDSEYE KNIT

Salt and pepper effect achieved by scrambling the colors used on the face design of the knit fabric.

KNIT JACQUARD CLOTH

All-over or sectional designs in color or sometimes texture are achieved by a Jacquard mechanism using a latch needle. As many as six colors can be incorporated in the designs.

POINTELLE

Eyelet-like patterns created in knit fabrics that are achieved by a rib or jersey stitch using the transfer method of needle loops.

ZIG-ZAG

A knit stitch that is produced by a construction called the "full cardigan," in which the needles knit and tuck and tuck and knit in alternating courses.

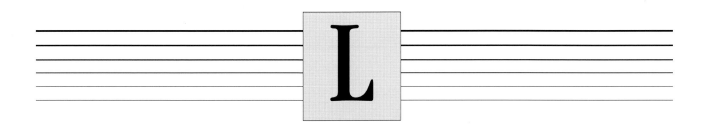

LABELING LAW

The Textile Fiber Products Identification Act, enacted in 1960, requires that a label be attached to textile products that clearly lists the fiber content. The percentages of the various fibers must be listed, e.g., 75% cotton 25% linen, in order of percentage. The act further requires that the manufacturer's identification number or name be included on the label as well. If foreign fibers are employed, the country of origin must be listed. The act is enforced by the Federal Trade Commission, in Washington, D.C.

LACE

The term lace is taken from the Latin word *laqueus,* which means loop, or snare. While not strictly a textile, the term covers any openwork that is created by looping, twisting or knotting threads or yarns by hand or machine. Machine laces, however, regardless of their degree of fineness, are often referred to as imitation laces. Handmade lace is recognizable when studied closely by its irregularities, as opposed to the regularity of machine lace.

The history of lace is vague. Though there are written references to lace as early as 4000 B.C., we cannot be sure that they refer to lace as it is known today. But as one studies the extant historic examples, the evolution of lace becomes clearer. For tangible evidence we turn to the 16th century, from which survive examples of drawn work (created by the pulling, removing and tying of threads) and cutwork (in textiles with cutouts and embroidery).

The removal of threads gradually became more pronounced until the ground of the textile itself was nearly totally diminished, leaving a space enclosed with threads of varying designs, creating an airy, lacey effect. In 1808, the Englishman John Heathcoat invented the bobbinet lace-making machine. In 1813 he also perfected a machine that would make narrow strips of lace. In 1813, another Englishman, John Leavers, invented a lace-making machine that was so intricate it could create a wide variety of lace types. Many of the principles employed in his very early machine are used today for manufactured lace.

While the methods of lacemaking are complex and could be the subject of an entire volume themselves, basically lace is created by hand with bobbins and pins, called bobbin or pillow lace; with needles, called needlepoint or point lace; and with a shuttle, such as tatting. Lace is also created by machine.

Bobbin or Pillow Lace. Bobbin lace is created by the use of bobbins to pull the many threads taut while they are being worked. It is more closely aligned with weaving than with embroidery. Bobbin lace is executed by outlining a pattern on paper, usually by pricking the paper with a pin. The pins are then pushed through the holes into a pillow and act as guides for the thread, while bobbins are attached to the end of each thread. The number of bobbins required depends on the complexity of the design; several hundred may be used. The

Bobbin or pillow lace Author's collection

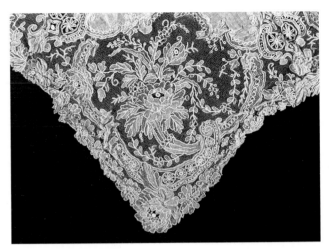

Needlepoint Author's collection

Tatting. Tatting is created by using a small shuttle and a continuous thread to form a series of small knots, called stitches, all tied together in circles or along a foundation thread. The only knot used is the "lark's head." Loops of thread are left between the knots. The loops vary in length and frequency creating the pattern known as tatting. Tatting evolved in the mid-19th century from the art of knotting.

LAMBSWOOL

Lambswool refers to the wool sheared from sheep before they are seven months old. In this first clip, the wool strands have a natural tip, which imparts special qualities

background of the design is called the reseau and the design itself is called the toile.

Four common types of bobbin laces include grounded lace, in solid designs which stand out from a light net background; tape lace, a design formed of a handmade tape; plaited lace, in which designs are made with one or two bobbins; and guipure, in which solid designs are connected by plaits and twists.

Other familiar examples of bobbin laces are: Genoese, Milanese, Maltese, Brabant, Binche, Valenciennes, Antwerp, Mechlin, point d'Angleterre, Bruges, duchesse, rosaline, Lille, Chantilly, Honiton and Cluny.

Needlepoint. Needlepoint lace is worked with a needle using the buttonhole stitch and resembles embroidery. Familiar needlepoint or point laces are: gros point, rose point, point de neige, point plat, coralline, reseau, point de France, argentella, argentan, Alencon, point de Colbert and point de Gaz. Needlepoint lace came into general use in Europe during the Renaissance.

Tatting Author's collection

to lambswool. It is extremely soft and smooth, and has superior spinning properties. Wool clips after the first shearing, which no longer have this tip, are called fleece wool. Lambswool yarns, also refer to a British term for wool yarn spun from a mixture of waste and low grade, shot, or defective, staple wool.

See also WOOL.

LAMÉ

The word lamé is derived from the French verb *laminer*, which means "to flatten." Today, lamé refers to fabric woven with metallic threads, which form either the ground or pattern of the textile. Originally, flattened metal was used, but now the term applies to a wide variety of metallic threads, including all metal, plastic-coated metal, metal wound around a core yarn or metal-coated plastic.

Originally, the threads of gold or silver used for lamé were made of pure metal that was pounded into thin strips. It was then wound around the core thread, usually of silk, or used without a core thread. (It is believed that the gold and silver threads were wrapped around the core threads using a device similar to the one now used to create bow strings.) Threads of pure gold and silver were still being used during the 19th century and continued into the 20th century until the advent of manufactured fibers, which could keep their luster and not oxidize as did the other metals.

In one technique used in the production of present-day lamé, aluminum is deposited on one side of a thin plastic sheet in a vacuum and transparent color is then applied to the silvery surface of the aluminum deposits, before they receive a protective covering of polyester film. Once the sheets of silver, gold or colored films have been made, they are slit into fine strips and wound around a core yarn, usually of cotton or silk.

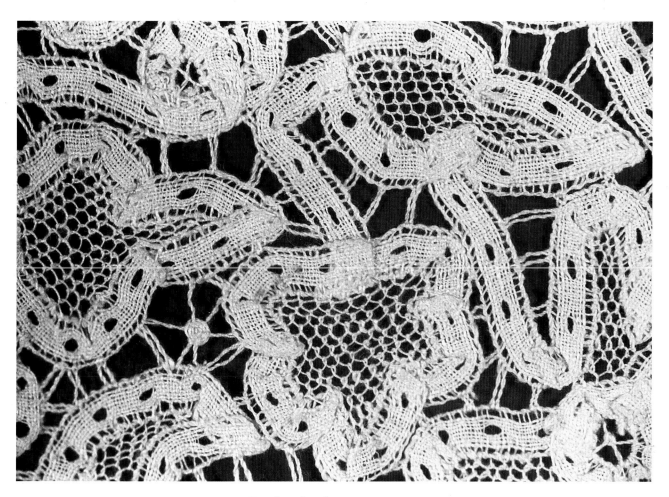

Tape lace (linen)   Author's collection

LANOLIN

Lanolin is a natural fatty chemical substance composed of a group of cholesterol esters obtained from WOOL in the grease (uncleaned wool). Lanolin is removed from the wool by washing. After it is put through a series of purification processes, it may be used as the base for medications, salves and cosmetics.

LATEX

Latex is the raw material from which natural and synthetic rubbers are made. Natural latex is a white, milky emulsion whose basic structural unit is the isoprene molecule. It is obtained from the roots, stems, and fruits of a variety of trees, shrubs and vines. The primary source of natural latex is the tree *Hevea brasiliensis,* which grows wild in the Amazon basin and which was later cultivated in Southeast Asia and Africa.

There are a variety of synthetic latices (aqueous suspensions of the basic structural units) from which synthetic rubbers are made by the polymerization process. The first synthetic latex which led to a commercially successful synthetic rubber was developed by the Du Pont company in 1931, following the research of Father Julius Nieuwland, professor of organic chemistry at the University of Notre Dame. Its basic structural unit is chloroprene, and the rubber based on it is called neoprene.

The latex of most importance in textiles is based on the urethane molecule. The elastomeric fiber based on this latex, SPANDEX, was first produced in 1959.

See also ELASTOMER, MANUFACTURED FIBER.

LAWN

Originally, lawn was made in a village in Laon, France near the textile center of Reims, and was made of linen.

Lawn (linen)   Author's collection

While linen lawn is still produced, lawn is now most often made of cotton. All lawn is known for the quality yarns used. It is a sheer, fine textile executed in a plain weave. The threads are usually combed. Lawn has the body, but not the stiffness, of an ORGANDY. Lawn can be bleached, dyed or printed.

LEA

A lea is a measure for the fineness of wet spun linen yarn, the number of 300-yard-lengths of yarn that weigh one pound. The finer the yarn, the more leas per pound. A *hank* of yarn consists of 12 leas, and a *bundle* refers to 200 leas, or 16⅔ hanks.

Lea also refers to a standard skein used in yarn strength tests. This skein contains 80 turns of yarn, each 1½ yards in length.

Lea also represents a unit of length of certain fibers: 120 yards of cotton yarn, 120 yards of spun silk and 80 yards of worsted.

LEE, WILLIAM (d. 1610)

The Reverend William Lee, a curate of St. John's College in Cambridge, England, invented a stocking frame that could knit woolen stockings in 1598. It was a flat bed machine that used needles with flexible hooks that ended in a point, a principle that is still applied in today's knitting machines. He later perfected the machine so that it could also weave silk stockings.

See KNITTING.

LENO WEAVE

Textiles created in the leno weave have a lace-like appearance because of their lightweight, open structure. It is thought that this weave originated near Reims, France, a linen textile center. Today it is generally executed in COTTON or MANUFACTURED FIBERS.

In the leno weave the warp yarns are arranged in pairs. The weft is shot straight across the fabric, but the threads are locked in place by twisting to the left and to the right of the warp threads by a device called the doup harness. (Leno is also referred to as a doup weave.) A well-known example of the leno weave is MARQUISETTE.

See also WEAVE.

LINE

The term line applies to the production of LINEN, and most specifically flax after it has gone through the hackling process. The term applies to fibers longer than 10 inches. Fibers shorter than 10 inches are called tow.

LINEN

Linen is a multicellular vegetable fiber that is extracted from the bark of the flax plant, belonging to the order Linaceae, species *Linum usitatissimum*. The flax plant bears a five-petaled flower of varying colors: blue, purple, and white. As flax must be raised in swampy, mild, moist lowlands, the number of countries capable of giving rise to a prosperous flax crop is limited.

The most valued variety of flax is Courtrai flax, raised in Belgium. Fine flax is also raised in France, Holland, West Germany, and Russia. In the United States flax is raised for seed rather than for its fiber, since a flax plant from which fine linen can be created does not produce good seed and vice-versa. The flax plant produces additional valuable products such as linseed oil, which is extracted from its seeds and used in cosmetics and varnishes.

History

It is claimed by many that flax or linen is one of the oldest textile fibers. It is known that linen fish nets and the earliest surviving linen textiles in Europe were used by the neolithic Swiss Lake Dwellers of the Stone Age at sites dated about 2940 B.C. Among the articles found at those sites have been bundles of flax, spun linen yarn, and fragments of linen fabric. The Bible also contains numerous references to the use of linen.

It is believed that linen may have been used for weaving in the Nile valley as early as 4000 B.C., for wall paintings in Egypt depict the art of spinning and weaving. It is known, as well, that the bodies of early Egyptian kings and nobles were wrapped in yards of delicate linen, a fact that indicates that the art of spinning and weaving had reached a high state of perfection in that country six thousand years ago. Pieces of linen cloth have been found in Egyptian tombs that date as far back as 2500 B.C. This cloth was finer than any linen woven today. Some of it contained 540 threads to the inch and was 60 inches wide and 6 or more yards long. Greek and Roman records also show that linen was of profound economic importance.

Flax flowers International Linen Promotion Commission

Evidence supports the theory that until the 18th century linen was the most important textile in the world. Finnish traders are largely given credit for disseminating linen to many parts of the globe, particularly to Northern Europe, and the Phoenician traders were pivotal in bringing the textile and fiber to other parts of the ancient world.

Structure

There are visual differences between the two predominant flax types. The flax plant that produces the fiber for linen has a very long, usually unbranched, stem. It bears very small seeds. The plants raised for seed or by-products are smaller in height, and bear larger seeds.

A cross section of the flax stalk reveals six roughly concentric rings.

1. The outermost ring consists of a layer of thick walled cells covered by the cuticle. There are openings in the cuticle, called stomata, which are large enough to permit the entry of bacteria during the retting process. This region is known as the epidermis, or simply outer layer.

2. Inside the epidermis is a region of one or two layers of circular cells known as the cortex, or bark. These cells contain pectins, which are a somewhat gummy substance that adhers to the fiber bundles.

3. Proceeding inward, the next layer contains the bundles of bast fiber that ultimately form the linen fiber. There are approximately 1,000 flax fibers per stem, arranged in up to 40 bundles.

4. The fiber bundles are separated from the woody cells by a ring of thin-walled cells called the cambium.

5. Inside the cambium is a ring of short, thick woody cells that give the stalk its strength.

6. The central part of the stalk is hollow. This central cavity is surrounded by thin-walled cells called pith.

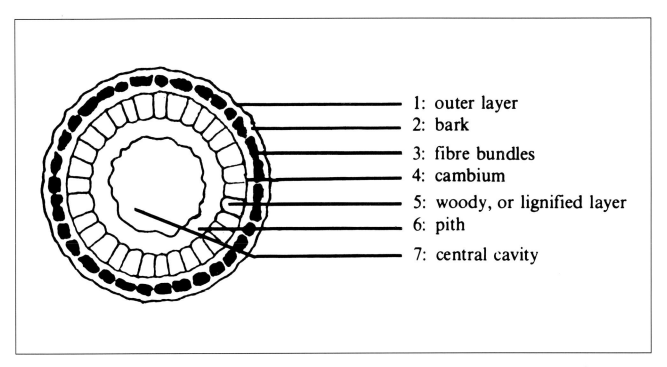

1: outer layer
2: bark
3: fibre bundles
4: cambium
5: woody, or lignified layer
6: pith
7: central cavity

Cross section of flax plant   International Linen Promotion Commission

This complex structure means that the extraction of the usable fiber bundles from the raw flax involves the removal of a considerable amount of extraneous material.

Cultivation and Production of Linen

It has been found that harvesting flax in late summer produces the best linen. The harvesting of flax differs from that of other types of natural fibers in that the plant is entirely uprooted during the process. After all of the stalks have been uprooted or "pulled," they are tied into bundles and allowed to dry, usually in the sun. After the stalks have been dried sufficiently they are combed to remove the seeds, which are used for other products.

Following the removal of seeds the plant goes through a retting process, which is actually a form of rotting or fermentation. This process is essential in the production of linen. Previously this stage was accomplished in

Harvesting flax   International Linen Promotion Commission

Drying flax International Linen Promotion Commission

several ways. One was dew retting, which entailed spreading the plants out in fields and allowing dew and bacteria to slowly decompose the exterior layers, or by placing the plants in slow moving rivers or bogs to achieve the same results. Another early method used was to soak the plants in a tank of warm water until a certain stage of fermentation set in. These fermentation processes were tenuous and unpredictable, for if fermentation extended too far the fiber for the linen was ruined. Today, chemicals are mainly used for the retting process, although the original method is still used on occasion. During the chemical process the plants are placed in a solution either of alkali or oxalic acid, pressurized, and boiled. This method is not only more predictable, but quicker. During this process, the outer, more soluble portions of the stalks soften and give way.

After the retting process, the plants are squeezed and allowed to dry in preparation for the next process, which is called "breaking." During the breaking process the

Retting   International Linen Promotion Commission

Scutching   International Linen Promotion Commission

stalks are sent through fluted rollers which break up the fiber, separating the soft exterior fibers from the bast fiber that will be used to make linen. The breaking process is followed by a beating process called scutching. Originally all scutching was done by hand, but today it is done primarily by machines. It is during the beating process that the final woody sections of the plant are removed.

The remaining fiber is then combed in a process referred to as hackling. The combing process is similar to

Seed pods   International Linen Promotion Commission

Opposite: Linen   International Linen Promotion Commission

Combed linen   International Linen Promotion Commission

properties that many fibers do, so linen textiles do not have as great an affinity for attracting lint, hair and other foreign particles that many textiles do.

Linen is soft, and the more it is washed the softer it becomes. It is strong as well as lustrous (nodes on the flax fibers reflect light). It can be manufactured so that it has great dimensional stability; in other words it will not shrink. The colors produced by dyeing linen are fast to washing, dry cleaning and light. Today linen is used for a wide variety of fashion apparel and household items, as well as for furnishings and wall coverings.

The linen industries of Austria, Belgium, France, Germany, the Netherlands, Italy, Spain, Switzerland and the United Kingdom, including Northern Ireland and Scotland, form an organization known as CILC (Confederation Internationale du Lin et du Chanvre). The members of CILC conform to a wide range of high technical and performance standards. The CILC issues a quality trademark to those who meet these standards. The international logo is a stylized "L." A blue "L" insignia is used for household linens. A similar brown insignia is used for furnishings, and a gray one for

that used in the preparation of the other fibers, causing the fibers to become parallel to one another. During this combing process the shorter fibers, called tow, are separated from the longer fibers, which are called line. The tow is used for a less expensive type of linen than the line fibers. At this stage in production the fine longer fibers will be a pale yellow or ecru. The shorter fibers will be off-white to gray in color.

Finally, the linen is spun into yarn, in a process not dissimilar from the spinning of cotton, and woven into linen cloth, often with a slubbed, rich texture.

Qualities of Linen

The flax fiber is hollow, causing it to absorb moisture readily. These absorptive qualities make it highly desirable for many household uses. This quality also causes it to absorb sound, thus it is often used effectively as a wall covering. Linen does not have the electrostatic

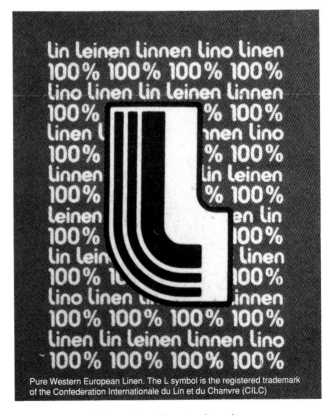

Pure Western European Linen. The L symbol is the registered trademark of the Confederation Internationale du Lin et du Chanvre (CILC)

International linen trademark

Linen threads International Linen Promotion Commission

apparel. For the consumer this trademark is a guarantee of the linen's origin and quality.

Care of Linen

As a natural fiber linen is washable, but finishing methods, dyes and trims may make the article non-washable, so one should always follow the manufacturer's instructions. If laundering is possible, as is usually the case with bed and table linens, it is usually the best cleaning process, for each time an article is washed a thin layer of pectic gum is removed from around the flax fiber, so the fabric becomes softer, whiter and more luminous with each washing.

When laundering linen, use mild soap or mild detergent. Never use soap or detergent with chlorine or sodium carbonate in them. White articles should be washed in warm water, colored articles in cold water. Harsh treatment, such as wringing and vigorous agitation, should be avoided, for linen fibers become more fragile when wet.

Whether the article is to be washed or dry cleaned, all stains should be pretreated quickly (see p. 127). Be sure to point out spots to a dry cleaner, who should pretreat them as well.

Caution should be taken with the drying of linen, which becomes brittle when dried out completely. Linen will recover its natural moisture and flexibility in time, however, by absorbing moisture from the air.

In pressing, the best results are obtained by ironing the article before it is entirely dry. Ironing should be done on the wrong side of the garment, unless a sheen is desired. The use of a pressing cloth over seams, hems and pockets will avoid lines. When ironing linens with embroidery, the placement of a soft towel under the embroidery or cut work will make it stand out in its original configuration. The article should be hung up when it is still slightly damp.

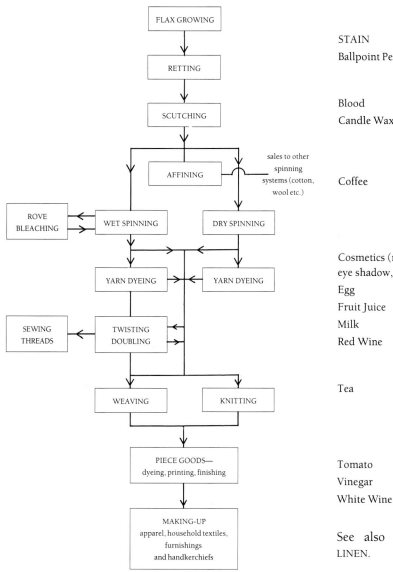

Linen production flow chart
International Linen Promotion Commission

═══

Opposite: Linen
International Linen Promotion Commission

═══

TREATMENT OF STAINS ON LINEN

STAIN	TREATMENT
Ballpoint Pen	Hold spot against a paper towel and spray with water closely from the back
Blood	Cool water rinse
Candle Wax	Chill with ice and scrape off as much as possible. Then iron out remainder between sheets of absorbent paper
Coffee	Stretch fabric over a bowl and pour boiling water (carefully) from one foot above. If the stain is old, use glycerine
Cosmetics (mascara, cream eye shadow, lipstick	Petroleum jelly/cold cream, followed with pre-wash
Egg	Cool water rinse
Fruit Juice	Cool water rinse
Milk	Cool water rinse
Red Wine	Pour salt to absorb the wine. If the wine has dried, rinse with club soda
Tea	Stretch fabric over a bowl and pour boiling water (carefully) from one foot above. If the stain is old, use glycerine
Tomato	Cool water rinse
Vinegar	Cool water rinse
White Wine	Rinse with club soda

See also LINEN CRASH; LINEN CRÊPE; NON-CRUSHABLE LINEN.   ═══

LINEN CRASH

Linen crash has a very rough feel due to the fact that it is woven with both line (fibers over 10" in length) and tow (fibers less than 10" in length) or, for the lesser grades, all of tow. Today some crash is also made in blends with manufactured fiber or with cotton and linen. The crash textile can be unbleached, bleached or dyed.
See LINEN.   ═══

LINEN CRÊPE

Linen crêpe is created by varying the length of the floats during the weaving process. (Despite the name, crêpe yarns are not used.) Linen crêpe has a rough pebbly character that is much in fashion. Linen crêpe comes in a

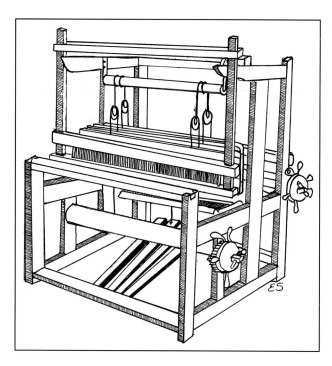

Basic treadle loom Elaine Swenson

variety of weights and qualities and is usually found in plain colors but occasionally may be printed.

See LINEN.

LODEN CLOTH

The term loden comes from the German word *Loda,* meaning hair cloth. The textile dates to the 16th century and is closely associated with the Tyrolean area of Austria, where the tradition of weaving loden cloth still exists. It was originally an all-wool textile made from the fleece of mountain goats. Today, it is usually a blend of alpaca, mohair, or camel with wool. Once the textile has gone through the weaving process it is shrunk, sheared and brushed. The fabric is known for its waterproof qualities and for its durability.

LOFT

Loft refers to the height and springiness of a fiber. Today it is used almost exclusively in the production of manufactured fibers particularly those used for blankets and sweaters. Acrylic fiber, for example, is known for its loft.

LONGCLOTH

Longcloth is a high-quality, soft textile, executed in a plain weave. It has a slight luster. Today it is both sized and calendered and is found in cotton and cotton-blends. Its name is derived from the fact that it is one of the first fabrics that was made in long pieces.

LOOM

A loom can be defined as a frame used for the creation of textile from thread or yarn by the process of weaving. The loom has crosswise threads, called the weft, and lengthwise threads, called the warp. It may or may not be equipped with heddle devices, which are guides for the warp threads.

History

The loom and its many varieties has a long history, beginning when weaving was done with the hands only. Hand weaving techniques include knotting, coiling, wrapping, twining, looping and braiding. It is thought that early looms might have been simple stakes driven into the ground, with warp threads stretched tautly between them. Most of the early peoples were nomadic and thus portability of the first looms or the ability to make them from simple, readily available raw materials was necessary.

In rudimentary looms, a simple frame holds the warp yarns rigid while the weft is interlaced between the threads. As the loom developed, elementary tools were developed to assist the weaver, such as crude needles that would pass the weft through the warp. A variation on this simple device is a hand loom with a slit piece of wood held apart by two vertical wooden props and tied at the ends to prevent separation.

Basic Parts of a Loom

In order to understand the development of the modern loom it is necessary to understand the parts of the basic loom and the equipment that is used to operate them.

FRAME	The structure of the loom that supports its moving parts
BREAST BEAM	A support at the front of the loom
BACK BEAM	Supports the warp and keeps it in a horizontal position
WARP BEAM	Holds the warp yarns. It is controlled by a ratchet that controls tension on the yarns

CLOTH BEAM	Holds the finished textile. It also has a ratchet that controls the warp tension
CASTLE	The uppermost part of the loom, which supports the harnesses
HARNESS	The frame on the loom which holds the heddles
HEAD MOTION	The device that controls the harness on a loom
HEDDLES	The section of the loom through which the warp threads pass
SHED	The space between spread warp threads through which the weft is thrown
BATTEN or BEATER	The part of the loom that swings back and forth, beating the weft into place. After each weft yarn passes through the shed, the beater moves against the textile, packing the weft against the previous one. The batten also holds the reed
REED	A device that resembles a comb. It is placed parallel to the harnesses. The warp yarns pass through this device after they leave the heddles. It keeps the threads aligned
DENT	The space between the teeth on the reed The spaces determine the warp count of the fabric
LAMMS	Bars that connect the harnesses to the treadles
TREADLES	Foot levers that raise and lower the harnesses

Warp-Weighted Loom

The next advancement in the loom was the creation of the warp-weighted loom. The vertical warp-weighted loom first appeared in Egypt during the second millennium B.C. and was eventually adopted by the Greeks, Romans, Scandinavians, and the Indians of North and South America. This loom consisted of a beam supported at either end by a vertical post around which the warp threads were tied. Each group of yarns was weighted with a stone or a piece of metal. A shed rod and a heddle rod facilitated changing of the shed. In the Greek version of the loom, weaving proceeded from the top downward, and the warp beam revolved so that as sections of web were completed, they could be rolled up over the beam.

Both the Romans and the New Kingdom (1550–1070 B.C.) Egyptians used a type of loom in which the warp yarns were weighted by another horizontal beam at the bottom. Weaving proceeded upwards, and the weft was beaten into place by a comb that was the ancestor of the modern-day reed. Herodotus referred to the making of cloth by "pushing woof upwards."

The Icelandic loom was an 18th-century version of the Greek warp-weighted loom. It was equipped with three heddle rods and two shed rods. When the shed was to be changed a heddle rod was lifted to raise selected warp yarns, and the movable shed rod was inserted, followed by a bobbin containing the weft yarn. Such a loom was quite practical for the nomadic Lapps. When they moved, they carried only the warp beam and heddle rods. Uprights were constructed from available timber at the new location. Warp-weighted looms are probably still used in isolated parts of Lapland and in other remote areas.

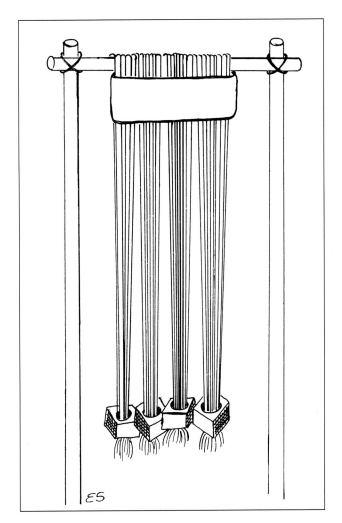

Warp weighted loom
Elaine Swenson

Backstrap Loom

Among the simplest of horizontal looms is the backstrap loom. It is one of the oldest and most common looms in the world. It consists of two bars around which a continuous warp is wound in a figure eight. One loom bar is attached to a permanent object such as a tree, and the other bar is attached to the weaver by means of a strap around the weaver's back. The weaver sits on the ground in a position that holds the warp in tension, and leans forward or backward to decrease or increase the tension. The weft is usually wound on a crude stick.

Originally, weaving was done with the fingers alone, but more advanced backstrap looms employ heddle rods and separators to create the shed, as well as a beater stick to pack the weft yarns into position. A shed stick is permanently placed under every other warp thread, and the alternate threads are strung with string heddles and can be pulled forward with a heddle stick. In this way the two sheds are formed. A smooth flat stick, called a battan or sword, is inserted in the sheds and turned on edge to hold the shed open, leaving the hands free to insert the weft. The battan is also used to beat the weft into place.

Other tools are used to beat in the weft also. These are wooden combs, or a pointed tool, called a pick, fashioned out of hardwood or occasionally deer horn or llama bone. A stretcher device is used to ensure a consistent width to the fabric. As the weaving progresses the fabric is rolled up on the front bar.

The backstrap loom was common among the Indians of Peru during the pre-Inca period. It is still used by native peoples of Southeast Asia and the Americas, including the Navajo of Arizona and New Mexico and the Indians of Mexico.

The fact that the body of the weaver controls the tension determines a maximum width of the textile of approximately 30 inches. For wider fabrics, narrow widths are woven and stitched together. Both warp-faced (more warp threads) and weft-faced (more weft threads) fabrics can be woven on this loom, as well as balanced weaves.

Horizontal Ground Loom

The origin of the ground loom is unclear, but it is the ancestor of the modern counterbalance loom, and has an advantage over the backstrap loom in that the body of the weaver was no longer strapped to the loom. This loom had treadles, and each warp thread had its own heddle. The heddles were suspended from two shafts, which could be raised or lowered alternately to change

the shed. A reed controlled the horizontal spacing of the warp yarns.

Such a loom provides for a fixed support at both ends of the warp, thus freeing the weaver physically from the loom. One early version of the ground loom was the pit loom, so called because it was designed to be placed over a pit dug in the ground. The weaver sat on the ground at a level with the loom, while his or her feet, in the pit, operated the treadles. Each warp yarn had its own heddle. The heddles were divided into two groups and suspended from two shafts that could be raised or lowered alternately to change the shed. A reed controlled the horizontal spacing of the warp yarns. Pit looms were used in India for weaving cotton. A variation of this loom is the tripod loom.

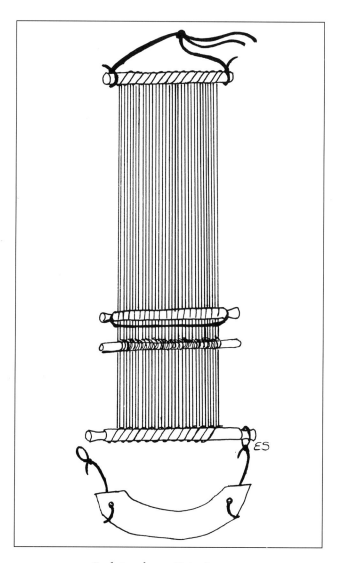

Backstrap loom   Elaine Swenson

Ground loom Biltmore Industries

Horizontal Frame Looms

The horizontal frame loom was known in ancient Egypt, but it may have been invented in China much earlier. Although many refinements have been added over the centuries, in operating principle it was identical to the common floor loom used today. A complex version of the horizontal frame loom, with treadle-operated harnesses, a reed beater and a movable warp beam, appeared in Europe by the 13th century, but its mechanisms must have been perfected long before. Even after the industrial revolution much cloth was woven on the horizontal frame loom in non-industrialized parts of Europe.

Draw Loom

The draw loom was invented in China about the time of the birth of Christ. It was a two person loom. The master

weaver (A) manipulated the heddle frames and threw the shuttle, while his assistant (the drawboy) (B), stationed at the top of the loom, controlled individual warp yarns independent of the heddle frames. This system permitted amazingly intricate patterns. Each warp yarn was attached to a cord run through a comber board to the top of the loom. On command from the weaver, the drawboy, in puppet fashion, could raise any warp or group of warps, thus providing infinite variety in the shed. When the knowledge of sericulture (the cultivation of the silkworm) spread westward out of Asia so did knowledge of this loom. The elaborate textile patterns of the Renaissance and Baroque periods were done on the European version of this loom.

Several improvements were made to the draw loom in the 18th century. In 1733, John KAY invented the fly shuttle, drawn through the shed with a cord, which made it possible to weave textiles wider than 22 inches and speeded the weaving process considerably. In 1760, Kay's son Robert KAY invented the dropbox loom. This device allowed one weaver to operate several shuttles simultaneously. Both improvements dramatically increased the loom's productivity. The draw loom was used in Europe until the end of the 18th century. In 1784, Edmund CARTWRIGHT invented the power loom in England, run by a steam engine, with a vertical warp.

Jacquard Loom

The JACQUARD loom represented a marked advance in the development of the automated power loom. Introduced by Joseph Marie JACQUARD in 1801, the Jacquard loom provides for the lifting or raising of individual warp ends without reference to adjacent warp threads. The ends are raised by means of hooks that form the top part of the shed of the warp in order to admit the passage of the weft pick through the opening that is formed. The apparatus is placed on top of the loom. Any combination of warp yarns can be raised, and through the use of this extraordinary invention intricate patterns can be created.

The Jacquard loom is often considered the precursor of the modern computer, for it operated through the use of punched cards. Each warp yarn is connected by means of a cord to a needle. The punched cards, one for each weft, have holes in accordance with the desired pattern. The cards are placed in a sequential manner. As each card passes through the machine and comes into position, only those needles corresponding to the holes in the card are released, thus raising the warp yarns. The weft thread is passed through and the card moves on, a

Draw loom Elaine Swenson

Air jet loom American Textile Manufacturers Institute

new card taking its place. Today, large Jacquards can operate more than 100 shots per minute, and state-of-the-art Jacquards are being equipped with special computerized heads that no longer require the punched cards.

Dobby Loom

The dobby loom is a power loom with a special attachment that allows the harnesses to be controlled by reading punched holes in a series of cards, thus allowing small designs to be created. The dobby loom is very useful in that it can create the designs less expensively than its sophisticated relative, the Jacquard loom. However, since the number of harnesses it can control is limited, it cannot produce the elaborate and intricate textiles that the Jacquard is capable of. Today, the dobby looms are controlled by punched cylindrical cards.

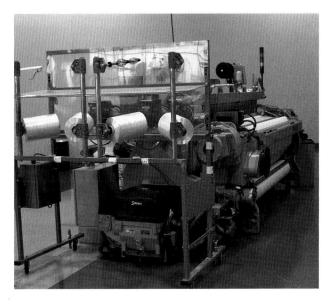

Dobby loom · SOMET of America, Inc.

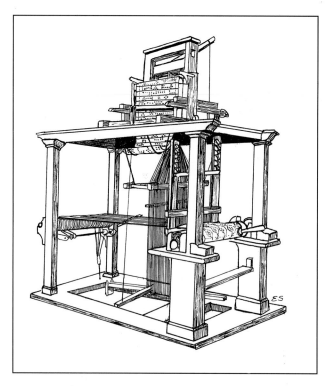

The original Jacquard loom Elaine Swenson

Modern Power Looms

New versions of power looms began to develop in the 1950s, advancing the technology of modern looms to a highly sophisticated state. Some modern looms are powered by streams of air or water. The water-jet loom uses a high-pressure jet of water to carry the weft yarn across the warp at rates up to 600 picks a minute, a pick

being a single insertion of the weft yarn. These machines operate at speeds up to five times faster than shuttle looms. The water-jet machines are not only faster but also quieter than previous looms.

The air-jet loom appeared in the late 1970s. It was developed by a Swedish textile engineer who got the idea while sailing. The air-jet loom uses puffs of air from nozzles to propel a strand of yarn through the warp, operating at up to 600 picks a minute. This loom is frequently called a shuttleless loom.

Another variation of the power loom are rapier looms, in which, instead of the wooden shuttle, flexible metal bands called rapiers are used to carry the weft through the warp. Rapier looms operate at 200 to 300 picks a minute.

Circular and triaxial looms are among the latest developments that have added speed and versatility to the weaving process. The triaxial loom operates with three sets of yarns set at angles of 60 degrees to each other, thus performing circular weaving to make tubular fabric. This results in strong and stable textile.

See also WEAVING.

LUSTER FABRIC

Luster fabric is a plain weave textile created by using weft yarns that have a high luster, such as a worsted or mohair yarn and some alpacas. The warp threads are usually cotton but today may also be of manufactured fiber. A special finishing process is given to the fabric during which it is stretched tightly enough to force the weft threads to the surface, imparting more luster.

MACKINAC

The term Mackinac originally referred to the blankets that were sold at Fort Mackinac, Michigan. The blankets were bright in color and often plaid in design. Lumbermen later adopted the blankets and had them made into jackets. Mackinac is still popular for hunting jackets today. The article of clothing made of Mackinac is often called a mackinaw.

Mackinac or mackinaw textiles frequently exhibit a long nap on both sides. The textiles are heavy and can be either a single or DOUBLE CLOTH made of wool or occasionally wool with cotton warp. When the fabric is executed as a double cloth, the patterns are often different on each side. Today the textile is made in many qualities, weights and colors and is further characterized by its strength, durability and warmth.

MACRAMÉ

The term macramé comes from the Arabic word *migramah*, which means veil. Macramé developed from the art of knotting. It is the precursor of WEAVING and is executed entirely by hand. It was spread from Turkey to Spain and Italy during the crusades. During that period, very fine thread was employed for the art, causing the work to become both delicate and intricate, even lace-like in appearance. During the mid to late 19th century the art enjoyed a revival, but the threads employed were much heavier and the work less intricate. The art of macramé is still popular today. Macramé is made of knots of yarn or string of varying textile fibers, including wool, hemp, cotton and silk that are arranged in various sequences.

See also LACE.

19th-century macramé　Private collection: Merle Sykora

MADRAS

The madras textile comes from the region of Madras, India. While today there are many imitations of the textile, the Federal Trade Commission has enacted strict rules regarding its labeling and a textile cannot be called a true madras unless it comes from the Indian region. The true madras is created of fine cotton on hand looms. The textile is executed in plain weave and the most common patterns are plaids, stripes and checks. Vegetable dyes are used on true madras, and they often have a tendency to bleed.

MALINE

Maline originated in Malines, Belgium. It is a very soft mesh NET with a hexagonal construction. Maline is available in silk on the market today, but not in the great quantity that nets of manufactured fiber and cotton are found.

See also ILLUSION; TULLE.

MANUFACTURED FIBER

History

The history of manufactured fibers is very short compared to that of natural fibers, which have existed for thousands of years. Manufactured fibers have been in use commercially only during the last 100 years, commencing in 1889 with the production of "artificial silk" by a Frenchman. Yet during this short span of time there has been an enormous amount of chemical research and development. The use of manufactured fibers has gone far beyond the dreams of its early

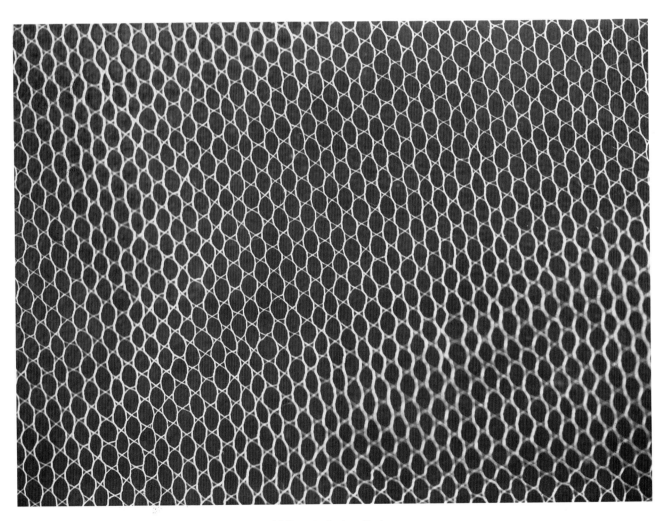

Maline Author's collection

Madras (cotton) Author's collection

discoverers, and we now find manufactured fibers not only being used for textiles and home furnishings but in a great variety of applications in medicine, aeronautics, aerospace, energy and industry.

The first patent for making "artificial silk," which subsequently became known as rayon, was granted in England in 1855 to George Audemars, a Swiss chemist, but the recorded history of the development of "artificial silk" dates back to 1644 when the Englishman and naturalist Robert Hooke declared that it would be possible to create a synthetic fiber some day that would be superior to real silk. It remained a prophecy, however, until Audemars dissolved the fibrous inner bark of the mulberry tree, thereby chemically modifying it to separate the cellulose. He was attempting to duplicate the process that the silkworm or caterpillar follows when it feeds on mulberry leaves. But rather than producing a fiber by extruding the liquid through a tiny hole, as the silkworm does, Audemars formed threads by dipping needles into the solution and drawing them out.

In the 1880s, an English chemist and electrician, Sir Joseph W. Swan, experimented with making carbon filaments for electric lamps in response to the demand created by Edison's invention. It was during his experiments that he struck upon the idea of forcing the cellulosic solution through fine holes into a coagulating bath, thus producing a fiber or thread. The idea then occurred to him that his filament could be adapted for textiles, and in 1885 he exhibited some of his fabrics in London. They did not create much excitement and since his main interest was in lamps, Swan never really pursued the textile possibilities of his project again.

The first person to produce a new fiber on a commercial scale was a French chemist, Count Hilaire de CHARDONNET. In 1889, his fabrics of "artificial silk" caused a sensation at the Paris Exhibition. Subsequently, he built the first commercial rayon plant at Besançon, France in 1891. His success with a cellulose fabric won him the appellation "father of the rayon industry."

Several attempts to produce "artificial silk" in the United States were made during the early 1900s but were commercially unsuccessful until the American Viscose Company, formed by Samuel Courtaulds and Co., Ltd., began its production of rayon in 1910.

Acetate, first produced in 1893 by Arthur D. Little of Boston, was first developed as a photographic film. In Basel, Switzerland, Camille and Henry Dreyfus also produced a solution, referred to as dope, from acetate that was used during World War I to coat the wings of English airplanes. Subsequently, when the United States entered the war, they were invited to build a plant in the United States, in Maryland, to create the same solution for American airplanes. It was not until 1924, however, that the Celanese Company began producing acetate fiber for the commercial textile market.

Dr. Wallace CAROTHERS, an American chemist working at the Du Pont laboratories in Delaware, presented a series of papers in 1931 to the American Chemical Society. It was in these papers that he revealed the research being carried out at Du Pont that was focused on finding out how certain organic molecules united to form "giant" molecules, or polymers. He referred at that time to a new fiber, which he called "66" because of its molecular structure. This synthesized polymer soon became known as NYLON, and marked the first development of a truly manufactured fiber, one that was not derived from plant cellulose.

In 1938, Paul Schlack of the I. G. Farben Company in Germany, discovered the polymerization of caprolactam, which became known as nylon "6," completing the nylon family of polymers, known as polyamides.

In 1950, a new fiber, ACRYLIC was added to the list of generic names by Du Pont. Acrylics are fibers in which the fiber forming substance is any long-chain synthetic polymer composed of at least 85% by weight of acrylonitrile units. The acrylonitrile is derived from elements taken from natural gas, air, water and petroleum.

In England, J. T. Dickson and J. R. Whinfield were conducting experiments based on the research that Dr. Carothers had initiated. Their interest was in the development of polyesters. The two men were able to produce a polyester fiber by condensation polymerization of ethylene glycol with terephthalic acid. The patent rights for this discovery were acquired by Du Pont in the

Extrusion   American Fiber Manufacturers Association, Inc.

United States and Imperial Chemical Industries for the rest of the world.

The development of polyester revolutionized the textile industry in a way quite apart from the fiber itself, for it was discovered that the textiles made from the fiber were wrinkle resistant, particularly when used in a blend with cotton. This revelation, which occurred in 1952, introduced the phrase "WASH AND WEAR" to the market, and created a revolution in the types of textiles that were used in clothing and home decoration.

During the 1960s and '70s many variations of these fibers were created, causing them not only to be wrinkle-free, but flame resistant as well as comfortable. It was discovered also that these fibers could be used for carpet that was soil resistant and more easily cleaned than carpets made of natural fibers. It was further discovered that the fibers could be extruded in different cross-sectioned shapes, offering greater flexibility and versatility in their uses. By the end of the 1960s a stretchable fiber, spandex, had come to the fore.

During the great period of space exploration and the Apollo missions to the moon, the astronauts wore clothing made of manufactured fibers, primarily of nylon and aramid. The flag placed on the moon was made of nylon, and the nose cone of the spaceship was also of manufactured materials. To this day, manufactured fibers continue to play a great role in aeronautics in general. Indeed, the exhaust nozzles of the two large booster rockets that lift the space shuttle into space are formed by 30,000 pounds of carbonized rayon. Carbon composites are also used in many of the structural components of modern commercial aircraft, adding strength while lowering weight and fuel costs.

Though the manufactured fiber industry was born just 100 years ago, it has been pursued with such scientific curiosity and zeal, and has produced an array of products with such a great range of properties, that it has in that short time affected every aspect of modern life.

FIRST COMMERCIAL PRODUCTION IN U.S.

1910	RAYON
1924	ACETATE
1930	RUBBER
1936	GLASS
1939	NYLON
1939	VINYON
1941	SARAN
1946	METALLIC
1949	MODACRYLIC
1949	OLEFIN
1950	ACRYLIC
1953	POLYESTER
1959	SPANDEX
1961	ARAMID
1983	PBI (Polybenzimidazole)
1983	SULFAR

OTHER GENERIC NAMES FOR MANUFACTURED FIBERS THAT ARE NOT PRODUCED IN THE U.S.

ANIDEX	NYTRIL
AZLON	TRIACETATE
NOVOLOID	VINAL

Production

All manufactured fibers are formed by forcing a thick fluid through tiny holes in a metal plate called a spinneret in the extrusion process. The spinneret is made of non-corrosive material and can contain from one to hundreds of tiny holes, and resembles a shower head.

Manufactured fibers can be grouped into two broad categories, cellulosic and non-cellulosic, based on the raw material they are derived from. The three cellulosic fibers (acetate, rayon, and triacetate) are made from modified wood pulp, which is dissolved in an organic solvent such as acetone so that it can be extruded through the spinneret. Non-cellulosic fibers are made from several polymers (large molecules) that are made chemically from petroleum crude. These polymers all contain carbon and hydrogen, and often contain additional elements, including oxygen, nitrogen and chlorine. They are generally melted or dissolved and then extruded through the spinneret.

Spinning. After the filaments emerge from the holes in the spinneret, they are hardened or solidified. The process of extruding and hardening the fibers is called "spinning." There are three methods of spinning manufactured fibers: wet spinning, which is the oldest of the spinning methods, dry spinning, in which solvents are used, and melt spinning, where the fiber is melted. During the wet spinning process the fiber-forming substances have been dissolved in a solvent. As the filaments emerge from the spinneret they are immediately immersed in a chemical bath where they become solidified. Acrylic, rayon, aramid, modacrylic and spandex are examples of the use of this method. In the dry spinning process the fiber-forming substances

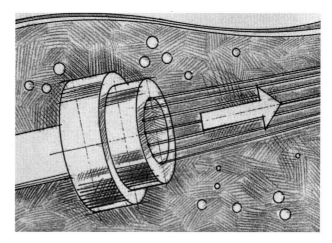

Wet spinning American Fiber Manufacturers Association, Inc.

have also been dissolved in a solvent. It differs from the process of wet spinning in that the fibers are solidified upon emerging from the spinneret by warm air. Examples of fabrics produced with the dry spinning process are acetate, acrylic, modacrylic, triacetate and vinyon. The melt spinning process requires the melting of the fiber solution prior to extrusion. Upon emerging from the spinneret the fibers are hardened by cooling. Examples of melt spinning are Nylon, olefin and polyester.

Stretching. All manufactured fibers are stretched in the manufacturing process, either while they are hardening or after they have hardened. Stretching reduces the fiber's diameter and rearranges the molecules in a more orderly pattern. This increases the fiber's strength and stabilizes its ability to stretch without breaking.

The terms denier and tex are used by the fiber industry to indicate thickness of fibers and yarns, respectively. Nine thousand meters of a fiber of one denier will weigh 1 gram,

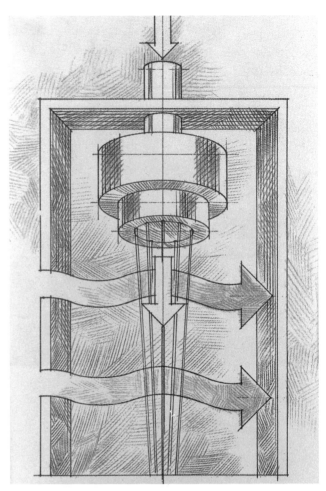

Melt spinning   American Fiber Manufacturers Association, Inc.

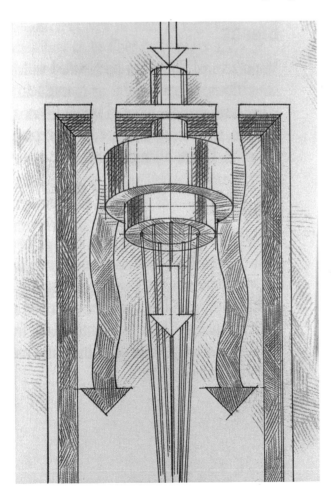

Dry spinning   American Fiber Manufacturers Association, Inc.

and 1000 meters of yarn of one tex will also weigh 1 gram. Depending on the design and hole size of the spinneret, as well as variations in the process, manufactured fibers can be extruded in a very great range of thicknesses. Examples of common applications are pantyhose (12 denier) and monofilaments used for automobile tires (840 denier).

Unlike natural fibers, which come only in the form nature provides, manufactured fibers can be extruded from the spinneret in different shapes or cross sections depending on the design of the spinneret hole. Such fibers might be round, trilobal, pentalobal, octalobal or even hollow.

Trilobal-shaped fibers reflect more light and give an attractive luster to textiles. Octalobal-shaped fibers also have a soft luster. Hollow fibers are bulkier and less dense in appearance.

A manufacturer can add various additives to the polymers or the solution before it is extruded. Such additives can produce colored fibers or can create a finished fiber that is anti-static, flame-resistant, less transparent, whiter, or more durable. Adding coloring material prior to extrusion is called solution dying and such fibers are often called "color sealed." The process gives the finished fiber and subsequent fabric a high degree of colorfastness.

Manufactured fibers are shipped to textile mills in different forms: as monofilament yarn (a single filament of continuous length), as multifilament yarn (two or more continuous monofilaments twisted together), as tow, as staple or as sheets. Tow consists of large untwisted bundles of continuous length monofilaments. Staples are then made by crimping the tow and cutting it into desired lengths. In some cases, polymers may also be extruded as a wide sheet of film, which is then slit lengthwise into narrow strips. These strips could also be described as monofilaments, and can be combined with other monofilaments to form multifilament yarns.

Manufactured staple fibers must be twisted or spun into yarn just as is the case with natural fibers. Depending on lengths and denier, various staples are spun in the cotton system, the wool system, or the worsted system. Staple that is not spun is called fiberfill, and can be used to fill pillows, mattresses, sleeping bags and jackets. A great variety of properties can be achieved by spinning manufactured staple together into a single yarn, bringing together the best properties of each fiber.

Yarns spun from staple fibers are more irregular than filament yarns. The short ends of fibers, projecting from the yarn surface, produce a fuzzy effect. Spun yarns are also more bulky and irregular than filament yarns of the same weight, and are therefore more often used for non-smooth porous fabrics, often used where good thermal insulation is desired.

Special machines can give manufactured continuous filament yarns different textures and stretch properties. These high-speed machines twist the yarns in such a way that the filaments no longer lie parallel to one another. The crimp and increased space between the filaments give the fibers greater bulk and stretch.

Laws require that the fiber content label must list all fibers that make up at least 5% of the fabric. A care label must also be attached to the garment.

This great variety of production methods combines with the variety of basic chemical structures to yield the almost endless variety of finished goods which use manufactured fibers today.

See ACETATE; ACRYLIC; ARAMID; LATEX; MODACRYLIC; NYLON; POLYESTER; RAYON; SPANDEX; TRIACETATE.

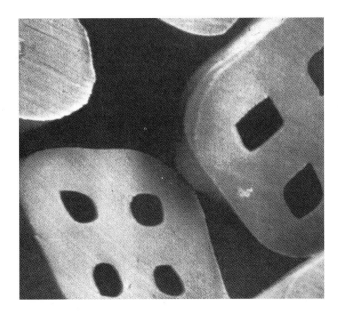

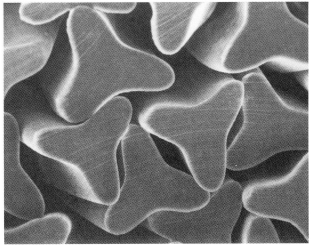

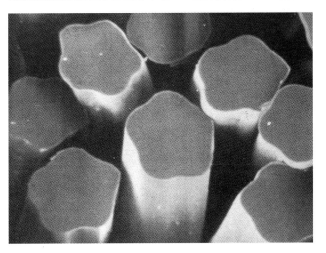

Micrographs of manufactured fiber shapes, hollow, trilobal and octolobal
American Fiber Manufacturers Association, Inc.

MAN-MADE FIBER GUIDE

GENERIC FIBERS	GENERIC TRADENAMES	MANUFACTURER	GENERIC CHARACTERISTICS
ACETATE	Ariloft	Eastman Chemical Products, Inc.	Wide range of colors and lusters; excellent drapability; fast drying; shrink, moth and mildew resistant.
	Celebrate	Hoechst Celeanese Corp.	
	Chromspun	Eastman Chemical Products, Inc.	
	Estron	Eastman Chemical Products, Inc.	
	Loftura	Eastman Chemical Products, Inc.	
ACRYLIC	Acrylan	Monsanto Chemical Co.	Soft, warm, resilient; wool-like, lightweight; retains shape; quick drying; resistant to moths, sunlight, oil, and chemicals.
	Bi-Loft	Monsanto Chemical Co.	
	Creslan	American Cyanamid Co.	
	Fi-Lana	Monsanto Chemical Co.	
	Orlon	E. I. du Pont de Nemours & Co.	
	Pa-Qel	Monsanto Chemical Co.	
	Remember	Monsanto Chemical Co.	
	So-Lara	Monsanto Chemical Co.	
	Zefkrome	BASF Corporation	
	Zefran	BASF Corporation	
ARAMID	Kevlar	E. I. du Pont de Nemours & Co.	No melting point; highly flame resistant. High strength; high resistance to stretch; maintains its shape and form at high temperatures.
	Nomex	E. I. du Pont de Nemours & Co.	
MODACRYLIC	Sef	Monsanto Chemical Co.	Soft, resilient, abrasion and flame resistant. Quick-drying. Resists acids and alkalies; retains shape.
NYLON	A. C. E.	Allied-Signal, Inc.	Exceptionally strong, supple, abrasion resistant. Lustrous. Easy to wash. Resists damage from oil and many chemicals. Resilient; low in moisture absorbency.
	Anso	Allied-Signal, Inc.	
	Antron	E. I. du Pont de Nemours & Co.	
	Blue"C"	Monsanto Chemical Co.	
	Cadron	Monsanto Chemical Co.	
	Cantrece	E. I. du Pont de Nemours & Co.	
	Capima	Allied-Signal, Inc.	
	Caplana	Allied-Signal, Inc.	
	Caprolan	Allied-Signal, Inc.	
	Captiva	Allied-Signal, Inc.	
	Compet	Allied-Signal, Inc.	
	Cordura	E. I. du Pont de Nemours & Co.	
	Courtaulds Nylon	Courtaulds North America Inc.	
	Crepeset	BASF Corporation	
	Cumuloft	Monsanto Chemical Co.	
	Hydrofil	Allied-Signal, Inc.	
	No Shock	Monsanto Chemical Co.	
	Patina	Allied-Signal, Inc.	
	Shareen	Courtaulds North America Inc.	
	Shimmereen	BASF Corporation	
	Tolaram	Tolaram Fibers, Inc.	
	Ultron	Monsanto Chemical Co.	
	Vivana	BASF Corporation	
	Zafran	BASF Corporation	
	Zefsport	BASF Corporation	
	Zefstat	BASF Corporation	
	Zeftron	BASF Corporation	

GENERIC FIBERS	GENERIC TRADENAMES	MANUFACTURER	GENERIC CHARACTERISTICS
OLEFIN	Avtex	Avtex Fibers Inc.	Unique wicking properties that make it very comfortable. Abrasion resistant; quick-drying; resistant to deterioration from chemicals, mildew, perspiration, rot, and weather. Sensitive to heat; soil resistant; strong; very lgihtweight. Excellent colorfastness.
	Elustra	Hercules Incorporated	
	ES Fiber	Avtex Fibers Inc.	
	Herculon	Hercules Incorporated	
	Nouvelle	Hercules Incorporated	
	Marquesa Lana	Amoco Fabrics & Fibers Co.	
	Marvess	Phillips Fibers Corporation	
	Patlon	Amoco Fabrics & Fibers Co.	
	Spectra	Allied-Signal, Inc.	
	Tolaram	Tolaram Fibers, Inc.	
POLYESTER	A. C. E.	Allied-Signal, Inc.	Strong; resistant to stretching and shrinking; resistant to most chemicals. Quick-drying; crisp and resilient when wet or dry. Wrinkle and abrasion resistant; retains heat-set pleats and creases; easy to wash.
	Avlin	Avtex Fibers Inc.	
	Ceylon	Hoechst Celanese Corp.	
	Comfort Fiber	Hoechst Celanese Corp.	
	Compet	Allied-Signal, Inc.	
	Dacron	E. I. du Pont de Nemours & Co.	
	E. S. P.	Hoechst Celanese Corp.	
	Fortrel	Fiber Industries, Inc.	
	Golden Glow	BASF Corporation	
	Golden Touch	BASF Corporation	
	Hollofil	E. I. du Pont de Nemours & Co.	
	Kodaire	Eastman Chemical Products, Inc.	
	Kodel	Eastman Chemical Products, Inc.	
	KodOfill	Eastman Chemical Products, Inc.	
	KodOsoff	Eastman Chemical Products, Inc.	
	Silky Touch	BASF Corporation	
	Strialine	BASF Corporation	
	Tolaram	Tolaram Fibers, Inc.	
	Trevira	Hoechst Celanese Corp.	
	Ultra Touch	BASF Corporation	
PBI	PBI	Hoechst Celanese Corp.	Highly flame resistant. Outstanding comfort factor combined with thermal and chemical stability properties. Will not burn or melt. Low shrinkage when exposed to flame.
	Arozole	Hoechst Celanese Corp.	
RAYON	Avril	Avtex Fibers Inc.	
	Avtex	Avtex Fibers Inc.	
	Beau-Grip	North American Rayon Corporation	
	Coloray	Courtaulds North America Inc.	
	Courtaulds Rayon	Courtaulds North America Inc.	
	Courcel	Courtaulds North America Inc.	
	Durvil	Avtex Fibers Inc.	
	Fiber 40	Avtex Fibers Inc.	
	Fiber 240	Courtaulds North America Inc.	
	Fibro	Courtaulds North America Inc.	
	Zanair	BASF Corporation	
	Zankare	BASF Corporation	
	Zankrome	BASF Corporation	
	Zantrel	BASF Corporation	

GENERIC FIBERS	GENERIC TRADENAMES	MANUFACTURER	GENERIC CHARACTERISTICS
SPANDEX	Lycra	E. I. du Pont de Nemours & Co.	Can be stretched 500 percent without breaking; can be stretched repeatedly and recover original length. Lightweight; stronger, more durable than rubber; resistant to body oils.
SULFAR	Ryton	Phillips Fibers corporation	High-performance fibers with excellent resistance to harsh chemicals and high temperatures. Excellent strength retention in adverse environments. Flame retardent; nonconductive.
VINYON	Hoechst Celanese	Hoechst Celanese Corp.	Softens at low temperature. High resistance to chemicals; nontoxic.

SOURCE: American Fiber Manufacturers Association, Inc.

MARBLE CLOTH

Originally marble cloth was produced in silk and wool, in England. Today it is produced worldwide and is made of manufactured fibers as well as natural fibers. Several colors are used in the weft, producing a variegated or mottled effect. Less frequently, the warp may be printed prior to weaving, causing a variegated effect.

MAROCAIN

Marocain is a ribbed textile with an undulating, wavy appearance similar to CRÊPE. The wavy look is created by using a spiral filling yarn during the weaving process. It is made of wool, silk and manufactured fibers. Occasionally it is made of blends of natural fibers and manufactured fibers.

MARQUISETTE

The word marquisette comes from the French word *marquise,* meaning entryway, alluding to the use of this sheer textile as a draping over entrances and doorways. Frequently, marquisette was used as mosquito netting and was made of silk. Today, marquisettes are lightweight, sheer, and have a lacy, open, mesh-like appearance and are made of cotton, rayon and manufactured fibers. The textiles are executed in a LENO WEAVE. They may be plain or have novelty effects. The yarns are often dyed in a variety of colors before the weaving process.

MARSEILLES

The marseilles textile, named after the city in France where it originated, is known for its raised woven patterns. It is a double-faced textile that is executed in on a Jacquard loom employing elaborately stitched patterns, giving the fabric a quilted appearance. During the weaving process two sets of heavy filling threads are usually employed. Juxtaposed against a plain ground, floats of the heavier filling form the raised figures. The best-known marseilles textiles are white on white and are known for their elegance. Occasionally a combination of colors may be used. Egyptian cotton (long fibers) is used in creating the yarn for marseilles.

See also MATELASSÉ.

MARVELLA

Marvella is created with a worsted warp and often employs a mohair and silk weft. Because of the mohair and silk the textile is noted for its silky luster. It is a PILE textile of high quality.

MATELASSÉ

The word matelassé is taken from the French noun *matelas,* meaning cushion or pad. Metalassé textiles are double or single weave fabrics with a definite three dimensional quality. Originally the textiles were made of silk, but today they are created in many fiber types, including manufactured fiber and metallic threads. A coarse filling yarn or stuffing thread is interlaced with the face and back of the fabric, not visible on either surface, causing the fabric to draw together, creating a padded or quilted effect. The textile is created in many weights, qualities, and variations. The term matelassé is also used to describe an ORGANDY with a crinkled appearance, called matelassé organdy, even though the textile is not a true matelassé fabric.

See also MARSEILLES.

MELTON

Named after Melton, England, where the textile originated, melton cloth is executed in a twill or satin weave and is heavily fulled and felted so that it has a smooth surface with a slight luster. It belongs to the family of face-finished textiles. The weave is totally obscured because the textile is sheared and the nap is brushed. Originally it was created only in wool but is now found in blends with manufactured fibers. Melton is always executed in plain colors.

See also FINISHES; FULLING.

MERCERIZATION

John Mercer, a calico printer in Lancashire, England, is given credit for the discovery of the mercerization process in 1844. The revolutionary process is of monumental significance in the world of textile production and is a result of the action of caustic soda upon cotton fibers. Mercer found that when a piece of bleached calico was placed in caustic soda it became stiff and translucent, but upon washing, it appeared to return to its initial state. Upon closer study, however, Mercer

Melton (wool)   Author's collection

Angora goats International Mohair Association

found that the fibers had become more rounded, the textile received dye readily and was stronger. The process was revolutionary and of great importance in the world of textile production. We now know that caustic soda (sodium hydroxide) causes a permanent swelling of the fibers. The swelling exposes more of the fiber to the light, thus giving the fabric a luster that was not possible before the process was discovered.

The mercerization process is carried out in two ways. In one process, the fabric is stretched tight and is washed in caustic soda. While the textile is still tight it is washed again with clean water. When it is relaxed it is smooth and has great luster. In the second process, the cotton is immersed in caustic soda without being stretched. The fabric is then removed from the solution, stretched beyond its original length, and washed until the tension lessens.

Yarn can also be mercerized by treating it with caustic soda and stretching it over rollers.

MERINO

Merino refers to a type of sheep, as well as a textile that is created from the wool of the sheep.
See WOOL.

MESSALINE

Messaline is thought to have been named after the third wife of the Roman emperor Claudius. A very compact warp-faced satin textile, generally made of silk, it originated in France at the end of the 19th century. It is a very lightweight, lustrous and soft textile.

MOHAIR

Mohair is a type of wool obtained from the angora goat (*Capra aegagrus hircus*). A major distinction between mohair and other types of wool is that mohair fibers lack the scales characteristic of other wools. This gives mohair the advantage of less shrinkage than other wool textiles.

The angora goat is a spiral-horned animal, delicate and graceful in its appearance. The mature male goat weights between 125–175 pounds and the female, between 80–125 pounds. Its hair is long and white and is known for its extraordinary luster, silkiness and fineness. The finest hair is from the young kid goats. The hair of the goats can grow as long as 12 inches in length, depending on whether the goat is shorn once or twice a year.

History

The angora goat can be traced to ancient times. It is thought to have originally come from Tibet and is believed to be one of the oldest surviving animals known to man.

It is said that the birth of the mohair industry began in Ankara, Turkey (from whence the name angora), after the goats were brought there from Turkestan, a distance of many thousands of miles. As Ghengis Khan drove Suleyman Shah out of the land of the Turkomans during the 13th century, he took the goats with him, moving his flocks a short distance each day. Ghengis Khan met his death on this long journey and his son succeeded him, eventually finding his way to Ankara. It was here in a favorable climate that the angora goat ended its long journey. Originally, mohair textiles were used only for the sultan's garments. Over a period of time mohair was discovered by the outside world and the demand for it became so great that the sultan of Turkey had to place an embargo on its exportation.

Many attempts to transport the goats to other countries met with total failure. The goats are delicate creatures that cannot tolerate a very wide range of environmental factors. If it is too moist they are subject to pneumonia; if it is too hot and dry, they die of thirst. Predators are always a problem. Indeed, today the

Raw sheared mohair International Mohair Association

WORLD MOHAIR PRODUCTION
(Thousands of kilograms)

YEAR	AFRICA	U.S.A.	TURKEY	ARGENTINA	LESOTHO	AUSTRALIA	NEW ZEALAND	OTHER	TOTAL
1970	4.1	7.8	4.1	1.1	0.9	–	–	–	18.0
1971	4.3	6.8	4.5	1.0	0.9	–	–	–	17.5
1972	3.7	4.6	4.1	1.0	0.8	–	–	–	14.2
1973	3.4	4.5	4.1	1.0	0.6	–	–	–	13.6
1974	3.7	3.8	4.1	1.0	0.6	–	–	–	13.2
1975	3.8	3.9	3.9	1.0	0.6	–	–	–	13.2
1976	4.1	3.6	4.0	1.0	0.6	–	–	–	13.3
1977	4.5	3.6	4.1	1.0	0.4	–	–	–	13.6
1978	4.9	3.7	4.5	1.0	0.5	–	–	–	14.6
1979	5.4	4.2	4.5	1.0	0.5	–	–	–	15.6
1980	6.1	4.0	4.5	1.0	0.5	–	–	–	16.1
1981	6.9	4.5	4.5	1.0	0.5	–	–	–	17.4
1982	7.6	4.5	4.5	1.0	0.5	–	–	–	18.1
1983	7.5	4.8	4.5	1.3	0.67	–	–	–	18.77
1984	8.1	5.1	3.5	1.0	0.75	0.5	0.05	0.05	19.05
1985	9.1	5.4	3.5	1.1	0.8	0.5	0.07	0.06	20.53
1986	11.0	5.6	3.5	1.25	0.8	0.6	0.14	0.07	22.26
1987	12.0	6.8	3.5	1.5	0.8	0.8	0.25	0.08	25.73
1988	12.5	7.0	3.0	1.5	0.5	1.0	0.35	0.1	25.95
1989	12.0	6.35	2.0	1.2	0.5	1.0	0.5	0.2	23.75

SOURCE: International Mohair Association, London. (1989 Figures projected)

greatest losses incurred by the breeders of angora goats are sustained because of "freeze loss."

In 1830, the goat was introduced to South Africa where the climate conditions were such that they prospered. Today South Africa is still the main producer of mohair. The goats later found their way to Texas as well, when Dr. J. B. Davis, conducting experiments on cotton growing in Turkey, returned to Texas with what he thought were 10 CASHMERE goats. They were, in fact, thoroughbred Angora goats. The Angora goats are also raised in Argentina, Lesotho, Australia and New Zealand, and a few other scattered locations throughout the world. At present there are 6.25 million Angora goats in the world, with approximately 1 million of them being in the United States. Each animal provides an average of 2 kilos (4.4 pounds) of hair when shorn. The total mohair production is less than 1% of all natural fibers, which qualifies it as a specialty fiber.

Production

If angora goats are raised on the range, it is necessary for the goats to be given supplemental feed such as alfalfa hay, cottonseed meal and corn, and the goats must also be given additional protein in their diets. Unlike some species, the goats are not scavengers and they respond well to good care, clean feed and clean surroundings.

Angora goats' hair grows approximately ¾ inch each month and the normal production is about 7 to 9 pounds per head per year. The goats are shorn in the United States about every six months: in February or early March, which is three to six weeks before kidding, and again in August when the kids are weaned. The shearing is done by power driven clippers similar to those used by barbers, which remove the fleece with long smooth strokes. It is then rolled separately, classified and packed into bags holding about 70 fleeces and weighing approximately 400 pounds when full.

Mohair requires skillful sorting, which is done in accordance with the fleece type. Kid fleeces are considered to be the first two shearings, at six months and one year. Young goats or yearlings are the fleeces produced at 18–24 months of age, and thereafter the fleeces are considered to be adult mohair. Each of the fleece types is sold separately, for they bear different values on the market.

The washing of mohair, which is called scouring, is achieved by moving it gently past rakes through a series

Opposite: Mohair (knit)   Mrs. William Hensler

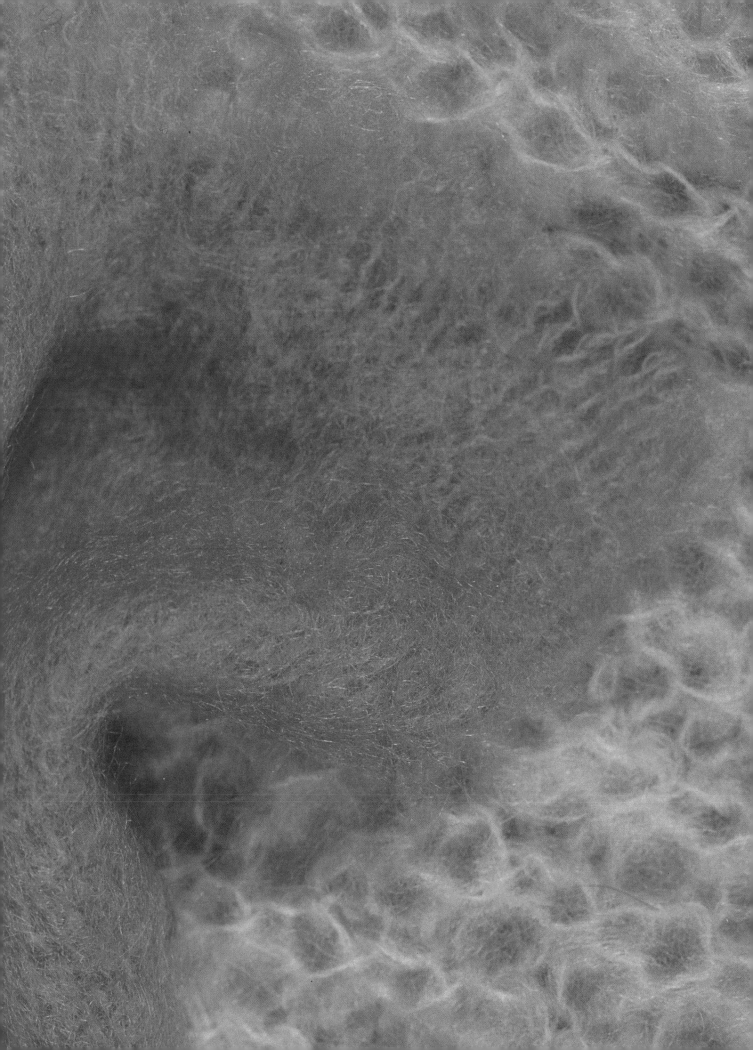

of tubs containing a soap-and-water solution, followed by rinsing. During the scouring process, as the natural grease (lanolin) and soil are removed, mohair loses about 20% of its weight. After scouring, the mohair is passed through a series of squeeze rollers and finally dried. The purified lanolin by-product is used in face creams, soaps and ointments.

The carding process blends the various types of mohair fibers, removes vegetable matter and straightens the fibers so they will lie in the same direction. This is done by passing the mohair through a system of rollers covered with wire teeth that form the fibers into a thin web. The web is then gathered into narrow strips that are joined to form the roving, or sliver.

In the spinning process, the sliver is twisted into single yarns. When two or more of these yarns are twisted together, they form ply yarns, which are stronger than singles. Yarns vary in size, twist, ply and novelty effects. After spinning, the yarn may be either knitted or woven.

If the fiber is to be used for a worsted yarn, the mohair sliver is combed to remove the short fibers, called noils, and to further straighten the long fibers for production of fine worsted yarns that are smoother than woolen yarns. The result is a thick strand that is called a "top." After combing, the number of fibers in the top is reduced by a series of processes called drawing. The drawn sliver is taken directly to the spinning frame where it is twisted to produce yarn.

After the weaving process the mohair fabric can be napped using a metal brushing process or sheared to give it a smooth uniform appearance. Various chemical finishes can be applied to make the textile mothproof, stain resistant, and washable. In order that the mohair retain its natural resilience, it is "rested" between each of the processes. The longer the lapse of time between the

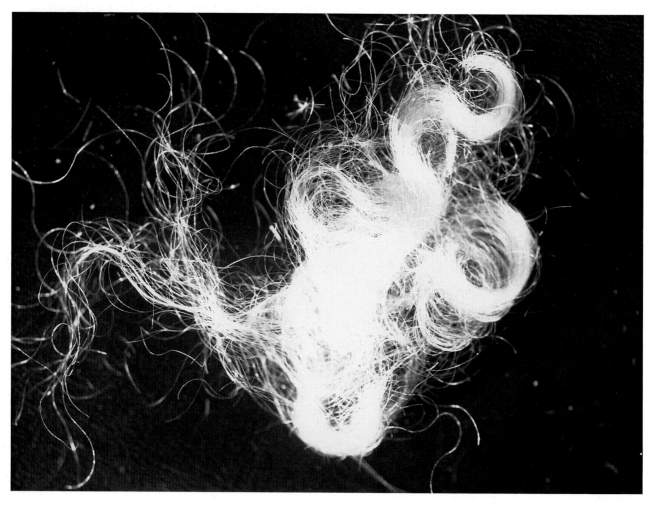

Scoured mohair International Mohair Association

Carded mohair   International Mohair Association

Mohair fabric   International Mohair Association

steps, the higher the quality of the mohair fabric that can be spun by the craftsman.

In another finishing process, mohair that is to be used for blankets and stoles is brushed with teasels, the flower head of a plant of the genus *Dipsacus,* similar to the thistle (especially the *Dipsacus fullonum,* known as the fuller teasel, with a head covered with stiff, hooked bracts). The teasel was used in ancient Egypt to comb the mohair garments to be worn by pharaohs and although much experimentation has been conducted to devise a utensil that would be as successful as the teasel, none has been produced. The teasel is grown for this purpose primarily in France.

Although mohair has a delicate look, it can be quite durable, though fabric made of kid mohair is much finer and thus less durable than a fabric made from the hair of an adult goat. Mohair remains an elegant luxury textile not often used for utilitarian garments.

The International Mohair Association has created labels to identify the quality of the mohair fiber. The gold marked label is awarded to yarns and fabrics containing a minimum of 70% mohair. The silver marked label is awarded to yarns containing a minimum of 40% mohair or fabrics containing a minimum of 35% mohair. All yarns and fabrics must be tested and approved before being awarded the mohair mark of guaranteed quality. The certification trademark is authorized by members of the relevant product group for tops, yarns, woven and knitted fabrics, men's and women's garments, and furnishing fabrics according to the separate rules of each product group.

Care of Mohair

Mohair is long lasting if treated with care. Always consult the manufacturer's instructions. In some cases, nonwashable linings and other materials may have been used in the manufacture of a mohair garment. After a mohair garment has been worn, it should be hung up to "relax." Brushing a suit will help prolong its life.

Mohair logo   International Mohair Association

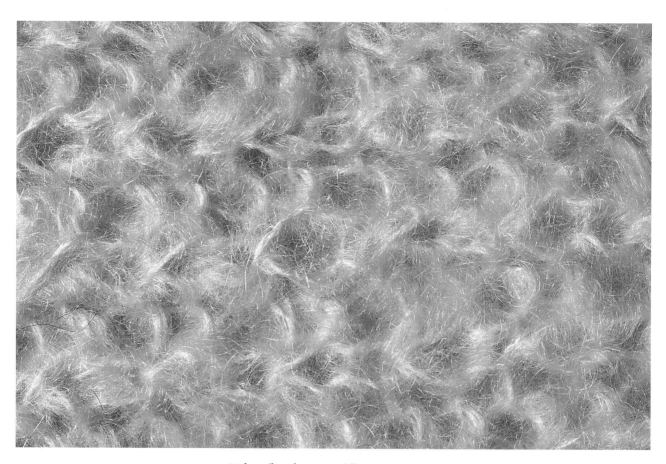

Mohair (knit [micrograph])   Dennis Sjoberg

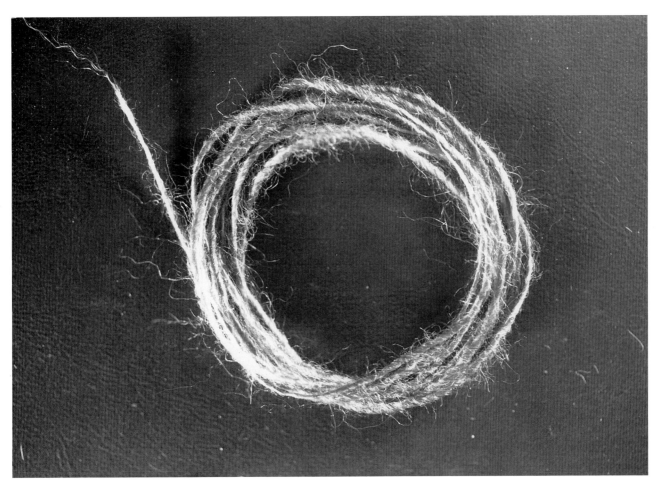

Mohair yarn (single ply)   International Mohair Association

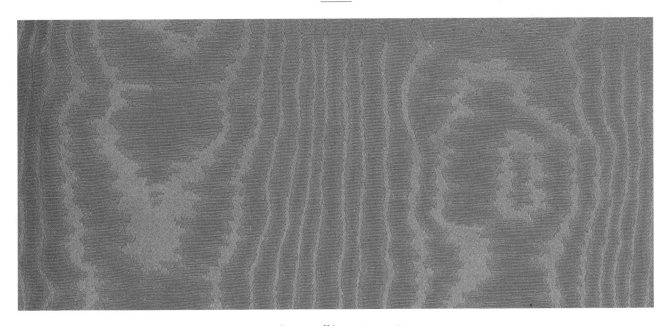

Moiré (woven silk)   Author's collection

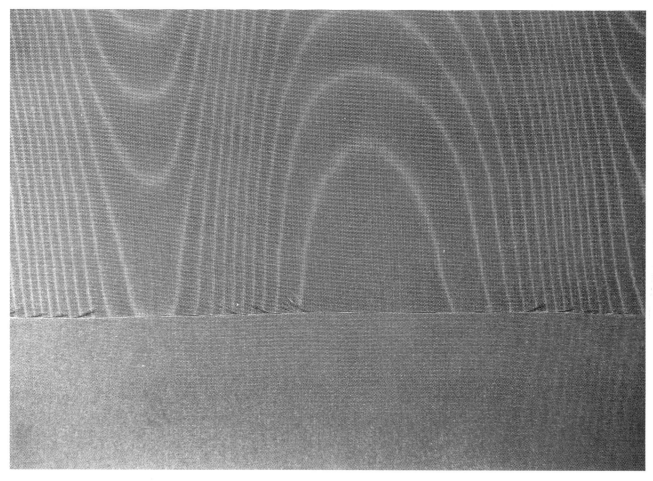

Moiré (calendered) front and back (manufactured fiber) Author's collection

If the manufacturer approves washing, follow these instructions:

- Use tepid water and a mild detergent, moving the garment in the solution with very delicate hand movements. Do not wring or squeeze.
- After thoroughly rinsing in cool water, dry the article flat on a towel. Do not wash the garment on a very humid day. High humidity prevents proper drying and increases the possibility of mildew.
- To speed the drying process encourage circulation in the room by setting up a small fan that does not blow directly on the garment.

See also WOOL.

MOIRÉ

Characterized by a wavy or watermarked effect, moiré has been popular since the 18th century. It was originally created in a silk taffeta, but now is also created in manufactured fiber. Originally the watermarked effect was created through a weaving process, today the weaving process is still used but the effect is also created through a special CALENDERING process.

MONK'S CLOTH

Monk's cloth is executed in a basket weave that incorporates double or quadruple threads in its construction. The result is a loosely constructed textile that is heavy and coarse to the touch. It is made of carded cotton yarn and nowadays is being imitated with manufactured fibers. Occasionally, the textile is called oatmeal because it often has a mottled beige tone. It is also found in a variety of colors and patterns.

MONOFILAMENT

A single filament (yarn) of continuous length extruded in the production of a MANUFACTURED FIBER.

MONTAGNAC

Originally created in France, montagnac is executed in a TWILL WEAVE with an extra set of weft yarns that FLOAT on the face of the textile. The floats are cut and brushed to a long nap. The textile is often created with cashmere or camel hair and is considered a luxury textile, due to its fiber content, softness and luster.

MOUSSELINE

Mousseline originated in France in 1826 and is the French word for muslin. The textile bears little resemblance to muslin, however. It is a very fine sheer textile made of silk, cotton, wool or manufactured fibers. It is executed in a plain weave.

There are many textiles in the mousseline family, named according to the fiber types that are employed, i.e., mousseline de laine (wool), mousseline de soie (silk), etc. The weights, sizings, finishes and qualities of the mousselines are wide and varied.

MULTIFILAMENT

A yarn made up of two or more fine continuous monofilament strands twisted together in the production of a MANUFACTURED FIBER.

MUSLIN

One of the earliest cotton cloths, muslin originated in Iraq. There are written records of its existence there as early as the 13th century. Today unbleached muslin is

Unbleached muslin (cotton)   Author's collection

the only member of the large muslin family to bear a resemblance to the original, in that it is not processed by bleaching and finishing and has a rough unrefined texture. It is known that in the 13th century, muslins were decorated with metallic threads in Iraq. By the Middle Ages the muslins were quite fine in texture and in India they were being printed with gold and silver. The first European muslins were created in Scotland in 1700. Muslins are always made of cotton and come in a wide range of weights, widths, qualities, and with various finishes.

NAINSOOK

The term nainsook is taken from two Hindu words: *nain,* meaning eye, and *sukh* meaning delight. It is known that the nainsook textiles existed as far back as the 17th century. Nainsook is executed in a plain weave. It is a lightweight cotton textile that is produced in a wide variety of qualities and finishes. Some finishes impart a crisp HAND to the textile, while others impart a softness. The textile is often mercerized, and when that process is employed, nainsook has a high luster. Occasionally cords are used in the warp and weft, and novelty effects include both stripes and checks. ≡

NAPPED FABRICS

Napped fabrics are processed so that they have either a slight or a dramatic nap on the face or both sides of the fabric. The napping process is accomplished by weaving loosely twisted yarns into the textile, which are then sheared and brushed to create the soft napped surface. Napped fabrics differ from PILE fabrics, in that they do not have extra threads incorporated in the textile.

Napping is considered a FINISHING process and is used on many fibers, including manufactured fibers, silk and wool, as well as specialty fibers such as camel hair and mohair. Occasionally the napped effect does not continuously cover the fabric but is executed in stripes or figures. ≡

NATURAL DYES

Natural dyes are dye materials obtained from bark, berries, insects, roots and other vegetable materials.
See DYES. ≡

NATURAL FIBERS

A natural fiber is any fiber that is made from natural materials and is not manufactured. They are generally derived either from plants (cellulosic fibers) or animals (protein).
See COTTON; FIBER; LINEN; SILK; WOOL. ≡

NEEDLEPUNCHED

Needlepunched fabric is created through the use of a machine that employs special hooked needles. The needles are driven through a thick web of fiber and then withdrawn. As they withdraw they disrupt the fiber, causing some of the fibers to intertwine and form a non-woven fabric referred to as stitch-bonded. The technique is rarely used for yard goods in the apparel

Net (cotton) Author's collection

market but is most often employed for household articles, such as blankets.

See also NON-WOVEN.

NET

There is a wide variety of net textiles on the market. They are always executed in a very open weave. Nets were originally created by hand and achieved by knotting, twisting, crocheting or knitting threads together to form the open web-like structures and are constructed so that there are knots at most corners. The ground of hand-made lace is also made of net. Today, nets are created by machine and vary in weight and quality. As nets are now made of silk, cotton and manufactured fibers, net is considered a generic term.

See MALINE; TULLE.

NINON

The origin of the textile ninon is not known, but it is thought that its name is a derivation of the French name Anne. Ninon originally was a very fine textile made of highly twisted thread, usually silk. It was diaphanous and had many of the qualities of a CHIFFON, although it was somewhat heavier. Today ninon is found in many weights and qualities. It is executed in a PLAIN WEAVE and constructed of silk or manufactured fibers.

NON-CRUSHABLE LINEN

Created by using a tightly twisted yarn in the weft, this versatile fabric is executed in plain weave. It is treated with a finish that imparts a resistance to wrinkling by making the textile more resilient and elastic. It is a washable and durable fabric.

See LINEN.

NON-WOVEN FABRICS

Non-woven refers to any textile that is not woven or knitted but is created by bonding fibers through the use of heat, chemical or mechanical means, or by a combination of these techniques. During the process the fibers may be placed parallel to one another or in a random manner. After the arranging of the fibers, usually in sheet form, they are bonded together with an adhesive, or by mechanical manipulation that causes the fibers to interlock. Non-woven fabrics are found most often in wool or manufactured fiber.

See also FELT; NEEDLEPUNCHED.

NOVELTY FABRIC

A textile created by using a NOVELTY WEAVE.

NOVELTY WEAVE

The term novelty weave applies to any weave or combination of weaves that deviate from the basic patterns of plain, satin and twill weaves. The novelty effects may be achieved by varying the numbers of ends (warp threads) and picks (weft threads) used in the weave or by weaving floats, puckers or other irregular patterns into the fabric. In the textile trade, the term fancies is also used, but is not regarded as an accurate definition of the novelty weave process.

See also FLOAT; PLAIN WEAVE; SATIN WEAVE; TWILL WEAVE; WEAVING.

NOVELTY YARN

YARN that embodies various unusual qualities, such as loops, crimps or varying thickness, that create unusual effects when woven.

NYLON

Nylon is a manufactured fiber that is extremely strong, elastic, abrasion resistant and lustrous. The first commercial production of nylon was begun in the United States in 1939 by the du Pont de Nemours Company. An American chemist, Dr. Wallace CAROTHERS, first synthesized nylon in 1931 as a result of his research to discover how and why certain molecules unite to form "giant" molecules, or polymers. It was through his efforts, and the efforts of his colleagues at Du Pont, that nylon was created.

The Federal Trade Commission defines nylon as "a manufactured fiber in which the fiber-forming substance

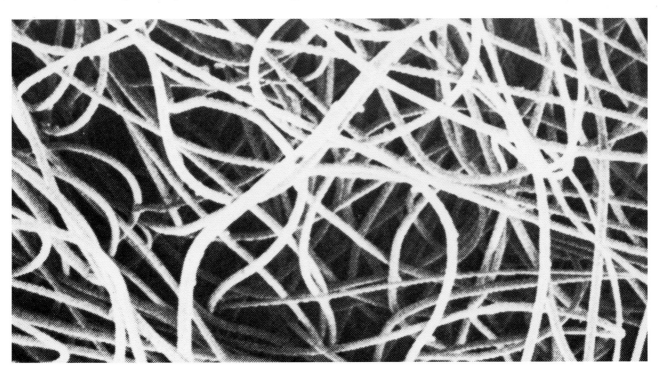

Non-woven fabric (micrograph)   American Textile Manufacturers Institute

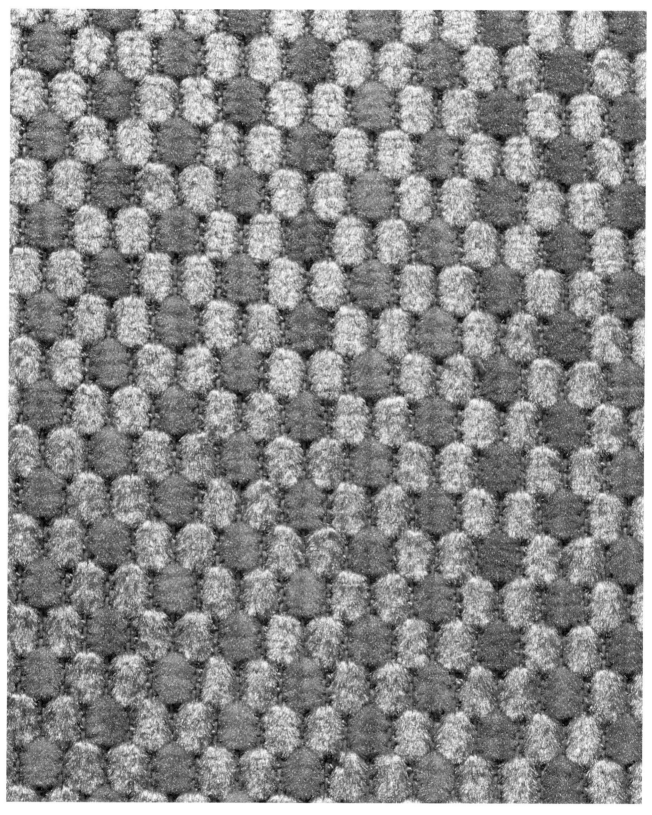

Left: Novelty cotton   Author's collection
Above: Novelty velvet   J.L. de Ball-Girmes of America, Inc.

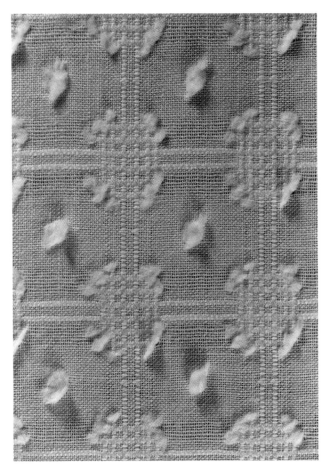

Cotton novelty weave Author's collection

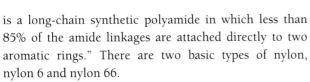

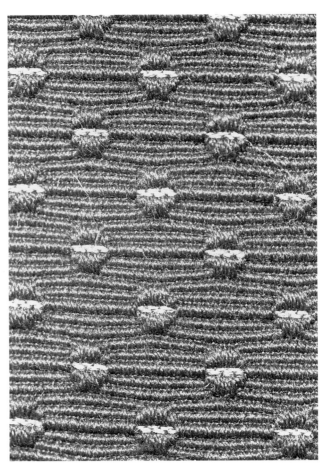

Wool novelty weave Author's collection

is a long-chain synthetic polyamide in which less than 85% of the amide linkages are attached directly to two aromatic rings." There are two basic types of nylon, nylon 6 and nylon 66.

The raw materials for creating nylon are obtained from four basic elements obtained from petroleum or natural gas (carbon and hydrogen), the air (nitrogen and oxygen), and water (hydrogen and oxygen). The elements are combined by chemical processes into compounds known as adipic acid hexamethylene diamine and caprolactam. These are reacted to form the long-chain polymers that constitute the fiber-forming substance known as polyamides. The polyamide is melt spun and drawn after cooling to give the desired properties for each intended use. For example, the production of industrial and carpet fibers of nylon begins with an aqueous solution of monomers, which proceeds through the polymerization, spinning, drawing, or draw-texturing processes. Nylon can be pre-colored, that is, coloring pigment can be added before extrusion, or it can be dyed after extrusion.

Care of Nylon

Always consult the manufacturer's label for care instructions. If the article is washable, it can be washed by machine. Warm, but not hot, water should be used, and a fabric softener can be used in the last rinse.

Nylon can be machine dried, but it is essential to use a low setting, and to retrieve the article as soon as it is just dry to avoid wrinkling.

Ironing nylon is rarely necessary. If it is required, it should be done at a very low temperature to avoid melting the nylon.

See also MANUFACTURED FIBER.

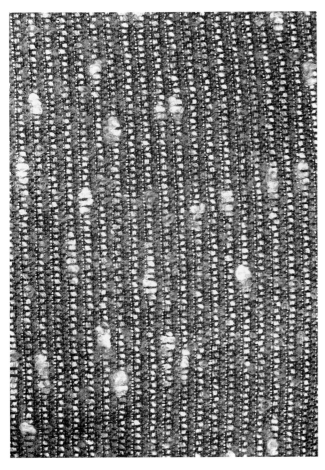

Wool blend novelty weave
Author's collection

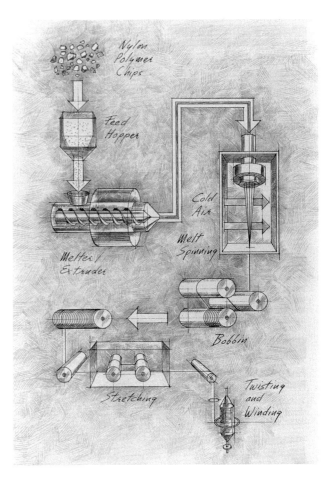

Nylon manufacturing process
American Fiber Manufacturers Association, Inc.

OILCLOTH

Originally, oilcloth referred to a textile such as cotton or linen that had been coated with oil to make it waterproof. It was known for its shiny outer surface, which had the look of patent leather, while the backing of the cloth had a brushed, soft surface. Today, oilcloth is coated with modern resins created from plastic derivatives rather than oil. The modern oilcloths are both versatile and flexible and are created in a wide variety of colors and prints.

OLEFIN FIBER

The Federal Trade Commission defines olefin as "a manufactured fiber in which the fiber forming substance is any long-chain synthetic polymer composed of at least 85% by weight of ethylene, propylene, or other olefin units, except amorphous (non-crystaline) polyolefins." The first commercial production of olefin in the United States began in 1958, when monofilaments were created for very specialized uses. In 1961 olefin multifilaments were created by Hercules, Incorporated, making the production of an olefin textile possible. Olefin is used for apparel, automobiles (particularly interior parts), home furnishings, and industrial uses such as carpets, ropes and bagging.

Olefin fibers (polypropylene and polyethylene) are petroleum products, derived from propylene and ethylene gases. Both fibers are characterized by their resistance to moisture. Of the two, polypropylene is the more favored for general textile applications. Olefin is

strong, abrasion resistant, quick drying, colorfast, resistant to deterioration from chemicals and mildew, and is stain and soil resistant. Its fibers have the lowest density of all manufactured fibers, giving olefin textiles a very lightweight quality. Color is added to olefin prior to or during the melt spinning process.

Care of Olefin

Always consult the manufacturer's care label. Stains can easily be removed from olefin textiles with lukewarm water and a mild detergent. Bleaches can be used on olefin without causing discoloration. Olefin dries very rapidly, but in order to ensure that the garment is not affected by heat, it should be dried on a line or at a very low heat in the drier.

See also MANUFACTURED FIBER.

ONDULÉ

The term ondulé is a French word meaning wavy or undulating. Ondulé is executed in a PLAIN WEAVE. The undulating effect is created by weaving the warp in an irregular or wavy fashion. A special reed is used to create that effect. Today, ondulé is created in silk, cotton and manufactured fibers.

ORGANDY

Organdy is a very sheer, crisp, lightweight cotton textile executed in a plain weave. The yarns or threads used for organdy are combed and the textile is given a clear finish.

Cotton organdy (front and back) Author's collection

Organdy was developed in Switzerland, by A. G. Wattwil for Heberlein & Company. The process he devised imparted a permanent finish to the textile, eliminating the need to sprinkle and iron the fabric. Although organdy is often white, it is now also available in a wide variety of colors.

ORGANZA

Organza belongs in the ORGANDY family. It is a transparent, crisp, PLAIN WEAVE textile of silk. Organza is now processed so that it has the same crisp texture that is characteristic of ORGANDY.

OSNABERG

Osnaberg originated in Osnabruck, Germany. It is executed in a PLAIN WEAVE and is characterized by its strength and durability. The texture of osnaberg is quite coarse and it is a medium to heavyweight textile. Osnaburg's characteristics are created by using the lower grades of cotton and by lowering the thread count. It can be found with or without a finish. When it is finished, it is usually called HOPSACKING or CRASH. Osnaburg can be obtained in a wide variety of colors and prints.

OTTOMAN

Ottoman originated in Turkey as early as the 13th century. During the time of the Ottoman empire, it was created solely of silk and was a luxurious fabric worn by sultans. Today, it is made of silk, wool or manufactured fiber. Occasionally cotton is used in the weft.

Ottoman is executed in a PLAIN WEAVE. It is very firm, has high luster and is characterized by horizontal ribs or cords. The cords are created by entirely covering the weft threads with the warp. Ottomans are also created in

DOUBLE KNIT fabrics, where the horizontal ribs are created by incorporating more stitches in the length of the double knit on one side than on the other.

Another type of Ottoman textile is a heavy ribbed fabric executed in a SATIN WEAVE.

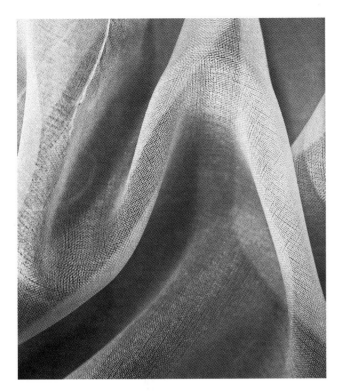

Organza (silk) Author's collection

OXFORD

Oxford cloth was originally made in Scotland during the late 19th century. The Scotch mill where the textile was produced created four types that were used primarily as shirting textiles.

Oxford cloth is executed in a plain weave using combed fiber and is given a finishing process that imparts a slight luster to the textile. Originally of cotton, it is now possible to find oxford in blends of cotton and manufactured fiber. Originally a dark gray color, today oxford cloth is available in white and a wide variety of colors, as well as in strips and other novelty effects. The lighter weight mixtures are sometimes called cambridge, after Cambridge University, Oxford's rival. Oxford is often treated with special finishing techniques making it wrinkle resistant.

Ottoman Loven Fabrics

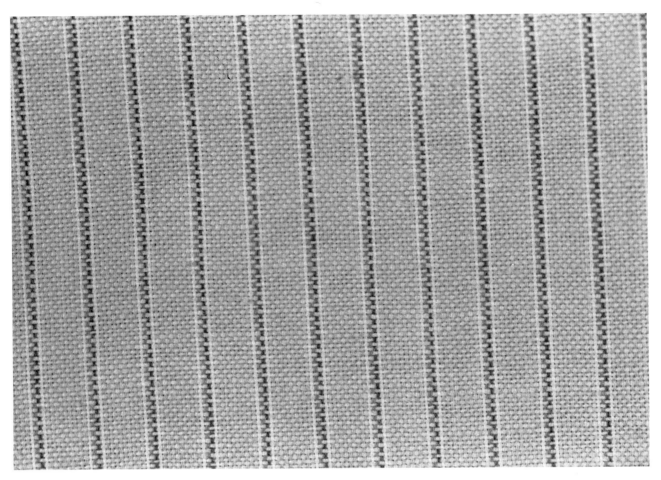

Oxford (cotton/manufactured fiber/blend)   Author's collection

P

PAILLETTE SATIN

Paillette satin is recognizable for its changeable color effects. The effects are achieved by using two colors in a five-harness warp satin weave that includes more ends (warp threads) than picks (weft threads) per inch. The textile is no longer made exclusively of silk, but is imitated in manufactured fiber, and is available in a wide range of colors.

PANNÉ

Panné is a French word that means plush. A textile known since the Middle Ages, it resembles VELVET but its pile is much longer than that of velvet. A technique employed in the creation of panné presses the pile in one direction during the finishing process and gives it a very high luster. Today, panné is created in silk, silk and wool blends, and is imitated with manufactured fiber.

PASTEUR, LOUIS (1822–1895)

A French scientist, Pasteur made contributions of worldwide importance in the areas of chemistry, medicine and industry. It was Pasteur's discovery that bacteria spread disease that he is best known for. In 1865 the silk industry in France was threatened by a disease called pebrine, which was killing hundreds of thousands of silkworms. Pasteur discovered that the cause of the disease was a microbe that attacked the silkworm eggs. By destroying the germ in the silkworm hatcheries the disease was eliminated. The disease had done so much damage to the industry, however, that it never fully recovered.

See SILK.

PAUL, LEWIS

An 18th century English inventor, Lewis Paul collaborated with John Wyatt in creating a drawing device that operated using rollers and the two men took out a patent for the device on June 24, 1738. The process involved pressing the fiber (cotton) between two rollers operating at different speeds. The two men also took out a patent on August 30, 1748 on a carding machine, although they did not invent the machine itself. On June 29, 1758 the men applied for and received a patent on a spinning machine.

See SPINNING.

PEAU de CYGNE

From the French phrase meaning "swan skin," peau de cygne is a silk textile woven of crêpe yarns, executed in a SATIN WEAVE that requires eight harnesses. Its characteristics are high luster, good body and a slightly slubbed texture.

PEAU de PECHE

Taken from the French, peau de peche, meaning "skin of the peach," is a silk textile executed in a TWILL WEAVE and undergoes a special FINISHING process that imparts a soft nap to the textile.

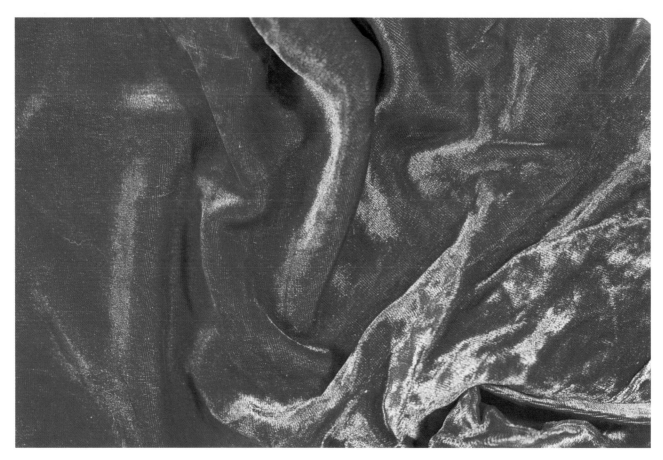

Panné velvet (manufactured fiber blend)

PEAU de SOIE

Peau de soie, meaning "skin of silk" in French, is a silk textile executed in a satin weave requiring eight harnesses. The characteristics of peau de soie are substantial body, good drapability and a dull luster. Today peau de soie is imitated in manufactured fiber.

PEKIN

Pekin is a textile with vertical stripes that are always of the same width and separated by the same width. Many varieties of the textile exist that incorporate NOVELTY WEAVEs and varying fibers. The textile can be of cotton, wool, or silk or made of elaborate velvet stripes separated by satin. It is known for its fine quality.

PERCALE

Percale come from the Persian word *pargalah*. Originally used to describe a cotton textile with an even higher thread count than the percales we know today, percale is now executed in a PLAIN WEAVE with carded yarn, and contains 180 to 200 threads per inch. The finest percales are made of combed fiber. Percale is an extremely important textile, used not only in the making of garments but in the production of household textiles such as sheeting. Today, percale comes in a wide variety of colors as well as prints.

PERCALINE

Percaline is created from combed cotton fabric with a high thread count. It is known for its luster, achieved by mercerization. During the finishing process percaline is frequently calendered so that it has a MOIRÉ effect. In some instances it is given a glaze of synthetic resin.

See FINISHING.

PERKIN, SIR WILLIAM HENRY (1838–1907)

William Henry Perkin, an Englishman, distinguished himself as a chemist when he produced the first synthetic dye in 1856. It rendered the color mauve, and was called mauvine.

Perkin attended the City of London school, where his abilities were quickly recognized in the subject of chemistry. He was sent to the Royal College of Chemistry where he became an assistant to the well known German chemist August Wilhelm von Hoffman. Hoffman was experimenting on a process he hoped would produce synthetic quinine. Perkin began to work on the process at home in his spare time. It was during those experiments that Perkin accidentally created mauvine by oxidizing aniline with potassium dichromate. When the black precipitate that was created was extracted with ethyl alcohol, a bright purple solution was produced. Perkin realized the potential of the solution as a dyestuff. He built a factory at Freenford near London to create the dye when he was only 18 years of age. Perkin's discovery had a profound effect on the worldwide community of chemists; there followed the discovery of a whole new series of synthetic dyes.

See DYES.

PICK

See WEFT.

PIECE GOODS

The term piece goods refers to textiles, that are not cut and that are specifically meant to be sold in textile retail stores.

PILE

Pile refers to any textile that has a plush, brushed surface of cut or uncut yarns. Many types of pile textile exist,

Peau de peche Loven Fabrics

Peau de soie (silk) Author's collection

such as warp pile, which is double woven with an extra set of warp threads, which are cut by special wires or knives and give the textile a textured surface. VELVET is another example of a warp pile fabric. Uncut pile is executed by weaving the extra yarns over smooth wires that are then withdrawn without cutting the threads, leaving raised loops.

Pile on pile textiles include patterns created by weaving pile of different lengths into the textile or shearing the yarns to different lengths. Knit textiles with a pile are called VELOURS and are usually created on a circular knitting machine.

See VELVET.

PIQUÉ

Piqué is a term taken from the French verb *piquer*, meaning to pierce. Piqué textiles are most often created

with combed and carded cotton that has been mercerized, but are also found in blends. There are many varieties of piqué. Some piqué has cords running vertically, some horizontally, and some have cords in both directions, creating a waffle effect. Piqués often take on an embossed look. Although white is usually associated with piqué, it often is available in colors and prints and is a very versatile textile.

PLAID

The word plaid is used to describe a particular pattern, but in actuality it does not refer to a pattern at all but rather to a type of a highland Scottish dress. It is a textile 2 yards wide by 6 yards long, pleated around the wearer. The kilt still worn today is an outgrowth of the plaid. The plaids were commonly patterned in stripes or bars that crossed each other at right angles. There are also

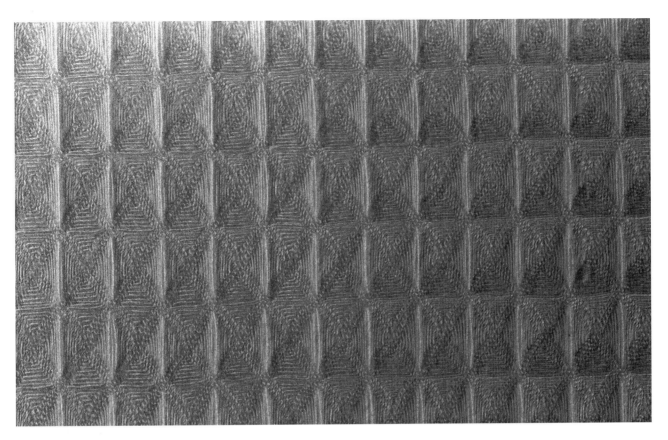

Novelty piqué   Author's collection

Plain weave (micrograph)   American Textile Manufacturers Institute

Plaid Jacquard   Valdese Weavers, Inc.

examples of patterns over patterns that are now called plaid on plaid. In Scotland each clan had its own pattern. Some of the most common patterns known are ARGYLE, TATTERSALL, GLENN URQUHART and harlequin.

See also TARTAN.

PLAIN WEAVE

One of the three basic weaves, plain weave is the most often used of the three. The plain weave repeats on two ends (warp threads) and two picks (weft threads). The first end passes over the first pick and under the second pick. The process is reversed by the second end and weaves one up. The basket weave is a form of the plain weave; it uses two up, two down. Occasionally, the plain weave is referred to as the linen weave, due to the fact that so much linen is woven this way. Linen weave is not a technical term, however.

See also LOOM; SATIN WEAVE; TWILL WEAVE; WEAVING.

PLISSÉ

The textile plissé gets its name from the French word meaning wrinkled. In the U.S. Plissé is a cotton textile that has been treated with a caustic soda solution, which shrinks part of the cloth. The shrinking of the textile produces a crinkled or wrinkled effect. In France, plissé is created by weaving tucks into the textile that form a permanent part of its structure. Plissé should not be confused with SEERSUCKER, which resembles it in appearance to some degree.

PLUSH

Plush is a term taken from the French word *peluche*, which means shaggy. The textile is constructed with a PLAIN WEAVE, similar to VELVET, but the pile is much longer and is usually less dense. Plush is often created using a combination of fibers, which may include MOHAIR, WOOL and MANUFACTURED FIBERS. Plush is often multicolored, and is also found in a variety of patterns.

Plissé (cotton) Author's collection

Plaid (linen) Author's collection

POLYESTER

Polyester fibers are produced from fiber forming material made from elements derived from coal, air, water and petroleum, and are melt spun.

Polyester is defined by the Federal Trade Commission as "a manufactured fiber in which the fiber-forming substance is any long-chain, synthetic polymer composed of at least 85% by weight of an ester of a substituted aromatic carbophylic acid, including but not restricted to substituted terephthalate units." The first production of a polyester in the United States was carried out by E. I. du Pont de Nemours in 1953.

Polyester fibers are strong and crease resistant, they retain shape and resist mildew. They also are abrasion resistant, and are readily washable.

Care of Polyesters

Always consult the manufacturer's label. Some polyester garments should not be washed, due to materials that are incorporated in the garment such as lining, interlinings and trims.

Launderable polyester textiles can be washed and dried by machine. Warm water should be used and it is advisable to add a fabric softener to the final rinse. In order to avoid wrinkles, the articles must be removed from the drier as soon as they are dry. If an article must be ironed, it should be done with a warm, not hot, iron to avoid melting the fiber.

See MANUFACTURED FIBER.

POMPADOUR TAFFETA

It is said that pompadour taffeta was named after Madame de Pompadour, mistress and confidante of King Louis XV of France. The distinctive textile most frequently has large floral designs in VELVET or PILE on a TAFFETA ground—if floral designs are not used, stripes are created of the pile or velvet—and is usually executed in rich jewel tones. Originally, pompadour taffeta was made of a rich silk, but today is copied in manufactured fibers as well.

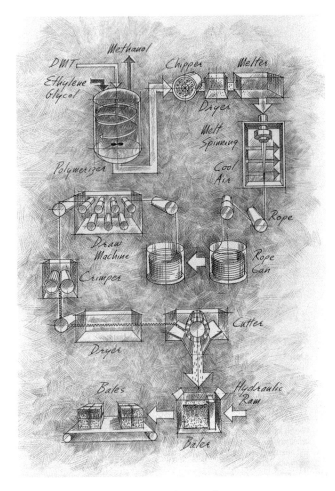

Polyester production chart
American Fiber Manufacturers Association, Inc.

PONGEE

Pongee is derived from the Chinese word *penchi,* which means "woven at home." The textile is executed in a plain weave in SILK and comes in many qualities and weights. The textile originated in China and India, where it was made of wild silk, which caused a nubby textural quality due to the irregularity of the yarn. Silk pongee is now imitated in both cotton and manufactured fibers. In order to attain the irregular slubby texture of true pongee, threads of varying weights and sizes are used in the weft. The textile dyes well and comes in a variety of colors.

POPLIN

The term poplin is taken from the French word *popeline* and was originally created in Avignon, France. Poplin constitutes a whole family of textiles that are created in a plain weave, characterized by crosswise ribs. The ribs are created by warp yarns that are much finer than the weft or filling yarns. Poplin is available in many weights and qualities, and may be constructed of WOOL, COTTON, SILK and MANUFACTURED FIBER.

POULT DE SOIE

Poult de soie is a French term taken from the Italian word *paduasoy* meaning silk from Padua. The textile of this name was first created in Padua, Italy, and was regarded by the Venetians as a luxurious fabric. It is of fine quality and made with heavier weft yarns that cause horizontal ribs. It resembles FAILLE, but is much more delicate in quality and hand. It is sometimes given a moiré finish by CALENDERING.

POWER LOOM

The power loom is the standard type of loom used today in the commercial production of fabrics.

See LOOM.

PRESSURE DYEING

See DYES.

Pages 178 and 179: Printed Italian silk adapted by the Metropolitan Museum of Art from a painting in the collections of the Princes of Leichtenstein. Made by Antonio Ratti, Como, Italy

PRINTING

As it applies to fabric or textile, printing (also called fabrography) is the surface application of design or pattern by hand or machine.

History

Because textiles are perishable and changes in temperature, humidity and light can destroy fabrics over the course of time, it is extremely difficult to trace the methods used to decorate textiles. Some indications of these techniques are given to us through writings and through cave and wall paintings, but we must theorize as to the actual origins of most techniques.

We do know that the Egyptians had printed fabrics. In the tomb of Beni Hasan, circa 2100 B.C., there are extensive wall paintings of figures wearing clothing that appears to have printed designs on them. There are also indications of print materials in early India, and in the early cultures of Indonesia, Java and Peru. Quite possibly the early Indian cottons were printed using a mordant and dye technique that was executed with a brush. Many feel that resist printing was probably the first type of printing developed. This technique involved painting the textile in a pattern prior to dyeing with a paste or chemical that would resist the dyes. After the dyeing process, the textile was washed, removing the paste or chemical and thus leaving a white design on a colored textile. Though simple in its beginnings, this technique has been highly developed in the textile industry today and is still used in roller printing.

In the 17th century, Germany became a center for an industry of printed textiles, which were executed using the block print method (see below). Other block printing industries also arose in Switzerland, France, and England during this same period.

By the 18th century, France had a vigorous industry in Jouy, where textile printing was truly raised to an art

Roller screen printing   J. L. de Ball-Girmes of America, Inc.

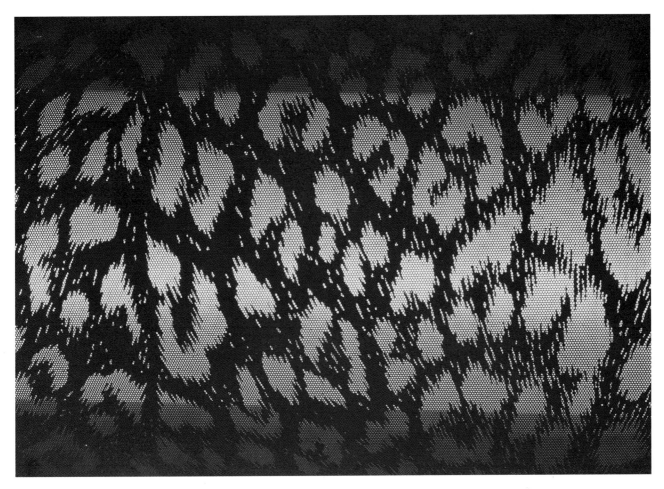

Roller screen   J. L. de Ball-Girmes of America, Inc.

form, in large part through the creativity of Christophe Philippe Oberkampf. Oberkampf was a Bavarian who had spent most of his life in France. He is often credited with the first roller printing, although there had been other attempts at the technique prior to his inventive use of it. In 1760 Oberkampf introduced his first TOILES DE JOUY. He had executed the design, the dyeing and the printing in a factory that he had established. The linen textiles were a tremendous success. By 1783 his factory was designated a Royal Manufactory, and his textiles were much sought after by ladies of the court. Oberkampf was clearly clever as well as highly creative. He capitalized on current events and very often incorporated them in central motifs of his work, thus creating a constant demand for his most recent textiles.

Screen printing, also called silk screening or serigraphy, is considered the most recent of the printing techniques. This method was first used commercially in Lyons, France, around 1850. Switzerland and Germany followed suit in 1870 though the method did not gain stature in the United States until the 1920s. Screening was still being done by hand until the 1960s when the firm of Fritz Buser, a Swiss company, developed an automatic machine capable of executing the process.

Printing Methods

There are several methods of printing fabric. The methods can be divided into two categories: hand application and mechanical application.

Hand Applications

Wood Block Printing. It is thought that the Chinese were probably the first to use wood block printing. This process is executed by hand using a block onto which a pattern has been made. The designs are usually cut out, but in some cases are built up with another medium. The designs are found only on one side of the block. The

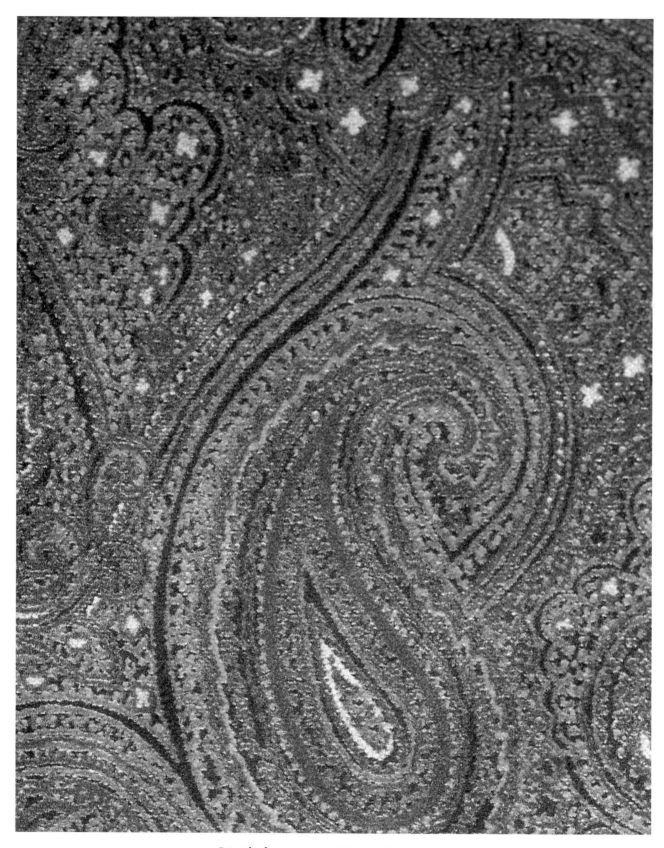

Printed velvet J. L. de Ball-Girmes of America, Inc.

artist places the design side of the block in a color medium that can be pigment or dye, prepared for textile use. The block is then pressed against the textile. The patterns imprinted can be all over, completely covering the fabric, or partial, depending on the desired composition. Often block prints have as many as six colors incorporated in the designs. Elaborate prints of this kind require a different block for each color. The block printing process is long and arduous, but is still used by artists today.

Stencil Printing. The forerunner of hand screen printing was stencil printing. The technique of stencil printing is most closely associated with the early Japanese. Stencil printing was accomplished by cutting a design out of a sheet of paper, placing the cutout over the textile and applying color to the area with a brush. Though the process appears simple, exquisitely elaborate

patterns were created in this manner. This technique eventually developed into the screen printing method.

Screen Printing. In screen printing, a sheer textile is stretched tight over a frame on which the inverse of the desired pattern is made by blocking out certain areas or lines, thus forming a type of stencil or mask. The material to be printed is placed in contact with and beneath the screen, usually held in place by means of a vacuum produced through small perforations on the print table. Dye or ink is spread across the entire surface of the screen by means of a spatula or squeegee, forcing it through the unblocked portions of the screen and forming the print on the material underneath.

There are two methods of producing the screen pattern. One is to cut the pattern by hand on laminated acetate film, cutting only through the top layer. This layer is then actually dissolved into the fabric and the

Roller-printed fabric Author's collection

Printed velvet (micrograph)   Dennis Sjoberg

backing layer is peeled off, leaving the pattern embedded in the screen fabric. The second method is to make an opaque mask in the desired pattern, usually on acetate film. The screen material is impregnated with a photographic emulsion and placed into contact with the mask and the arrangement is exposed to a strong light source. Exposure to light hardens the emulsion in the screen, but the areas masked by the pattern remain soft. The screen is then washed with a solvent, which removes the emulsion only where it has remained unexposed, creating the same pattern on the screen that was on the mask.

Patterns of great refinement can thus be made, limited only by the fineness of the fabric used for the screen. Silk was originally used, and hence both its commonly used name, silk screening, and the technical term for the process, serigraphy (from the Latin *sericus,* meaning silk). Today there are many manufactured textiles that are more durable than silk that are expressly made for this purpose in a variety of mesh sizes. Individual artists

still practice the hand method of screen printing and many fine examples are available in galleries.

Mechanical Applications

Screen Printing. Screen printing has been adopted by the commercial textile industry and is considered to be one of the most important methods of textile printing. The methods are essentially the same as those used in hand printing, but commercial print tables have automated squeegees and conveyor belt dryers that facilitate fast and consistent printing. In multicolor printing, a different frame (and pattern) is used for each color. If the pattern is not very large, this can be done on turret presses, where four frames rotate into place in succession, locking into automatic registration. The size of the repeat for a screen printed textile is limited only by the size of the screen frame and the print table used.

Rotary Screen Printing. This method is a variation on screen printing in which a design is made with perforations on hollow metal cylinders through which the dye or ink is forced as the textile passes beneath the rotating cylinder. As many as 12 to 16 cylinders can be used in succession, each imprinting a different color and part of the design to the textile in perfect registration. State-of-the-art rotary printing machines can print up to 100 yards of fabric per minute, creating designs of high quality and complexity.

Roller Printing. The roller printing method has become highly developed today. It is a process that incorporates the techniques of engraving and color printing, except that fabric is used instead of paper. The designs are transferred onto metal rollers through the use of a photochemical process that etches them on the surface. The rollers are then polished so that the dye will spread evenly over the surface of the fabric when it is applied. The rollers on the machine are kept at a carefully regulated, even pressure. As the fabric moves around the roller, dye is applied from a trough. The textile is run through the machine over another textile that absorbs any excess dye. Printing in this manner is an exacting and precise process. An offshoot of this method is duplex printing in which both sides of the textile are printed at the same time. So sophisticated has duplex printing become, and so accurate are the registrations on both sides, that it is hard to discern without a microscope that the pattern isn't woven into the textile.

Many other methods of printing have been developed. See individual entries for APPLIED PRINTING; BLOCK PRINTING; DISCHARGE PRINTING; DUPLEX PRINTING; ELECTROSTATIC PRINTING; FLOCKING; ROLLER PRINTING; ROTARY PRINTING; SCREEN PRINTING; TRANSFER PRINTING.

QIVIUT

Qiviut, pronounced KI-VEE-UTE, an Eskimo word meaning "down" or "underwool" refers to the underwool obtained from the rare arctic musk ox (genus *Ovibus*, species *moschatus*). Textiles made from qiviut are characterized by their softness, luster, durability, and the lack of oils or lanolin, even in its harvested state. Qiviut's warmth (eight times warmer than sheep's wool of equal weight), fineness and delicate lightweight quality are superlative.

The adult male musk ox stands about 5 feet high and is about 7 feet long; females are somewhat smaller. The adults weigh between 400 and 700 pounds. They have short, stocky legs with hooves similar to cattle, and a short tail. The animal bears a long shaggy coat that is dark brown, with an undercoat of grayish brown or taupe. It feeds on grass, willows, and lichens. The name for the musk ox favored by native Alaskans is "oomingmak," which means "the bearded one."

History. Musk oxen are survivors of the ice age, and have few natural enemies save man. By the end of the 19th century they had been hunted almost to extinction. A large effort was undertaken in the 1930s to reintroduce the animal to Alaska from herds that still existed in Greenland. The effort was largely successful, and as a result there are approximately 2,000 wild musk oxen in Alaska today.

In the 1950s Dr. John Teal, professor and director of the Institute of Northern Agricultural Research at the University of Alaska-Fairbanks, sought a way in which the musk ox and the Eskimo could join forces for mutual survival. Dr. Teal placed a few of the animals on his farm in an effort to determine whether or not it was possible to domesticate them. He concluded that it was, for the musk oxen demonstrated a peaceful, even docile, nature. They seemed to thrive when provided ample nutritious food, and the qiviut was not affected by domestication. As a result, 33 calves were brought to a farm from Nunivik Island in 1964 and became the nucleus of a herd that now numbers around 100.

Removing qiviut Oomingmak, Inc.

A musk ox producer's co-op, Oomingmak Inc., was started in Anchorage exclusively to provide additional income to native Alaskans. The basic motive in the qiviut industry is not in making large corporate profits, but rather to help sustain the villages and their culture. The musk ox is also a beneficiary of this effort, since it is the goal of Oomingmak, Inc. to establish herds of the animals at many remote villages, where they will be cared for by village members, creating a self-sustaining enterprise.

Production. Musk oxen lose their undercoat (qiviut) every spring, usually in May. In the wild, the undercoat is found on bushes and rocks where the oxen rub themselves during the molting season. Native Alaskans occasionally gather the "wild" qiviut and knit with it, but exposure to the extremes of weather dry the fiber out. Most of today's qiviut is from the domesticated herd.

During the molting season the musk oxen are brought into pens where the undercoat is coaxed out of the long guard hairs of the outer coat by gently massaging with fingers, or by using combs to bring the qiviut gently to the surface. No shearing is necessary. The qiviut emerges in soft puff balls that are almost entirely devoid of foreign materials such as twigs, burrs, etc. For this reason, qiviut needs no carding (combing) prior to spinning.

The qiviut underlies the entire outer coat, which results in a high annual productivity of approximately 5 pounds per animal. This figure is all the more remarkable since an entire scarf can be knit from only 1.5 ounces of qiviut.

Spinning. Originally, native Alaskans hand spun the qiviut in the same way that they made thread from sinew, by gently twisting and plying two threads simultaneously with their fingers. Qiviut is now machine spun, however, by the village women, for if both spinning and knitting were done entirely by hand, the time required to produce finished articles would cause their price to be prohibitive.

Knitting. Knitting with qiviut was a natural development, since the native women were already knitters, rather than weavers. At present, approximately 198 native Alaskan women knit all the articles made from qiviut, using patterns indigenous to each of their villages. Some of the patterns date back to the 11th and 12th centuries. The women are paid by the stitch, not by the finished piece. Finished articles are flown from the remote villages to Anchorage, where they are marketed by Oomingmak, Inc.

Some of the patterns that are made are:

Mekeryuk (harpoon)   Oomingmak, Inc.

Bethel (butterfly)   Oomingmak, Inc.

Nelson Island's nightmute (diamond) Oomingmak, Inc.

Shishmeref (star) Oomingmak, Inc.

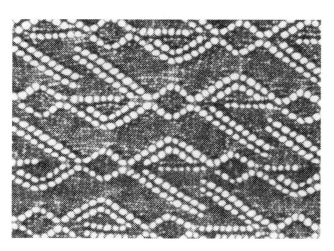

St. Mary's (dancer) Oomingmak, Inc.

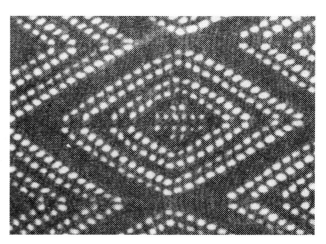

Marshall (grass basket) Oomingmak, Inc.

R

RADIUM

Radium originated in Lyons, France, where it was created with the weft thread of silk that alternated in twist from left to right. Today, the textile is created in a plain weave with a weft of a different color. Occasionally the textile is executed with a very tightly twisted yarn in the weft that gives it a SHOT effect when it moves in the light. The silk textile is characterized by its luster and smooth, soft hand.

RAJAH

Rajah originated in India, where it was made exclusively of silk. Today, it is imitated in manufactured fiber as well. It is executed in a plain or twill weave and employs weft threads that are heavier than warp threads. It resembles SHANTUNG because of its slubby surface. Rajah is a strong compact textile, available in a wide range of colors and prints.

RAMIE

The word ramie is Malay for China grass. It is the fiber that comes from the inner bark of a plant of the genus *Boehmeria* of the family Urticaceae. The plant stands between 5 and 8 feet in height and has dark green foliage and non-stinging nettles. The fiber obtained from the plant is white to cream-colored and is 83% cellulose. The average fiber length is 6 inches, is very strong, dyes well and has a high luster. It is processed much as flax is processed in the production of LINEN, with the exception that the fiber is removed from the ramie plants prior to drying. Textiles created with ramie are executed in a plain or twill weave. They are strong, smooth and moderately durable.

RATINÉ

The textile ratiné originated in Italy as early as the 17th century, but its name comes from the French word *ratiné* meaning rough. It is a PLAIN WEAVE textile executed in NOVELTY YARNS that give it an uneven pebbled surface. Because the pebbly surface may look like grains of rice, ratiné is often called "rice cloth." Ratiné is created in SILK, COTTON and WOOL, and is available both in solid colors and prints.

RAYON

Rayon is a cellulose fiber used to make fabrics characterized by high absorbency, softness, dyeability and drapability.

The Federal Trade Commission defines rayon as "a manufactured fiber composed of regenerated cellulose, as well as manufactured fibers composed of regenerated

Rayon Author's collection

cellulose in which substitutes have replaced not more than 15% of the hydrogens of the hydroxyl groups."

The first rayon fiber was produced by Count Hilaire de Chardonnet, an inventive Frenchman, referred to as the "Father of rayon." It was his dream to produce an artificial silk. In 1884, he did create a fiber by chemical means, which he presented at the 1889 Paris Exhibition. It proved to be a sensation, and was called "artificial silk" until nearly half a century later, when the term rayon was coined.

This first fiber was discovered to be highly flammable however, and more experimentation was necessary to remove the flammable nitrates from the fiber. Chardonnet also built the first commercial plant to create manufactured fibers at Besançon, France, in 1891. The original Chardonnet silk is no longer in use, having been superseded by rayon fibers that are superior, but his pioneering contribution was of great significance in the development of manufactured fibers. The first rayon was produced in the United States in 1910 by Avtex Fibers Inc.

Production

Rayon is produced by passing a solution of purified cellulose through a spinneret to form soft filaments that are then converted or "regenerated" into almost pure cellulose. Because of the reconversion of the soluble compound to cellulose, rayon is referred to as a regenerated cellulose fiber.

There are several types of rayon on the market today. Viscose rayon is made by converting purified cellulose to xanthate, dissolving the xanthate in dilute caustic soda, and regenerating the cellulose from the solution as it emerges from the spinneret. Other varieties of rayon include high wet-modulus rayon, which is highly modified viscose rayon that has greater resistance to stretching when washed, and cuprammonium rayon, which is made by combining the cellulose with copper and ammonia, after which it can be dissolved in caustic soda. This material is passed through the spinneret and the cellulose is regenerated by wet spinning in solutions that remove the copper and ammonia and neutralize the caustic soda.

Care

Always consult the manufacturer's instructions. Most rayon must be dry-cleaned. If the garment is washable, a mild soap and lukewarm water should be used. Chlorine bleaches should never be used on rayon. Do not twist or wring rayon. Hang the garment on a rust-proof hanger to dry and iron on the wrong side before the garment is entirely dry. It is essential that the iron not touch the right side of the garment directly. It will score the fiber and cause it to shine.

See also MANUFACTURED FIBER.

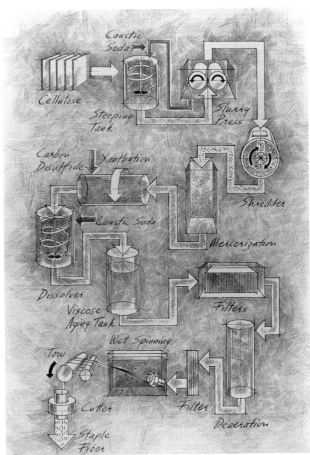

Rayon production chart American Fiber Manufacturers Association, Inc.

Count Hilaire de Chardonnet—"Father of Rayon" American Fiber Manufacturers Association, Inc.

REP

Rep textiles are characterized by indistinct ribs and are created in a variety of fibers and fiber blends as well as in various weaves. They can be created in a rib weave, or a plain weave in which fine and coarse yarns are alternated in both the warp and weft. Occasionally, they are created by employing a very low count of coarse threads in the weft. Today, reps are created in a wide variety of fibers, including SILK, WOOL, COTTON and MANUFACTURED FIBERS.

REPEAT

Repeat is a term that describes the size or dimension of a pattern, either woven or printed, which is repeated on a textile. When the pattern is woven, the repeat refers to the number of picks necessary to make one complete pattern cycle. When referring to printing, the repeat is the length of one complete pattern block, such as the circumference of a roller, or the length of a stencil, etc.

RESIST DYES

See DYES; PRINTING.

ROLLER PRINTING

See PRINTING.

ROMAINE

Romaine is executed in a plain weave that employs crêpe yarns in every other end, causing an uneven textural appearance similar to that of CRÊPE. The textile is lightweight, has low thread count and is lustrous. Originally romaine was executed in silk, but now it is found in RAYON, ACETATE, WOOL, SILK and MANUFACTURED FIBERS.

ROTARY PRINTING

See PRINTING.

Repeat pattern Valdese Weavers, Inc.

S

SANGLIER

The word *sanglier* is French for wild boar. The textile was named for its texture, which is very compact and wiry. Sanglier is most often constructed of worsted and mohair, in a plain weave with tightly twisted yarns. The textile is given a very rough surface finish.　　≡

SATEEN

Sateen was originally called satine. The terms distinguish between a silk textile (satin) and cotton textile (sateen). Sateen is constructed in a SATIN WEAVE and is characterized by its durability and its lustrous quality. The textile is available in many weights and qualities, and in the heavier textiles carded yarns are employed. It is MERCERIZED and has a slightly crisp hand.　　≡

SATIN

Satin gets its name from the port of Zaytoun, China, which exported satin during the Middle Ages. Satin is a highly lustrous textile constructed in a SATIN WEAVE. The luster is derived from the long floats used in the weave, which act as prisms in reflecting light. Satin was made exclusively of silk fibers during previous periods in history, but today it is constructed in manufactured fiber as well. Satin is occasionally used as a backing for other textiles such as CRÊPE. In some cases, when manufactured fibers are employed, dull yarns are used to produce a non-lustrous textile.

Satin Textiles and Variations

PANNÉ SATIN	A heavy satin, given a highly lustrous finish. It is done in silk, rayon, cotton, or manufactured fiber
CRÊPE BACKED SATIN	A reversible textile with one smooth surface and one crêpe surface. It is executed in satin weave and constructed of a wide variety of fibers, including manufactured fibers
SATIN MERVEILLEUX	A satin weave textile that is often shot, producing variations in color. It is a very soft textile, usually of silk
SATIN ROYAL	A double faced silk satin that is given a highly lustrous surface
SATINET	Constructed in a satin weave, it is unlike satin in that it employs a cotton warp and a wool weft. The weft or filling threads form the face of the textile. Satinet is finished as a wool and undergoes the fulling process

≡

SATIN WEAVE

One of the three basic weaves. The face of the fabric has more warp or weft floats than the back, causing the textile to have a very smooth reflective surface.

See also PLAIN WEAVE; TWILL WEAVE; WEAVING.　　≡

SCREEN PRINTING

See PRINTING.　　≡

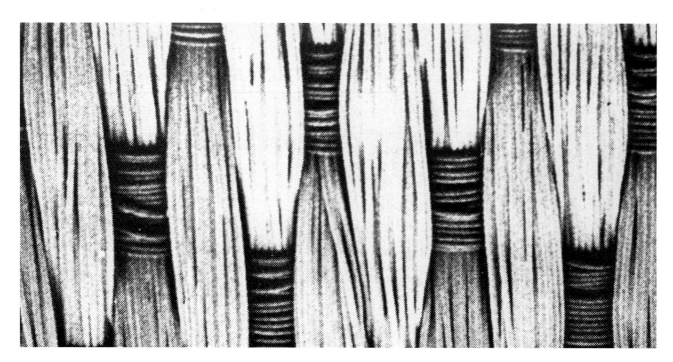

Satin weave (micrograph)   American Textile Manufacturers Institute

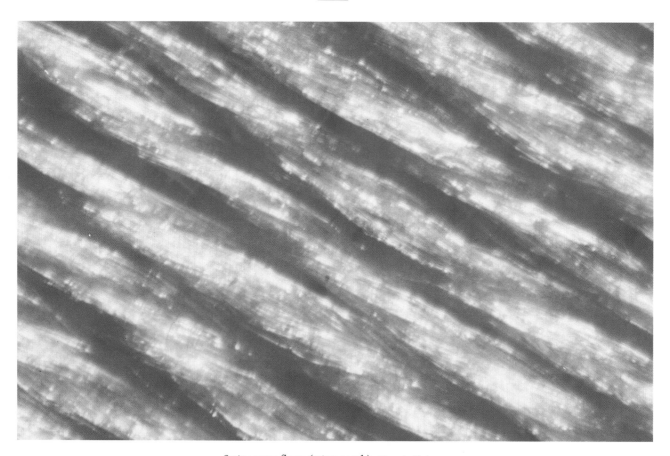

Satin weave floats (micrograph)   Dennis Sjoberg

Seersucker (cotton blend) Author's collection

SCUTCHING

See LINEN.

SEERSUCKER

The word seersucker is taken from the Persian term *shirushakar,* referring to the blistered appearance of this textile. Seersucker is a lightweight textile that employs woven stripes running with the warp. The ground is woven with regular tension and the stripes are allowed a certain slackness, causing a permanent, blistered effect in the stripe. The textile is made in a wide variety of weights and qualities. It is done in a PLAIN WEAVE, usually of cotton, but it is also made with MANUFACTURED FIBER. Occasionally, it can be found with different patterns such as checks or stripes, but the same techniques of construction are used.

See also PLISSÉ.

SELVAGE

The word selvage is derived from the expression self-edge. It refers to the woven edge of the textile, running with the warp in the direction of the grain. The selvage is created with stronger yarns and its purpose is to keep the textile from fraying. Originally, the selvage was used to identify the quality of a textile and sometimes the manufacturer. Today, it is frequently printed with the company's name and often the individual colors used in the textile are imprinted as well, making coordination with the pure colors of other textiles easier.

SERGE

The term serge is taken from the Latin *serica,* meaning silk. In Italy, where the textile was created from a silk and wool blend, it was called *sergea.* It is known through written records that the textile existed as early as the

Seersucker (cotton) Author's collection

12th century. Today, serge is such a popular textile that it is considered a staple of the textile industry. It is created by employing a right hand twill weave and is characterized by a diagonal wale that moves from lower left to upper right. It is further characterized by its excellent draping qualities and a wide variety of textures. It is given a range of finishes and can be found finished, unfinished or semi-finished. Today, the textile is constructed of wool, worsted, cotton, rayon, silk and many blends. It is also found in numerous qualities and weights.

SERICIN

See SILK.

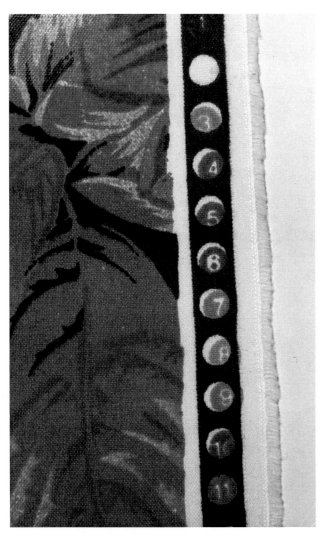

Selvage showing color spectrum of textile
Author's collection

Shantung silk Author's collection

SERPENTINE CRÊPE

Serpentine crêpe employs a crêpe (twisted) thread in the weft or filling that creates the crêpey effect. It is executed in a plain weave. The texture of serpentine crêpe varies greatly depending upon the size of the crêpe thread used in its execution and may take on the appearance of a ribbed textile. Today, the textile is found in a wide variety of fibers including MANUFACTURED FIBER.

See also CRÊPE.

SHADOW ORGANDY

Shadow organdy is a textile that is printed in a self color, such as white on white, producing a shadowy effect. It is a lightweight, crisp textile that is further characterized by its sheer quality. The same shadow technique is used on many other textiles today.

SHADOW WEAVE

Shadow weave refers to a pattern in which part of the threads are twisted in the opposite direction, creating a shadow effect in the textile, partially due to the reflection of light upon the twisted threads. Occasionally a HERRINGBONE is called a shadow weave because of the repeating pattern, but it is not considered true shadow weave.

SHANTUNG

Shantung derives its name from the Chinese province where it originated. Shantung is created from a reeled SILK from the tussah moth or caterpillar. The silk from the tussah is characterized by its uneven qualities that create a slubbiness in the weaving process, giving the textile great character. Shantung is executed in a plain or twill weave. Imitation shantung is created in cotton, rayon and manufactured fibers. To produce the slubbiness in those textiles, variations in yarn size are used in the weaving process.

SHARKSKIN

Sharkskin is executed in a plain or twill weave. Two types of sharkskin are produced, both characterized by their sleek, delicate, faintly pebbled surface. The pebbled surface is caused by a subtle rib achieved by using a weft yarn that is slightly larger than warp. Those characteristics are found in the most popular sharkskin, which is done in plain colors, very often of wool, although manufactured fibers are also employed today. The second type of sharkskin uses threads of two colors in both warp and weft, which are alternated, causing the ribs to have color lines that run right to left. Sharkskin is characterized by its durability and fineness and comes in many qualities and weights.

SHATUSH

Shatush is created from the white or silver-gray hair of a wild goat, the ibex (*Capra aegagrus*), found in Kashmir and northern India and the upper slopes of the Himalayas. In Persia, *Shah* means ruler and *toosh* means cloth, thus "cloth of the king." Shatush is unquestionably one of the finest textiles extant.

The fiber comes from the neck hair of the wild goats. The animals descend to the timberline in the spring to forage on the tender leaves of the low growing trees, brushing against the branches. The native women gather

Sharkskin (manufactured fiber and wool) Author's collection

the hair and spin it into yarn, from which the sheer cloth is handwoven.

It is possible to weave the yarn into the thinnest and warmest of all fabrics. Made in 5- to 7-yard shawls that serve wealthy Indian women as winter wraps, they are said to be the Indian woman's equivalent of the mink coat and make other luxury cloths seem almost coarse by comparison. A 54-inch-wide shawl can be pulled through a wedding ring, hence it is often called "the ring shawl." The supply of shatush fiber is limited and the demand has made it one of the most expensive fabrics in the world, and one of the most rare.

SHETLAND

Originally, shetland came from the sheep raised on the Shetland Islands off the coast of Scotland. The wool from the Shetland sheep is particularly fine and imparts a soft hand to the textiles. Today, the Shetland textiles, which include knitted fabrics, are not necessarily restricted to fibers from the Shetland sheep, but are found in combinations of wool from many types of sheep. The

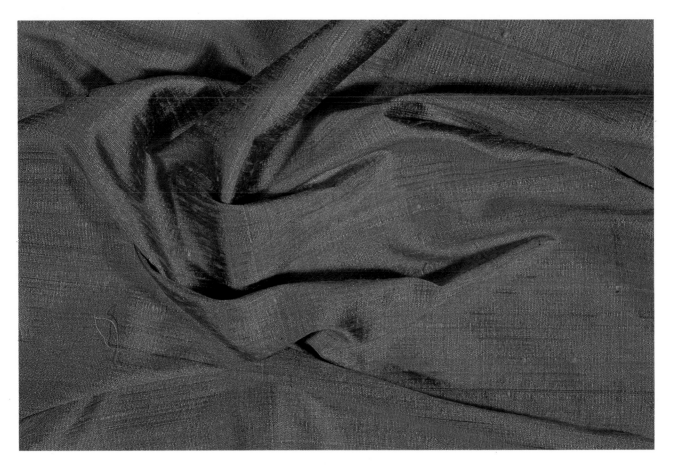

Shantung (silk)   Author's collection

fabrics are distinguished by their lightweight soft qualities, and are further characterized by a raised textural surface.

See WOOL.

SHOT CLOTH

Shot cloth refers to any textile that uses two or more colors in the weaving so that as light reflects from the textile various color changes are apparent. Shot cloth is also referred to as irridescent or changeable.

See also CHAMELEON.

SILK

Silk is obtained from the cocoons of certain species of caterpillars, often, but erroneously, referred to as silkworms. All of the silk-producing caterpillars belong to the insect family called Lepidoptera.

There are over 500 varieties of wild silk-producing caterpillars, which feed on oak leaves, the castor oil plant, mulberry leaves and various other shrubs found in the wild. The silk obtained from them is called wild silk, although the term is largely a commercial classification, since these caterpillars have been cultivated in China and India for many centuries. The best known of the wild silkworms is the tussah, which is one of the larger varieties, sometimes reaching a length of 6 inches and laying very large eggs. The tussah produces silk that is stronger and more durable than cultivated silk. It has a slubbed or nubby surface that is desirable because of the uneven texture it imparts to the silk fabric. China produces 80% of the world's supply of silk from the tussah.

The bulk of the world's silk is now obtained from a domesticated variety, *Bombyx mori*, although silk does come from other wild varieties of caterpillars as well. *Bombyx mori* has been reared systematically under controlled conditions, dating back to the Chinese before recorded history. The process of rearing the caterpillars and obtaining the silk fibers they produce is called *sericulture*.

History

As early as the 12th century B.C. silk was mentioned in Chinese texts. In 2640 B.C. Confucius recorded that silk was first reeled from a cocoon. From that point on for 3,000 years China shrouded its silk industry in secrecy and held a monopoly on silk production. The use of silk was not confined to apparel but was used as well for bow-strings, stuffing and fish-lines. There were periods in China history when silk was so widely used that it was cheaper than any other textile.

It was during the third century B.C. that the famous silk routes came into use, over which silk textiles were transported by traders to the West. The routes began at what is now Xi'an in the Shanxi province of China and proceeded through the mountains and desert to Antioch and Tyre. They were then transported to Europe and Egypt by sea. At the same time, silks found their way to Japan by sea. The journey overland along the Silk Roads was a treacherous one over difficult terrain inhabited by

maurauders who preyed upon the caravans as they conducted their arduous journey. Many caravans did not reach their destinations.

The history of silk is filled with colorful stories and mythical lore. One of the stories that has come down to us tells of the Byzantine emperor Justinian sending two monks to China in A.D. 552 with the mission of bringing back the long-held secret of silk. When the monks returned to Byzantium, they brought with them the eggs of the silkworm. They had, the story goes, placed them in hollow walking sticks. Some authorities have stated that if the temperatures and environment were correct, it is indeed possible that the eggs could have survived such a journey. Whether or not the story is true, it gives us some insight into silk's romantic past.

Once the secrets of sericulture became known, the practice spread with migrating tribes, such as the Arabs, who conquered Persia in the seventh century. This knowledge was further spread by the Arabs as they swept through Africa, Sicily and Spain. The spread of sericulture was aided by the crusades in the 13th century, and with Marco Polo's journeys to China in the 14th century, leading to commercial ventures with

Silk and metallic fibers (micrograph) Dennis Sjoberg

China. It is also known that the Italian silk industry started as early as the 12th century. The Italians still have a flourishing silk manufacturing business centered around Como, Italy.

In 1466, the French king Louis XI declared his intention to create a weaving center for silk textiles in Lyons. The undertaking was further aided when King Francois I gave Lyons the monopoly on silk importation and trade. These events were responsible for creating the great silk industry that still exists in Lyons today. When the Edict of Nantes granting religious freedom to French Protestants was revoked in 1685, French Huguenots were once again subject to religious persecution and they fled to Germany, Great Britain, Italy and Switzerland, taking their expertise in silk weaving with them.

Throughout the 18th century, the silk industry continued to prosper in France. From this period such a profusion of silks of extraordinary quality were produced that scholars and students alike still study its unique

Bombyx mori   International Silk Association

Silk Road   International Silk Association

WORLD PRODUCTION OF RAW SILK, 1938–1986
(in tons)

PRODUCER	1938	1978	1983	1985	1986
CHINA	4855	19000	28140	32000	35700
INDIA	690	3475	5691	7029	8277
JAPAH	43150	15960	12456	9582	8240
USSR	1900	3240	3660	3999	4000
BRAZIL	35	1250	1362	1458	1780
REP. OF KOREA	1825	4235	1944	2088	1650
OTHERS	4045	2200	2738	2748	2875
TOTAL:	56500	49360	55981	58914	62622

SOURCE: International Silk Association

achievements. The French Revolution very nearly devastated the silk industries of France when its drive toward social equality dictated the replacement of silk by cotton.

The 19th century brought many changes in the silk industry. One remarkable change occured in 1804 with the invention of the JACQUARD loom, named after its creator, Jean Marie JACQUARD. The Jacquard loom, with its use of punched cards, operated on the same principle as the computers that we now use (and indeed may be the earliest computer system known). This remarkable invention allowed elaborate designs to be created mechanically and gave great impetus to the weaving industry in Lyons and throughout the world.

The art of sericulture began to decline in Europe after the opening in 1872 of the Suez Canal, which facilitated

Bombyx mori *caterpillar*   International Silk Association

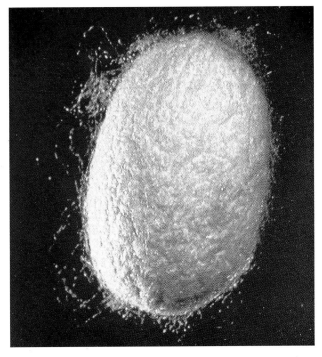

Bombyx mori *cocoon*   International Silk Association

the shipment of raw silk from Japan, which became highly competitive in the silk trade. In 1865, the French silk industry was further threatened by a disease called pebrine, which killed hundreds of thousands of silkworms. In his important work in the areas of chemistry and medicine, the French scientist Louis Pasteur (1822–1895) discovered that the cause of the disease was a microbe that attacked silkworm eggs. By destroying the germ in the silkworm hatcheries the disease was eliminated, though the silk industry never fully recovered. The Second World War also greatly affected the silk industry as the supply of raw silk was cut off from the United States and Europe. At this time, the introduction and acceptance of manufactured fibers also reduced the importance of European sericulture.

After World War II, silk production resumed in Japan. The Japanese had made great technical advances, particularly in reeling silk, and Japan became the biggest producer and exporter of raw silk until the 1970s when Japan entered a period of rapid industrialization and interest in sericulture declined. China then regained its historic role as the world's largest silk producer.

Moth and cocoon   International Silk Association

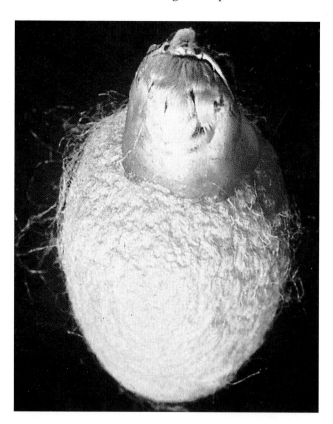

Emerging Bombyx mori *caterpillar*
International Silk Association

Cultivation

Today, the *Bombyx mori* accounts for the major part of the world's silk production. It feeds exclusively on mulberry leaves, which means that it can be raised only in those regions where mulberry trees can be grown. As a result of research carried out mainly in Japan, the mulberry tree is now cultivated in shrub form, which facilitates the harvesting of the leaves. The Japanese have also created an artificial food composed of mulberry leaves, soybeans and cornstarch that is produced in large bars each capable of nourishing thousands of the caterpillars. The waste of the silkworm is called frass and is used for fishfood and fertilizer. The *Bombyx mori* moth is blind, and although it has wings, is incapable of flight. It also has no digestive system and dies after three or four days.

The eggs are raised in a room called the Magnaneric and are prepared for hatching at a temperature of about 22 degrees C (71–72 degrees F) to coincide with the appearance of the shoots of the mulberry leaves that will feed the newly hatched larvae. The eggs are frequently cold stored so as to arrest their development awaiting the proper hatching time. Each egg, called a "grain," is the size of a pinhead, and produces a tiny caterpillar about 3 mm long.

After three or four weeks, the caterpillars are fully developed and have shed their skin four times. The caterpillars are now 8–10 centimeters long and are 10,000 times as heavy as at birth. They now begin to search for a place to spin their cocoons. With rhythmic movements of its head, the caterpillar lays the silk filament in figure-eight form, building up 20 to 30 concentric layers of thread, creating the cocoon from the outside in. Gradually, the caterpillar disappears inside its cocoon, which remains porous to enable the caterpillar to breathe. At this stage the cocoons often have pastel colors that are caused by the sericin, also known as "silk gum," which is the substance that holds the cocoon together. The sericin also protects the fiber itself. The colors, as well as the sericin, are completely or partially removed later by a process called "boiling off."

The caterpillar produces the silk filament through a tiny hole in its lower lip, which is called the spinneret. The spinneret is connected to two canals of the silk glands, which run alongside its body. Liquid silk is

Reeling silk International Silk Association

ejected at the rate of a foot a minute. The semi-liquid silk solidifies into a continuous filament on contact with the air at the outlet of the spinneret.

The silk thread, or bave, is made up of two filaments, or brins, extruded from each of the two silk glands and bonded together after passing through a spinneret. A cross section of the thread looks like an electric cable. The bave is composed of two main ingredients: fibroin (75–80% of the weight), which forms the textile fiber itself, and sericin (20–25%), which forms a protective sheath around the fibroin, and which is important in protecting the silk filament during the mechanical stress and strain of throwing and weaving.

The diameter of the bave is about 30/1000 mm, too fine for it to be used alone as a thread. For a silk thread to be used as a textile fiber, it must be composed of at least four baves, i.e., the product of four cocoons. The operation of assembling the baves is known as reeling, in which four, five, six or more baves are bonded together to give a thread of appropriate thickness for the ultimate end-use.

When it has finished spinning its cocoon, the caterpillar then changes into a chrysalis, and ultimately into a moth, if the natural cycle is allowed to continue. The moth emits a brownish liquid to soften one end of the cocoon, allowing itself to emerge by pushing its way through the threads forming the cocoon. Since at this stage these cocoons can no longer be used for reeling, most chrysalids are stifled by hot air. Those male and female moths that are allowed to reach maturity for reproduction are mated, and almost immediately afterward the female lays between 300 and 500 eggs. These eggs are preserved in cold storage until the incubation period, and the whole cycle starts again, in the next season.

Processing

After the chrysalis has been stifled and dried, three more operations are required before reeling. First, the cocoons are cooked in water near boiling temperature, so as to soften the gum on the outer layers. Second, mechanical brushes then beat the cocoons to loosen the floss, which is a mass of short fibers on the outside of the cocoon. Third is the process of purging, in which the floss is removed and the end of the continuous filament forming the cocoon, which can be up to 1,200 meters (3,960 ft) in length, is picked out.

In the past, after the cocoons had been thoroughly prepared in this way, they were placed in a reeling-basin, in which water at a temperature of 50 degrees C (122 degrees F) was constantly replaced. Today, the reeling-basin is often replaced by an automatic reeling machine, which is equipped with sensors allowing for the immediate replacement of the empty cocoons or broken filaments. The reeler will assemble the baves of four, five, six or seven cocoons, according to the desired thickness of the thread. The thread thus assembled is fed over a series of pulleys, and at the same time is very lightly twisted, thus ensuring good cohesion between the baves. It is then taken up on a reel or swift, which is a sort of very large bobbin. The yarn obtained after the reeling stage is known as raw silk. It is packaged in the form of skeins. The yarn attained in this manner is used for fabrics to be dyed after weaving.

The process of twisting and assembling the single-ply yarns is called throwing.

The Qualities of Silk

Among fibers, silk possesses many superlative qualities. It is noted for its softness to the touch and its brilliant sheen. The basic silk filament has incredible fineness, a single 3-gram cocoon yields 1,000 meters of fabric (it takes 110 cocoons to make a tie, 630 to make a blouse), yet a silk yarn only 1 mm in diameter will support a weight of 100 pounds (45 kilos). Its resilience is

Twisting silk   International Silk Association

noteworthy: a creased silk fabric will uncrease simply on contact with air. In addition to textile applications, the strength and fineness of silk has been a lifesaver in the hands of surgeons, who have used its easily knotted threads in sutures. During the spinning process small uneven pieces of silk fiber are separated and this by-product is referred to as silk noil. Silk noil is spun into lesser quality yarn and is used in inexpensive blends.

Silk fibers are triangular and so reflect light like prisms. Layers of protein build up to a pearly sheen, giving silk fabric a luxurious, sensuous appearance. Silk has high absorbency, enabling it to readily absorb dyestuff, allowing for a great range of deep and brilliant colors. This property also enables it to absorb perspiration, making it a traditional favorite type of clothing in hot weather. This absorbency also makes silk a good insulating material for its weight, keeping the wearer warm in winter and cool in summer.

When properly cared for, silk will resist degradation, an important characteristic for sewing-thread, and it is non-conductive, making it an excellent electrical insulator.

Care of Silk

Washing. Many silks can be hand-washed, and some even become brighter after washing. There are three basic rules to be observed:

1. Wash silk in lukewarm water with a gentle detergent or soap
2. Wash silk articles separately
3. Wash with a delicate hand movement

Rinsing. This should also be done delicately in lukewarm or cold water.

Ironing. Silk should be ironed on the reverse side while still damp at a low temperature.

In addition, to preserve the life of silk articles:

1. Never spray perfume or deodorant directly onto a silk fabric
2. Never soak silk in water for a long period
3. Never wring silk before drying. Excess water should be removed by rolling the silk article in a towel, after which the garment can be ironed

SILK NOIL

Silk noil refers to waste products from spinning during the creation of silk yarn. It is often combined with other fiber types to create blends, or used in the creation of yarns for knitting. It is not considered to be of superior quality and often has a very textured surface.

See also SILK.

SINGLE KNIT

Single knit fabrics are usually executed on a circular knitting machine, which interlocks one set of loops with another.

See KNITTING.

SIZING

Sizing refers to any chemical or compound that is added to a textile to change its innate qualities, causing it, for example, to become more rigid or crisp.

See FINISHING.

SLATER, SAMUEL (1768–1835)

Samuel Slater, called the "Father of the American cotton textile industry," was an Englishman, whose father William Slater, was a well-known timber merchant and land agent in Derbyshire, England. Jebediah Strutt (who invented the knit stocking machine) was a neighbor of the Slater family. As a child Samuel was greatly influenced by Strutt and spent a great deal of time at the Strutt factory in Derbyshire, apprenticing there at the age of 14. He studied the art of cotton spinning and also became a master machinist. At a very young age Slater proved to have creative genius as well, for within seven years he had invented a device to enlarge bobbin capacity for Strutt's machines, which greatly increased the productivity of the factory. In 1789, at the age of 21, Samuel Slater came to the United States and began to search for a suitable site for a mill. He selected Pawtucket, Rhode Island, where he located a site that had been used as a fulling mill earlier and had water power. In Pawtucket, Slater had the good fortune of lodging at the home of Wilkinson, who was an accomplished blacksmith. Early in the relationship, he perceived Slater's intentions and was able to help him in the tooling of what was to become the first cotton mill in the United States. Without the expertise of Wilkinson, Slater might have been thwarted in his efforts, for he was reconstructing machines from memory. Though the task was monumental he was able to accomplish it in a mere 14 months, giving rise to the first New England mill. Samuel Slater's efforts served as inspiration to others and by the year 1812, there were 53 cotton factories and 48,030 spindles, within 30 miles of Providence, Rhode Island.

SLIVER

During the spinning process, sliver is a loose continuous strand without twist produced during the carding stage. After carding, the sliver is drawn into thread or yarn.

See SPINNING.

SOLUTION DYEING

See DYES.

SPANDEX

Spandex is an elastomeric fiber defined by the Federal Trade Commission as "a manufactured fiber in which the fiber-forming substance is a long-chain synthetic polymer comprised of at least 85% of a segmented polyurethane." It was first produced in 1959 by E. I. du Pont de Nemours & Company. Today spandex fibers are

A Flyer assembly
B Drive band
C Drive wheel crank arm
D Drive wheel
E Axle

F Uprights
G Treadle arm (footman)
H Table (or stock)
I Treadle
J Treadle bar

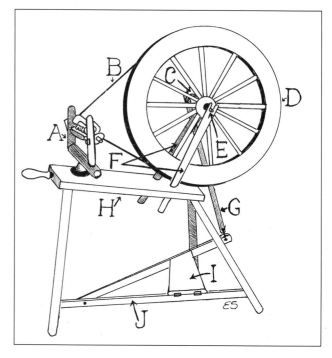

Saxony flyer wheel Elaine Swenson

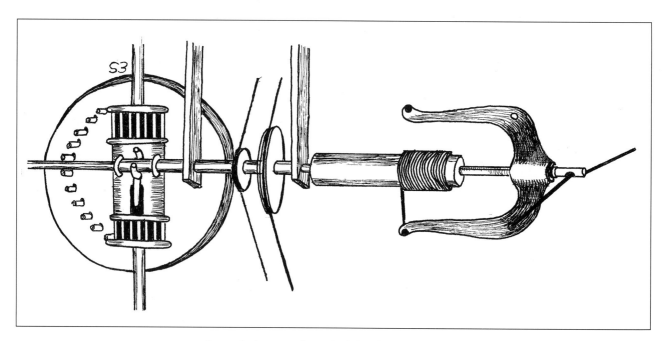

Leonardo da Vinci's flyer wheel design Elaine Swenson

marketed by a number of manufacturers under a variety of trade names.

This type of fiber can be extended up to five times its unstretched length without breakage. Lower deniers produce greater stretchability. Core-spinning of spandex yarns, in which the spandex is fed into the spinning process under controlled tension, has become increasingly important. The spandex forms the core around which are spun any of the basic textile fibers. Yarns containing even relatively small percentages of spandex (5 to 10%) exhibit great stretchability and recovery. Spandex core diameters of as little as $\frac{1}{150}$ of an inch are used to create very fine, soft, and sheer fabrics.

Spandex fabrics are lightweight, they allow freedom of movement, and are resistant to deterioration from perspiration and detergents. Major uses include athletic apparel, foundation garments, and support and surgical hose.

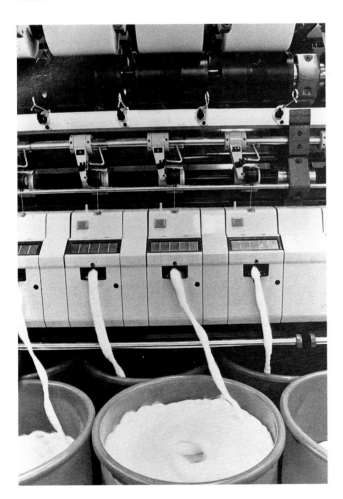

Open end spinning
American Textile Manufacturers Institute

SPECIALTY FABRIC

A textile created using a NOVELTY WEAVE. Also called novelty fabric.

SPINNERET

A spinneret is an aperture through which a solution is forced during the creation of manufactured fibers, in a process called extrusion.

See MANUFACTURED FIBER.

SPINNING

Fibers are spun to form continuous lengths so that they can be used for weaving. During this process the fibers are drawn, which causes them to be parallel with one another, and twisted together. The continuous workable strands that are formed in this manner are called threads or yarns.

History

The history of spinning has been obscured by time. The earliest examples of implements used for spinning come to us from Stone Age man. Spindles, whorls and thread have been found in the Swiss Lake Dwellings, which existed during the New Stone Age. The Bible refers to spinning and there are written references to spinning in Roman writings of the first century B.C. There exist as well murals on the walls of ancient Egyptian tombs that show the spinning process.

The early methods of spinning were confined to the spindle and the distaff. It is known that the first spinning wheels were created in India, but that innovation did not reach Europe until some time in the late 14th century. The basic principle of the spinning wheel is to import a rotary motion to the spindle by means of a belt or cord. In 1519 Leonardo da Vinci created a device called a flyer to provide a continuous movement in the spinning process. This device twisted the yarn before it was wound onto the bobbin, and it also caused the thread to be wound and evenly distributed onto the bobbin.

In 1533 a spinning wheel with a treadle was invented in Nuremberg, Germany, incorporating Leonardo's flyer. It became known as the flax, or Saxony, wheel.

The next important development in the history of spinning took place in 1737, when Lewis Paul and John Wyatt invented the roller method of spinning, which made possible the spinning of yarn without working it with the fingers. Several years later, in 1764, James HARGREAVES invented the famous spinning jenny, named after his wife, which operated by drawing the fiber using a carriage that could accommodate up to eight spindles at a time. By 1766 he had improved the machine so that it could accommodate 100 spindles, vastly speeding up the spinning process.

Between 1769 and 1775, Sir Richard ARKWRIGHT developed the water twist frame and made further improvements to the carding and drawing processes. In 1779, Samuel CROMPTON incorporated the spinning jenny and Arkwright's frame in the mule spinning frame (flyer spinning frame) that drew fibers through the use of carriages and rollers. Further improvements were made when Charles Danforth invented the cap-spinning frame in 1828. That same year, John THORPE patented the ring-spinning device, which afforded continuous spinning and produced a higher twist yarn. These early spinning wheels remained in used until the industrial revolution, when commercial ventures developed the technology for faster methods of spinning.

Process

Natural fiber undergoes a number of processes before it becomes thread or yarn. (Manufactured fiber, which is produced in long filiments, may also be spun to resemble

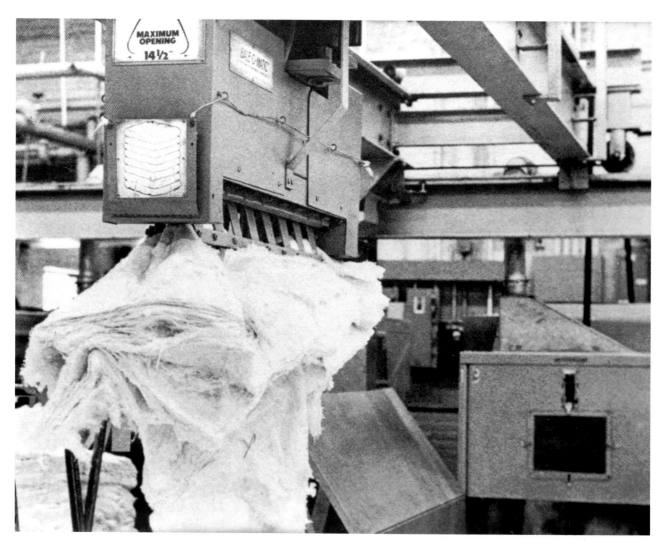

Blending cotton American Textile Manufacturers Institute

Carding machine   American Textile Manufacturers Institute

natural fibers, but it does not undergo these preliminary steps.) The first step is the blending process, during which various types, qualities and grades of fiber are brought together in a machine called a blender, depending on the desired end product and purpose.

After the fiber has been blended, it is further cleaned of impurities and any remaining clumps of fiber are separated. The fiber is then distributed into rolls called laps.

The laps are processed in a carding machine to make the fiber strands more parallel to one another. The laps of fiber are moved over revolving cylinders with sharp metal teeth, causing the laps to form rope-like strands. These strands are called slivers.

At this juncture, if a very fine yarn is desired, the strands are sent through a combing machine. The teeth on the combing machine are much finer than those of the carder. After the carding and combing, several of the slivers are combined to form one strand during a process called drawing. The slivers are then twisted slightly and drawn into an even finer strand in a process called roving. The resultant strands are also called roving.

The fiber is then ready for the spinning process, during which the roving is refined into even thinner strands and is twisted, thus adding further stability. It is during the spinning process that the yarn is placed on bobbins.

Air jet spinning   American Textile Manufacturers Institute

The weft or filling yarns are usually used in this state for weaving, but it is necessary for the warp threads to be further processed to attain greater strength and stability. They are further twisted, and two or more yarns or threads are then twisted together and wound onto bobbins for the weaving process.

The two most prevalent methods of commercial spinning today are open-end spinning and ring spinning. The ring spinning method patented in 1828 by John Thorpes constitutes the bulk of the present commercial spinning industry. It is a very rapid continuous method. During this process a ring is used that drafts, twists and winds the yarn or thread onto the bobbins in a continuous effort, producing a very strong yarn.

Open-end spinning is a newer system of spinning, and is three to five times faster than ring spinning. During this type of spinning, fibers are fed by a stream of air into a rotor unit. The fibers pass through a combing wheel where they are broken down into individual fibers. The fibers are drawn into layers by centrifugal force, then twisted and drawn off.

In 1981 the air-jet spinning method was introduced, a process used on wool, manufactured fiber or blends. The method is seven to 10 times faster than ring spinning. During this process one air jet pulls the fiber while another twists it into yarn. This method, while rapid, has not yet been widely implemented in the industry.

Hand Spinning

Artists and home craftsmen continue to spin their own yarn by hand. In preparation for spinning, the fibers are placed in a more parallel position by plucking and straightening with the fingers in a process called teasing. While the fibers are placed in a more parallel position they are also pulled apart or separated so that they form a flat lap or roll. Sometimes the fiber is carded, but the color contrasts and textures of individual yarns become more visible when the fiber is teased and not carded. Only short fibers are carded in any case. When the carding is done, wire brushes are used. Hand teasing and carding is a long and laborious process.

SPINNING WHEEL

The spinning wheel is a simple tool used since early times to join fibers into long continuous yarns.

See SPINNING.

STAMPED VELVET

See FINISHING; VELVET.

STAPLE

When used accurately, the term staple refers to the length of a fiber. It is essential to know the length of fibers for the most effective and efficient weaving processes. Nowadays the term staple is also used instead of the term fiber. There are frequent references, as well, to a staple fabric, one that enjoys such popularity and thus demand that it is in continuous production.

STRUTT, JEDEDIAH (1726–1797)

In 1758, Strutt created a machine that produced a lacy, ribbed textile. Not long thereafter he founded a mill in Derby, England, that specialized in the creation of hosiery using his invention. The stocking frame operated on the principle of dropping stitches. Strutt is credited not only for his invention but also for triggering a whole chain of inventions in the field of weaving. When Strutt

Spinning room American Textile Manufacturers Institute

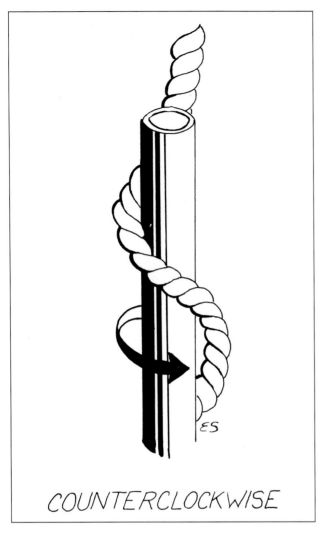

S-twist Elaine Swenson

S-TWIST

S-twist refers to the counterclockwise direction of the twist in a yarn or thread. It is also called the lefthand or reverse twist.

See also YARN; Z-TWIST.

SUEDE CLOTH

Suede cloth is characterized by a soft, napped surface with the nap cut close to the textile. It can be executed in either a woven or knitted fabric and may be made of a wide variety of fibers, including manufactured fiber. Suede cloth is created in many qualities and weights. Suede cloth is sometimes called DUVETYN although it is much heavier.

SURAH

Surah is named for the city of Surat in India. Originally, the fabric was created exclusively in silk but today is found in manufactured fibers as well. It is created in a twill weave and is characterized by luster and soft hand. Occasionally it is printed.

SWISSING

Swissing is a finishing technique that originated in Switzerland. The process creates a smooth surface with luster.

See FINISHING.

SYNTHETIC DYES

See DYES.

died in 1797, the mills that he and his brother-in-law, William Woollatt, had established were considered the greatest in England.

T

TAFFETA

The earliest written records of taffeta date from the 16th century. The textile derives its name from the Persian word *taftah,* which referred to a fine, plain weave silk textile.

Today, taffeta textiles are created using a tightly twisted yarn. The fabric has a slight crossribbed effect which is caused by using filling yarns that are slightly larger than the warp yarns. Taffeta has a very firm, close weave and usually has a luster, although it is occasionally executed with a dull finish. The hand of taffeta is crisp and smooth.

The textile is found in plain colors and prints and frequently is calendered to create moiré effects. A wide variety of fibers are used in its production, including manufactured fiber, silk and blends. It is such a popular textile that it is regarded as a staple in the textile industry.

TARTAN

The tartan is a plaid fabric that originated in the Scottish highlands and figured prominently in the history of Scottish dress. The word is derived from the Gaelic *tarstin* or *tarsuin,* meaning across, describing the cross stripe pattern. Scottish literature first refers to tartan in the 13th century. Different designs, specific as to both color and stripe or check width, were developed by the various prominent clans and districts of Scotland. A tartan can be made in any size, depending on the use of

Tartan plaid (wool)   Author's collection

215

Tattersall Author's collection

the fabric. However, the proportions of the widths of the stripes in the design, called a sett, must always be kept the same regardless of the size of the pattern. Tartans may be worn by men as a pleated knee length skirt, called a kilt, and as a shawl or mantle fastened with a brooch at the shoulder, which is called a plaid. Colors range from bright primary hues for special occasions to more subdued colors for hunting and ordinary wear.

Traditionally, tartans were made of wool or worsted, but now are made of blends, including manufactured fibers. There are hundreds of different tartans today, and the term has become a generic one referring to bright plaid woven designs.

Some of the most familiar plaids bearing clan names are: Buchanan, Cameron, Campbell, Cumming, Ferguson, Graham, Grant, Innes, Lindsay, MacDuff, MacGregor, MacLeod of Lewis, and MacTavish.

TATTERSALL

The origin of the tattersall pattern is unclear, but it is thought that it was inspired in England by the famous auction house in London of the same name and that the check was derived from those seen frequently on horse blankets. Today, the tattersall check is made in many different fabrics such as WOOL, SILK and MANUFACTURED FIBER and the checks vary in size as well. Although the traditional colors of tattersall are black and white it also is found in other colors.

TERRY CLOTH

Terry cloth is a fabric that has a looped pile on one or both sides. Today, it is constructed of cotton, manufactured fiber or, most commonly, a blend of the two. Ply yarns are used in its construction. Terry cloth is

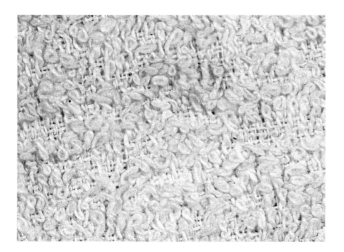

Terry cloth (cotton/manufactured fiber/blend) Author's collection

produced on either a Jacquard or a dobby loom and is known for its absorbent qualities.

TEXTILE FIBER PRODUCTS IDENTIFICATION ACT

The Textile Fiber Products Identification Act was passed in 1960. It requires that a label with generic fiber (not tradename) content be affixed to every article that is for sale. It further states that the percentages of each fiber be listed on the label in descending order. The manufacturers name and the country of origin must also be included on the label. The FEDERAL TRADE COMMISSION administers these regulations.

THERMAL WOVEN OR KNIT FABRIC

The term thermal is applied to a textile woven so that portions of the textile are held away from the skin, such as in a waffle weave or ribbed knit. Air is trapped in these pockets and warmed by the body, offering an increased degree of insulation. Thermal woven or knit fabric are found in both cotton and manufactured fibers or blends of the two.

THORPE, JOHN (1784–1848)

John Thorpe, an Englishman, invented the ring spinning frame about 1828. The actual date is unclear and it is thought that the invention may have been as late as 1830. The ring spinning frame was used particularly in the production of warp yarn of very high twist and provided continuous spinning, required fewer workers and increased production. It was a revolutionary contribution to the textile industry and the principles that Thorpe introduced are still used in the industry today. See SPINNING.

TICKING

Ticking refers to fabric originally used to make bed ticks, which are the cases or coverings for pillows, mattresses and mattress foundations. It is generally a strong and closely woven fabric, done in any of the three basic weaves. Very often, ticking is finished at the mill in striped patterns with dyed yarns (usually blue), using a greater density of warp yarns than picks, thereby imparting greater strength. It also can have Jacquard effects in the weave, or can be printed in various patterns. Ticking is usually done in cotton or linen, and in blends with manufactured fibers. The use of ticking today has expanded to include casual and sports apparel.

TIE DYEING

See DYES.

TISSUE FAILLE

Tissue faille is created primarily in silk in a plain weave with a low thread count giving it a diaphanous quality. The hand of tissue faille is smooth and soft and it is further characterized by a deep luster. It is always created in plain colors. See FAILLE.

TOILE DE JOUY

Once used to refer exclusively to the famous printed textiles produced in Jouy, France, the term now applies to fabrics with classic floral or scenic designs on cotton, linen or silk. In response to the popularity in the late 18th century of printed cotton fabrics imported from India, the German Christopher Philip Oberkampf established a factory at Jouy, near Versailles, where he printed elaborate, beautiful designs on fabric using etched copper plates, usually in a single color. He was also the first to achieve any success in producing fast

Pages 218 and 219: Taffeta (silk) Author's collection

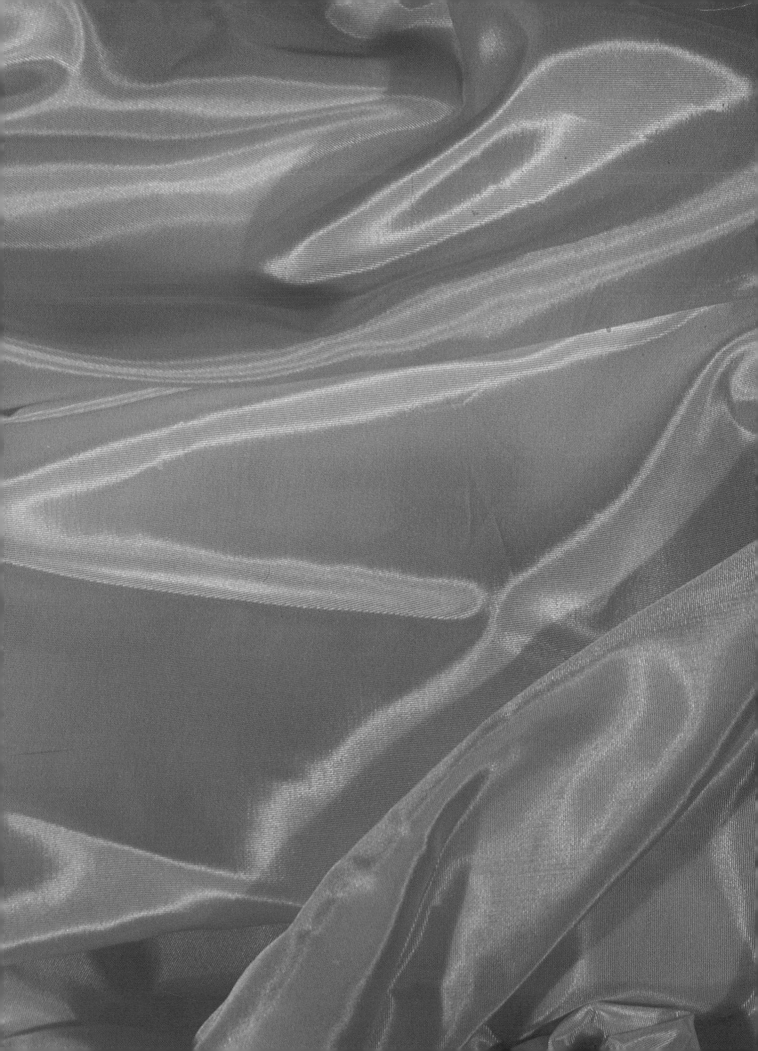

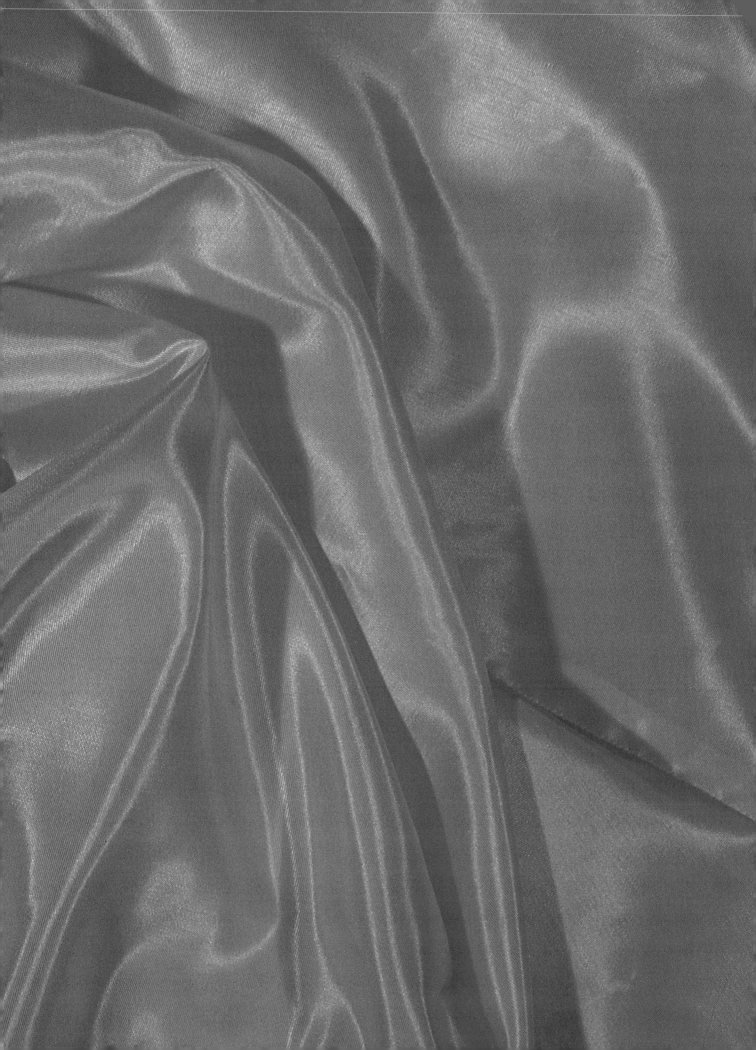

Twill (wool) Author's collection

Micrograph of twill weave
American Textile Manufacturers Institute

dyes, to produce a solid green color in a single operation and to apply steam during the dying process. Ever since Oberkampf's time, the name Jouy has been associated with finely printed fabrics of the types he developed, characterized by beautifully engraved and finely colored motifs.

TOW

The term tow can apply to both manufactured fibers and flax bast fibers. In the production of LINEN from flax, tow is used to describe any fiber that is shorter than 10 inches. Fibers longer than 10 inches are called line. In the production of manufactured fibers, tow refers to long extruded continuous filaments that have not been twisted.

TRANSPARENT VELVET

See VELVET.

TRIACETATE

Triacetate is a MANUFACTURED FIBER that differs from ACETATE in that it has been completely acetylated while acetate has only been partially acetylated. Acetylation is a chemical process that changes CELLULOSE into acetate. Triacetate has many superior qualities in that it can resist higher temperatures and does not wrinkle to the degree that acetate does.

TRIAXIAL WEAVING

While the conventional method of weaving incorporates two yarns, one warp and one weft, the triaxial method of weaving employs two yarns in the warp interlocked with one weft thread, producing a textile that is stronger than those executed using the conventional method. This method is most often used for textiles that must be resistant to stress, such as tents and other sporting equipment.
See WEAVING.

TRICOT

The term tricot is derived from the French word *tricoter*, meaning to knit. It can be used to describe a group of weaves employed in the execution of woolen and worsted fabrics. The tricot or knit effect is created by alternating a thread of right twist, or Z-TWIST, with one of left twist, or S-TWIST, in both warp and weft in a plain weave. The direction reversal of the twist causes a ridge or rib in the textile. The ribs are very narrow and are so uniform and delicate that the fabric resembles a knit textile. When tricot has a horizontal, or weft, rib effect on the face, it is called "tricot cross." When the ribs run vertically or with the warp the fabric is called "tricot long."

Tricot also refers to a knitting stitch that can be executed either by hand or machine. When it is executed by hand it is called the stockinette stitch, which is worked by alternating one row of knit with one row of purl. When it is constructed by machine it is called either the jersey stitch or tricot stitch. A circular knitting machine is used most often to produce tricot knit, requiring two sets of needles. The needles are arranged in a circle on a rotating cylinder and the fabric is created in tube form. The stitch incorporates one row of loops on the face of the textile alternating with one row of loops on the back of the fabric.

See KNITTING.

TULLE

Tulle refers to a machine-made fine cotton or manufactured net with a hexagonal mesh. Prior to the 18th century, tulle was created by hand. Tulle was first created by machine in Nottingham, England, in 1768; however, it wasn't until improvements had been made on the machine many years later that the textile was produced in any quantity. The first record of factory production of the fabric was in 1817 in Tulle, France, from which the textile derives its name.

TUSSAH

Tussah is a strong silk produced by caterpillars which are living in a wild or semi-domesticated state called the tussah worm (*Anthereae paphia*). The caterpillar feeds largely on oak leaves, which cause the silk to be beige to brown in color (due to tannin in the leaves). The silk yarn is usually left in its natural color, for it does not receive dye easily. There is considerable production of the silk in Manchuria and India. The silk is irregular and thus the textiles have a slubbed character. Textiles made from the silk are called "tussor" in China, or "tassar" or "tussah" in India.

TWEED

The term tweed is derived from the Scotch term tweel. It is uncertain when it originated or how it came to be called tweed. Some believe that a London merchant, Mr. Locke, misread the word tweel when placing an order and called the textile tweed (1831). Another theory claims that the name was applied because the fabric was produced by hand on the Tweed River which runs between Scotland and England.

Today, tweed is associated almost exclusively with machine woven textiles with the exception of HARRIS TWEED, which is still handwoven on the islands of the Hebrides. Tweeds are characterized by a rough textural surface, that can be found in twill, plain and herringbone weaves. Although wool is most commonly the fiber found in tweed it is also made of manufactured fiber, blends of wool, and manufactured fiber and wool.

TWILL WEAVE

Twill is one of the three basic weaves, characterized by a diagonal alignment of FLOATS, either in the weft (weft-faced twill) or in the warp (warp-faced twill). For each successive weft thread, the float pattern is advanced to the right or to the left by one warp thread. This creates a diagonal rib, called the twill line, running either from left to right or right to left up the fabric.

There are a great number of variations in the twill weave, determined by the basic float-span ratio and changes in the direction of the diagonals. The float-span ratio specifies the number of warp ends crossed over by the weft followed by the number of warp ends the weft then passes under. Examples are E2/1, 2/2, 3/1, etc. If the over-under order is even, i.e., 2/2, the weave is said to be an even twill. If the order is uneven, as in 3/1, the twill is said to be uneven.

Plain or regular twills are those in which the direction of the diagonals does not change. Changing the direction of the diagonals creates what are called broken twills. This can result in diamond patterns, herringbones, chevrons, and zigzags.

TWO-PLY

Two-ply is used to describe either the construction of yarns, made of two single strands twisted together, or of textiles consisting of two layers. Examples of these textiles include DOUBLE CLOTH, whose layers have been woven together, or fabrics whose layers have been joined in any other way.

Page 222: Toile of Juoy print on linen Author's collection

Harris tweed (wool)   Author's collection

Harris tweed (micrograph)   Dennis Sjoberg

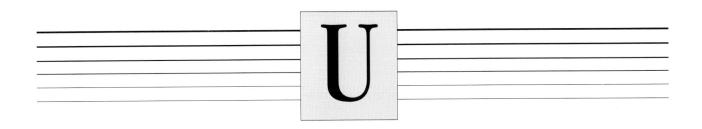

UTRECHT VELVET

Utrecht velvet was first created in Utrecht, Holland during the 17th century by Daniel Havart, a Frenchman and political refugee. The textile was constructed using the traditional velvet production methods except that mohair was used instead of silk. Havart also employed a process called gauffering, a pressing and crimping of the textile to produce raised relief effects, which cause it to have great reflective qualities. Today, Utrecht velvets are still manufactured in both MOHAIR and SILK.

See VELVET.

VELOUR

The word velour is a French derivation of the Latin word *vellosus*, meaning fuzzy or hairy. The term velour is used to describe a pile textile. It is much heavier than VELVET, having a very dense, soft pile, but though it has a lustrous soft texture, it is does not have the drapability of velvet. Originally made of wool, velour is now found in many fibers and may also be created in a knit fabric.

VELVET

The precise origin of velvet is not known. Many authorities believe that it originated in Italy during the

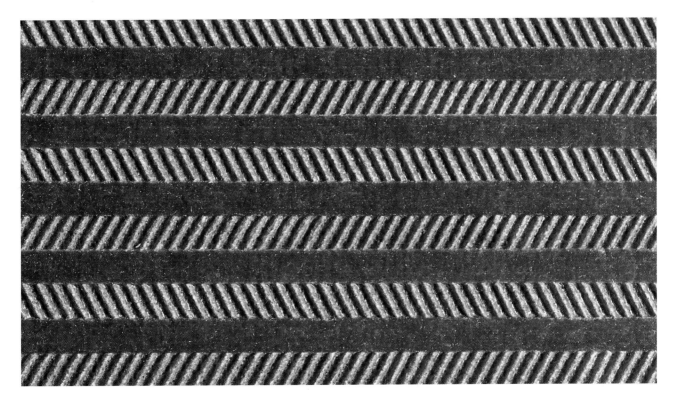

Embossed velvet J. L. de Ball-Girmes of America, Inc.

W pattern J. L. de Ball-Girmes of America, Inc.

V pattern J. L. de Ball-Girmes of America, Inc.

Cutting knife and sharpener J. L. de Ball-Girmes of America, Inc.

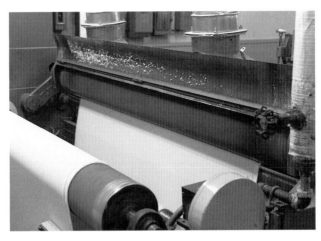

Brushing of velvet J. L. de Ball-Girmes of America, Inc.

Trimming cylinder J. L. de Ball-Girmes of America, Inc.

Brushes J. L. de Ball-Girmes of America, Inc.

Trimming of velvet J. L. de Ball-Girmes of America, Inc.

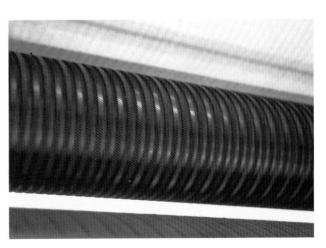

Embossing cylinder J. L. de Ball-Girmes of America, Inc.

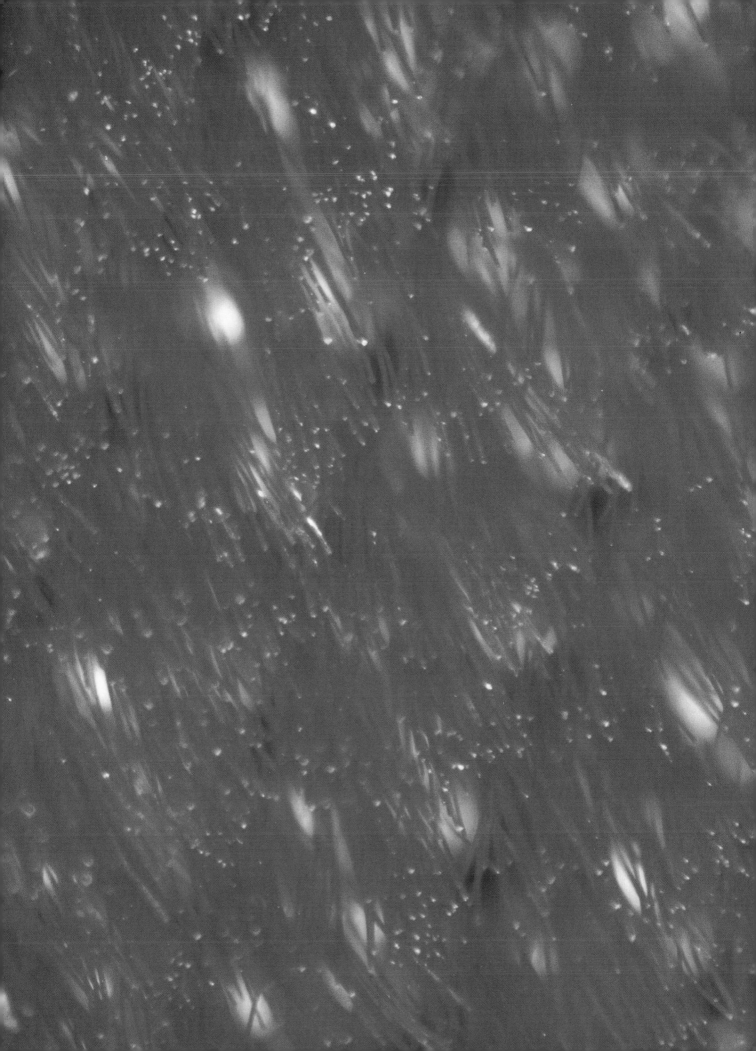

Above: Printed velvet J. L. de Ball-Girmes of America, Inc..
Left: Velvet (micrograph) Dennis Sjoberg

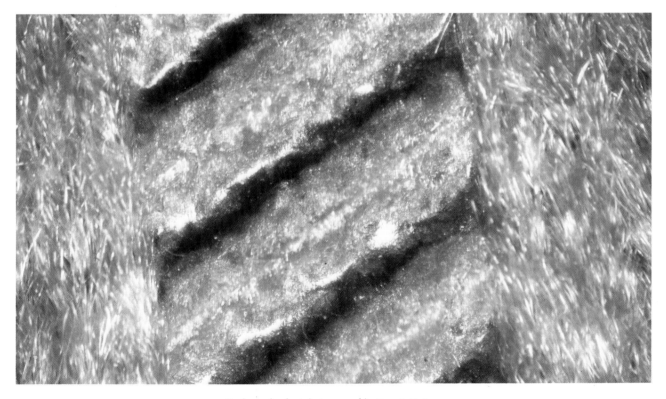

Embossed velvet (micrograph) Dennis Sjoberg

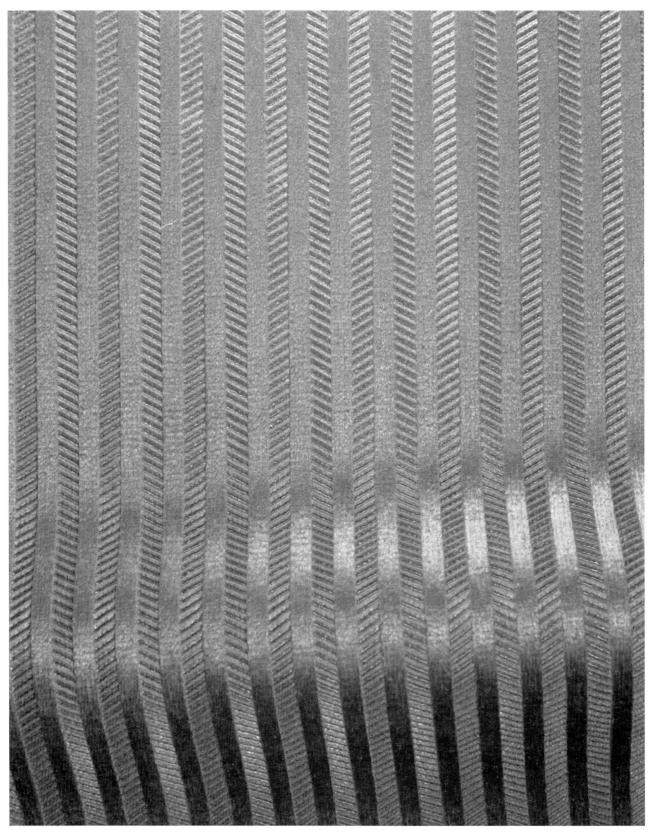

Embossed velvet J. L. de Ball-Girmes of America, Inc.

Voile (silk) Author's collection

Renaissance, while others feel that it was first produced in the Near East. Though its roots are obscured by time, velvet is still one of the most popular fabrics and today is created in many forms and executed with great sophistication, employing a wide variety of fibers.

Sometimes confused with velour or velveteen, a true velvet is classified as a pile fabric and is created in two ways. The first and most prevalent is the double cloth method. This method is executed by weaving two cloths face to face with separate pile threads joining the two. The cross threads are placed either in a straight "V" pattern by alternately looping around warp threads of each cloth, or by weaving the cross thread into three warp ends in each cloth alternately, making a "W" pattern. The latter method creates a more stable pile. After weaving, the pile ends are cut by a knife, thereby creating two fabrics.

The second method to produce velvet is an intricate procedure in which cutting wires are inserted in the weft. The wires cut the pile when they are withdrawn.

After the textile is woven and cut, the velvet is trimmed. The trimming process is executed by a roller containing razor-sharp knife edges in a helical pattern. As the cylinder spins it trims the fabric to the desired length in much the same way as a reel-type lawnmower trims grass. The pile is trimmed in various lengths, but a true velvet is never longer than ⅛". If it exceeds that length it is called a plush. Each cylinder can be used for approximately four months before it must be sharpened again.

The trimming process is followed by brushing to remove loose fiber and give the velvet a smooth, soft, lustrous finish. The brushing occurs on special rollers that are equipped with brushes that resemble needles and yet are flexible enough not to damage the textile. The brushing of the textile is crucial in its final refinement. Velvets can also be given a wide variety of finishes to make them washable, crush resistant, water repellent and soil resistant.

Today the production of velvet has reached new creative and technological levels. A new proprietary technique has been perfected by one company that

Pages 234 and 235:
Cut velvet with metallic threads
Author's collection

allows discharge printing of velvets. Specialty velvets include velvet pile on satin ground, called jardinière velvet, and velvets with cut and uncut loops. Panné velvet is characterized by flattened pile, giving it exceptional luster. There are also figured velvets in satin and plain weaves with motifs created by cutting and pressing some of the pile. Velvets can also be embossed by passing the fabric between etched cylinders, permanently pressing the pattern into the pile. The resulting textiles are a tactile and visual delight.

Other popular velvets include: bagheera, which is uncut, fine and crush resistant; burnt out velvet, in which patterns are created by chemical destruction of one of the yarns used in its creation; chiffon velvet, with notably soft and fine cut pile; ciselé, with patterning achieved with areas of cut and uncut pile; crushed velvet, with an irregular surface due to the pressing of the pile in various directions; cut velvet, in which patterns of velvet are executed on a sheer ground, such as chiffon, giving a brocaded appearance; épinglé, a soft, fine velvet with pin dot patterning and ribs; Lyons, a rigid velvet with a thick erect pile; mirror, with pressed pile giving the textile greater reflectivity and brilliance; panné, a lightweight, lustrous velvet with pile pressed in one direction; and transparent, a soft, transparent velvet, usually made of pure silk, known for its drapability.

See also individual entries for CUT VELVET; UTRECHT VELVET.

VELVETEEN

Velveteen is a weft-faced pile weave always created in cotton. Velveteen embodies long floats placed at even intervals, so that when they are cut, the fabric becomes very smooth. The fabric is frequently given a finish to improve its luster. Velveteen is most commonly found in plain colors that have been piece dyed, but it is also often printed. A form of velveteen called velveteen plush is made by cutting the floats at longer lengths than usual.

VINYON

The Federal Trade Commission defines vinyon as "a manufactured fiber in which the fiber-forming substance is any long chain synthetic polymer compound of at least 65% by weight of vinyl chloride units." It is a generic name. Vinyon was first produced commercially in the United States in 1939 by the FMC corporation, Fiber

Division (formerly American Viscose). Vinyon fibers are commonly used in industrial applications as bonding agents for non-woven products, since they have high resistance to chemicals. ≡

VISCOSE

See MANUFACTURED FIBER; RAYON. ≡

VOILE

Voile is executed in a PLAIN WEAVE and is loosely woven. A true voile is very lightweight and very crisp. The yarns used in the creation of voile have a very hard twist and are usually gassed (or singed) so that the fabric has a high luster. Voile is most often made of cotton, but is also made of RAYON, SILK and WORSTED. Today voiles are found in plain colors, stripes and prints. ≡

Cut velvet with metallic threads (micrograph)   Dennis Sjoberg

WAFFLE PIQUÉ

See PIQUÉ.

WALE

A wale fabric is readily identified by lengthwise ridges or ribs (wales). The wale is found in both woven and knit fabrics. In knit fabrics they are created by loops. Waled fabrics are found in a variety of weights and qualities, in both wide and narrow wales. The most common fabric characterized by this technique is CORDUROY.

WARP

Warp refers to the yarns that run lengthwise on the loom. They are also referred to as ends. The warp yarns undergo an extra process of twisting before the weaving process.

See LOOM; WEAVING.

WARP EFFECTS/WARP PATTERNS

Patterns in fabrics that are formed mainly by the WARP threads. Threads of varying colors are often used, making the patterns very complex.

WARP FACED

Warp faced refers to a textile that has more warp threads (ends) than weft threads (picks) visible on the face.

See also WEAVING.

WASH AND WEAR

Wash and wear fabrics were introduced in 1952. The term originally described textiles that had a blend of cotton and acrylic fiber, which caused the textiles to be wrinkle resistant. The creation of textiles with this quality caused a revolution in the home, for they diminished the need to sprinkle and iron clothing and also gave rise to the introduction of the automatic clothes dryer. Today, wash and wear is a generic term and refers to any textile that is free from wrinkles and retains its original shape after washing and drying. The textiles have these qualities not only because of the types of fibers or fiber blends used, but also because of the application of any of a wide variety of resins. The many corporations currently producing wash and wear fabrics have adopted a wide variety of tradenames or trademarks to denote this quality.

WATT, JAMES (1736–1819)

James Watt, a Scotsman, patented the first steam engine in 1769. In 1785, he applied steam power for the first time in a cotton mill. Watt also perfected a technique of bleaching linen and cotton fabrics with chlorine.

See COTTON; LINEN.

WEAVE

The term weave refers to the methods of interlacing threads, yarns or fibers on a loom in the weaving process, producing a length of textile or cloth. The three basic weaves are the PLAIN WEAVE, the SATIN WEAVE and the TWILL WEAVE.

See also LOOM; WEAVING.

WEAVING

Weaving is simply defined as the art of intertwining of threads, yarns or fibers on a loom at right angles to create a length of textile or cloth. The yarns, threads or fibers that run lengthwise on the loom are called warp threads, or ends. The crosswise threads, yarns or fibers are called the weft threads and are also referred to as the filling.

Although weaving is simply defined, it is much more difficult to describe the methods used to execute the various methods of weaving, the weaves that are created and the equipment that is used for the weaving process. It is thought that the first weavers were probably basket makers who used long fibers that did not need spinning for their interlacing. Later, the early weavers began to twist natural fibers such as wool and cotton to create a primitive yarn that was then woven on a loom.

There are four operations to weaving on a basic hand loom. First, the warp or lengthwise threads, the ends, are strung on the loom. The threads are then separated vertically to form a channel for the crosswise threads in a process called shedding. The phrase "up," or "down," refers to lifting and lowering of the shed. The weft, or filling, is then passed through the shed in an operation called picking. The carrying of the weft thread across the cloth one time is called a pick. Each pick is pushed against the previous pick in a process called battening. The warp threads are then released from the beam in a process called letting out; the fabric is then moved onto another beam in a process called taking up and a new shed is formed. These processes are continued until the fabric is complete.

The warp threads along the exterior edges of the fabric are usually heavier and more closely woven, creating bands of more stable textile, called selvages, to prevent raveling.

There are three basic types of weave: In the PLAIN WEAVE, the most common type of weave, the weaving pattern is repeated on two ends and two picks. The first end passes over the first pick and under the second pick. The process is reversed by the second end, producing an even cross-hatched pattern. In a variation of this pattern, called the BASKET WEAVE, two ends are woven over two picks.

In the SATIN WEAVE, the face of the fabric has more warp or weft floats than the back, causing the textile to have a very smooth, reflective surface.

In the TWILL WEAVE, a diagonal rib, or twill line, is created in the fabric, generally running upward from left to right.

Today, more advanced textile manufacturing processes are also able to create a great variety of NOVELTY WEAVES, which differ from the basic patterns by varying the number of picks and ends. In TRIAXAL WEAVING, a third end is incorporated into the textile at a 60-degree angle, producing a fabric of great strength.

See also LOOM.

WEIGHTING

Weighting is the process of adding materials to a fabric to produce greater body. The process is executed either chemically or mechanically. Historically, weighting has been applied for the most part to silks, making them heavier and more crisp, and in certain cases, creating very subtle color tones. Today cottons are also weighted. Eventually strict laws were passed to prohibit the use of excessive amounts of weighting materials, particularly lead, when it was found that the substances could be absorbed through pores in the skin. Tin salts are still used as a weighting material. Other permanent sizings, such as resins, are pressed into the fabrics as well.

Weighting has also been referred to as loading or dynamiting in the past.

See also FINISHING.

WEFT-FACED

A weft-faced is a fabric that has more weft threads (picks) than warp threads (ends) visible on the face.

See also WEAVING.

WOOL

Wool is a fiber made from the fleece or hair of various animals such as sheep, Angora goats, camels, llamas and alpacas. Hair from the Angora rabbit is also used for fabric, but the fiber is not classified as wool for labeling purposes. Wool fiber is also found on the buffalo, cow and horse, but though the entire hide of those animals may be used for articles of apparel, the fiber is not sheared and spun separately for fabric use.

Wool is composed of protein in the form of a substance called keratin. Chemically, protein fibers such as keratin are composed of carbon, hydrogen, oxygen, nitrogen and sulfur, whereas the cellulosic fibers from which many textiles are made do not contain the latter two elements. When viewed through a microscope, wool fiber looks like a rod that gently tapers from root to tip, and is unmistakably characterized by scales, which are called epithelial scales. The scales are important, because they act as a protective covering for the fiber, which causes wool to be very resistant to wear. The scales are covered with two membranes: the epicuticle and the exocuticle, which greatly affect the manner in which dyes are received by wool. Until the advent of the scanning electron microscope, the presence of these two very thin membranes was unknown. Now, as a result of their discovery, much progress has been made in the

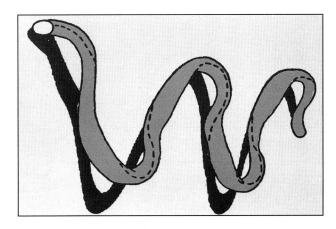

Crimp   The Wool Bureau, Inc.

washing and dyeing procedures that are possible with wool.

In contrast to cotton and other cellulosic fibers, wool is distinguished also by crimps in the fiber, sometimes as many as 30 per inch of length. These crimps create many tiny air pockets which impart to wool a resilient, spongy texture. This in turn gives wool a great degree of thermal insulation per weight of fabric. It also gives wool the ability to absorb a great deal of water before it becomes saturated. This is a source of additional warmth in a garment, since the wearer remains dry until the fabric reaches saturation.

Wool has been valued for centuries because of its unique characteristics that set it apart from other fibers. It resists dirt, it is flame resistant, and because of its absorptive qualities for water it resists the build-up of static electricity. Further, it resists both tearing and abrading, as well as snagging, pilling and crocking.

History

There is historical evidence that wool is one of the first fibers to have been made into textiles. It is well known that wool existed in Babylonia as early as 4000 B.C. Indeed, it is interesting to note that the word Babylonia means Land of Wool. Sheep were raised and sold in ancient Mesopotamia to such a large extent that wool making could be described as a major industry. Also of note is the fact that the Sumerians sold wool throughout the known world in these early times. Around 2000 B.C., the Phoenicians not only traded wool but also introduced the art of weaving in the Mediterranean area.

In A.D. 45, the Romans are credited with having bred a new strain of sheep that would come to have great and

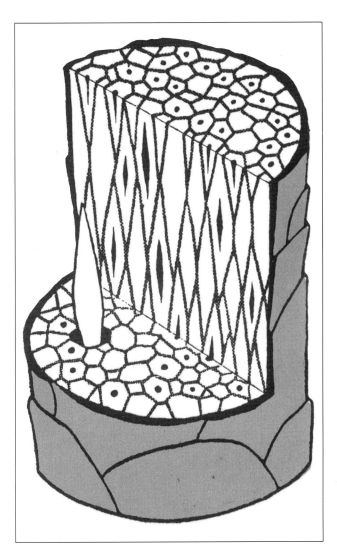

Wool cross section   The Wool Bureau, Inc.

lasting importance in the development of wool textiles. This was the merino sheep, a cross between the Roman Tarentine sheep and the African ram, accomplished in Spain, which was possession of the Romans during that period. The merino sheep then produced what is still considered to be the finest wool.

For several hundred years during the Middle Ages, Spain's breeding of merino sheep gave it leadership and control of the world wool market. The industry was so important that taking a single merino out of Spain was punishable by death. The sheep were inevitably dispersed throughout the world, however, because they were given as prized gifts, and sometimes taken into conquered lands for food and a source of wool for clothing.

In 55 B.C. when the Romans occupied England, they introduced wool to the country, thus setting into play the rich history that England has had in the creation of wool textiles due in part to the damp cold climate. By the year 1600, wool exports had grown to the point where they played an important role in the economy of Britain. Because of wool's importance, laws were enacted in Britain to prevent the importing of wool and to prevent the wearing of articles of wool clothing that had come from foreign markets.

The original British colonies in America used sheep not only for clothing but as an essential source of food. After the American Revolution, merino sheep were imported from Spain and soon the quality of the wool produced in the United States improved.

In 1752, patterns were first printed on wool in the United States, using a method that employed copper plates. Beginning in the latter part of the 18th century, a number of inventions aided in the mechanization of the wool industry, thus speeding up production. In 1773, John Kay invented the flying shuttle. Other notable inventions included the spinning jenny, the water frame, the mule loom and the power loom. In 1810 there were 24 wool mills in the eastern United States, mostly in New England. By the end of the 19th century, the United States was producing enough wool to meet all domestic consumer demand. Today sheep are raised in every state in America.

To better serve today's international wool industry and hence the consumer, an International Wool Secretariat was formed in 1937. This unique organization is dedicated to promoting and improving the standards of wool all over the world. With offices in 32 countries, the secretariat has a broad international network to transfer new and emerging technology to the industry.

Woolmark label   The Wool Bureau, Inc.

The Wool Bureau carefully controls and licenses the use of the woolmark and the woolblend mark on woolen products. Companies must meet very high quality-control standards in order to place either mark on a fabric or product made of wool or a wool blend.

Production

The leading wool-producing countries are Australia, New Zealand, South Africa and Uruguay. Other major producers include the United States, Argentina, Turkey, India, Pakistan, Iraq and the Soviet Bloc countries.

Although the merino sheep is still considered the finest and most luxurious wool on the market, selective breeding of sheep has produced over 30 major varieties

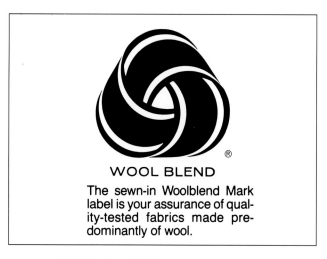

Woolblend mark label   The Wool Bureau, Inc.

WORLD PRODUCTION OF RAW WOOL (in Thousands of Tons)

	1977–78/ 1981–82	1982–83	1983–84	Average 1984–85	1985–86	1986–87	1987–88
COMMONWEALTH							
Australia	702	702	728	814	830	887	917
New Zealand	347	371	364	373	358	350	355
United Kingdom	49	50	54	56	58	59	62
India	35	35	35	35	35	30	33
Lesotho	2	3	3	3	3	3	3
Canada	1	2	2	2	2	1	1
Falkland Isles	2	2	2	2	2	2	3
Other	4	5	5	5	5	5	5
TOTAL COMMONWEALTH	1142	1170	1193	1290	1293	1337	1379
OTHER COUNTRIES							
Argentina	170	162	162	150	152	150	152
South Africa	105	113	108	105	98	90	92
United States	49	49	47	44	41	39	40
Uruguay	69	82	82	71	87	90	90
Turkey	59	62	62	60	61	61	61
Spain	28	30	31	32	31	32	32
Brazil	30	28	25	30	28	28	30
Pakistan	37	41	45	48	49	50	51
France	24	25	25	24	24	24	24
Chile	20	22	21	21	21	20	22
Iran	16	16	16	16	16	16	16
Morocco	18	13	16	15	15	15	15
Iraq	18	18	17	17	17	17	18
Yugoslavia	10	10	10	10	10	10	10
Italy	12	13	13	13	13	13	14
Portugal	9	9	9	9	9	9	9
Peru	11	12	12	12	12	12	12
Irish Republic	8	7	7	7	7	8	8
Greece	10	10	10	10	10	10	10
West Germany	5	5	5	5	5	6	6
Other Asia (Ex. China)	60	63	64	66	61	69	69
Other Africa	71	71	74	86	94	93	93
Other America	20	21	21	21	22	21	21
Other West Europe	10	11	11	11	12	12	12
TOTAL	2013	2063	2086	2175	2188	2232	2286
SOVIET UNION, CHINA, AND EAST EUROPE							
Soviet Union	470	474	485	488	468	492	477
Romania	36	39	39	42	44	44	44
Bulgaria	35	35	36	36	34	33	32

WORLD PRODUCTION OF RAW WOOL (in Thousands of Tons)

	Average						
	1977–78/ 1981–82	1982–83	1983–84	1984–85	1985–86	1986–87	1987–88
Hungary	11	13	13	12	11	11	10
Poland	13	12	13	15	17	18	19
East Germany	11	13	12	15	15	16	16
Czechoslovakia & Albania	7	8	8	8	8	8	8
China	160	202	194	183	178	183	208
Mongolia	20	21	20	20	19	19	19
TOTAL	763	817	820	819	794	824	833
WORLD TOTAL	2776	2880	2906	2992	2982	3056	3119
SOURCE FOR APPAREL							
Merino	1159	1183	1197	1255	1306	1363	1392
Crossbred	805	824	834	840	807	828	839
TOTAL APPAREL	1964	2007	2031	2095	2113	2191	2231
NON-APPAREL	816	873	875	897	869	865	888

SOURCE: The Wool Bureau, Inc.

which has resulted in various grades of wool. In the unfinished state wool is yellow or off-white, but there are wide variations that can include grays, browns and blacks. The fibers can vary in size from 15 to 40 microns in diameter, and from 1 to 15 inches in length.

The following is a summary of the numerous steps in the processing of wool from animal to finished product.

Shearing. Shearing is the first process undertaken in the production of wool fiber. Research is now being conducted on a substance that, when injected into the sheep, will cause the fleece (wool fiber) to die at the root without hindering the growth of new fleece. This would allow the fleece to be plucked from the sheep without shears. At present, however, the shearing is done by hand, and the fleece is sheared off the sheep using long, smooth strokes so that the fiber appears to roll off the animal. The shearing process is usually undertaken in the spring, and is done either once a year or once every two years. All of the wool taken from one sheep is referred to as its fleece, in the plural. The shearing is most commonly done at a shearing plant where the fleece from 20 to 40 sheep are bagged together in preparation for sending to a warehouse, and in some cases directly to the mill for further processing.

Shearing The Wool Bureau, Inc.

THE MAIN BREEDS OF SHEEP AND PROPERTIES OF THEIR FLEECES

WOOL TYPE	BREED	ORIGIN	12 MONTH WOOL LENGTH (inches)	WEIGHT OF FLEECE (lbs.)	% SHRINKAGE
FINE	Merino	Spain	1.5–4	5–35	50–80
	Rambouillet	France	3–5	8–25	50–60
MEDIUM	Southdown	England	2.5–3.5	5–12	45–50
	Shropshire	England	2.5–3	8–16	45–50
	Hampshire	England	2–2.5	5–10	45–50
	Oxford	England	3–4	7–20	45–50
	Suffolk	England	2.5–3	7–9	45–50
	Dorset	England	2.5–3	7–10	45–50
	Cheviot	England-Scotland	3.5–4.5	5–10	45–50
LONG	Lincoln	England	12–18	10–18	35–40
	Cotswald	England	10–14	12–16	35–40
	Leicester	England	7–10	8–15	35–40
	Romny/marsh	England	5–10	8–20	35–40
CROSS BRED	Corriedale	New Zealand	3–4	8–30	45–55
	Columbia	United States	3–4	8–30	45–55
CARPET	Scotch Blackface	Scotland	5–15	6–18	25–30
	Navaho	New Mexico	5–16	6–18	25–30
	Karakule	Asia	5–16	6–18	
	Fat Tail	Africa-Asia	5–16	6–18	25–30

SOURCE: International Wool Bureau

Grading and Sorting. Grading refers to the process by which fleece is evaluated by type. It is judged by fiber length, fineness and color. After the grading process, the raw wool, known as grease, is then sorted. The sorting process is executed by hand and calls for close inspection to determine the average length and diameter of the fibers. The two predominant ways of sorting the wool are the trap method and the bench method. The trap method is the easier of the two methods, and usually results in less expensive wool. The bench method is a more careful method of sorting. The fleece from a single sheep has many varying qualities within it. The best fibers are found on the shoulders, sides and back. During the sorting process the fleece is pulled apart and the various qualities of wool within one fleece are separated into various quality groups.

Washing. The lanolin, or grease, is removed from the wool by a washing process, which also removes other impurities. The washing process frequently is referred to as scouring. Three alternative methods are the use of soap and water, naphtha, or a process called frosting. During the frosting process the wool is frozen, thus embrittling the oils in the wool, which can then be brushed out in a dusting machine. The wool is then washed.

Blending. At this stage blends are sometimes created by mixing various varieties of wool. This is done mechanically, and allows a wide variety of qualities to be achieved. The Wool Bureau states that by using this method "2,000 different combinations" are possible.

Dyeing. As mentioned, the scales on wool cause it to receive dye readily, making a wide range of colors as well as printed patterns, possible. Wool absorbs dye so readily

COMPARATIVE TABLE

Wool Grades, Fiber Lengths, Diameter, Crimp

Type	English Number System	American Blood System	Fiber Diameter in Microns	No. Crimps per Inch of Fiber Length	Minimum Combing Length in Inches	French Combing Length in Inches	Clothing Length in Inches
FINE	80	Fine	18.1–19.5	28–32	2	1¼–2	0–1¼
	70	Fine	19.6–20.0	22–28	2	1¼–2	0–1¼
	64	Fine	21.1–24.0	14–22	2	1¼–2	0–1¼
MEDIUM	60	½ Blood	24.1–25.5	10–14	2¼	1¼–2¼	0–1¼
	58	½ Blood	25.6–27.0	10–14	2¼	1¼–2¼	0–1¼
	56	⅜ Blood	27.1–29.0	8–10	2½	1½–2½	0–1½
	50	¼ Blood	29.1–31.5	5–8	2¾	1½–2¾	0–1½
COARSE	48	¼ Blood	36.1–33.2	5–8	2¾	1½–2¾	0–1½
	46	Low ¼ Blood	33.3–34.7	2–5	3	2–3	0–2
	44	Common	34.8–36.5	0–2			
CARPET	40	Braid	36.6–38.7	0–1			
	36	Braid	38.8–41.3	0–1			

SOURCE: The Wool Bureau, Inc.

that it is possible to dye it at many stages in its production. It is often dyed in the bulk stage immediately after washing, which is known as "stock dyeing." Dyeing the wool in yarn stage is called "yarn dyeing," while dyeing after the wool is in fabric form is called "piece dyeing."

Carding. Carding is the process that prepares the fiber for spinning. The fiber is passed through a series of rollers to which teeth are attached. The teeth brush and pull the fibers, untangling them and causing them to be more nearly parallel to one another. At the end of the process, the fiber resembles a very fine web in appearance and texture. The fine webs are then divided into narrow strips that are referred to as "slivers." The slivers may still have fibers in the web that are not absolutely parallel. The slivers may go through a second carding process or the crossing fibers may be left that way so that the resulting yarn will have more texture to it. That is the case with the wools that are destined to become tweed. The woolen slivers are then twisted by the "roving" machine into rope-like strands. After this "roving" process, the fiber is wound into balls in preparation for spinning.

Combing. The combing process is used when a smoother wool is desired, as is the case with gabardine and crepe. Short fibers still remaining in the sliver are referred to as noils. During the combing they are removed. Later the noils or short fibers are used to create wools that are not as refined as some woolens, or they are blended with longer fibers. They are also used to some extent to create felt.

Drawing. The drawing process is an additional step that a WORSTED wool is undergoes. During this process the fibers are (drawn out) in order to ensure that all the fibers are parallel to one another, and a specific uniform fiber diameter is selected before the fibers are twisted and rolled into balls for spinning.

Spinning. When loose fibers are twisted they become stronger. That essentially is the purpose of the SPINNING process, which is applied to both woolens and worsteds. Spinning draws the wool fibers out even more, and then twists them. The result is an unbroken thread, which is necessary for weaving. Today, power machines are used for the spinning process. The roving is fed through large rollers, which draw it even further in extension. It is then wound onto revolving bobbins to give the yarn a final twist.

Weaving. WEAVING is the process by which the actual fabric is produced. Power looms are used exclusively for commercial production.

After the weaving process, the fabrics undergo FINISHING, which may include brushing, shearing or "clear finishing", fulling, decating, crabbing, sponging, and then a final pressing.

Care of Wool

First and foremost before washing wool, one should consult the care label that is required by federal law in the United States. The label must tell the fiber content as well as care requirements.

Wool has a great deal of resilience and thus resists wrinkling, and with proper care retains its original shape. Since wool is renewed by moisture, it needs only to be pressed with a steam iron using a pressing cloth to rejuvenate the fiber. There are very many wools on the market today that can be washed and even machine dried due to new technological advances.

Wool must be dry-cleaned if it is not washable. However, it is possible to remove stains yourself, and sometimes is very important to do so, so that the stain is not allowed to set in the fiber. It is important to remember that excessive rubbing can abrade wool. The very delicate wools created of mohair, cashmere and alpaca can be severely damaged by even slight rubbing. A dabbing or sponging action must be used.

The following chart gives stain removal suggestions as well as methods to be used. All of these methods are "emergency" methods. If you are close to a dry cleaner, and can take the garment there immediately, do so. This chart applies to pure wool only and not to blends.

TREATMENT FOR SOME COMMON STAINS ON WOOL

STAIN	MATERIALS TO USE	PROCEDURE
Alcohol	Soda Water	Place a towel under the stain. Gently dab the stain with the soda, working from the outside in. Using a dry towel, gently dab from the center of the stain outward, thus blending the wet edge with the dry surrounding fabric.
Blood	Powdered Starch	Mix the starch with water into a concentrated paste. Gently dab the starch mixture onto the stained area. Using the rounded side of a spoon, gently rub the entire area. Let stand for 2 minutes. Reverse the fabric, placing the stained area on a towel. Using an eyedropper, rinse with clear water, using a small amount at a time. Reverse once again. Gently dab the area with a towel moistened with cool clean water. Continue to dab until the starch and blood are gone. To ensure that a ring does not remain, moisten the edge of a towel with cool water and gently dab from the center of the area outward, blending the wet area with the dry.
Butter	Perchlorethylene	Turn a glass upside down and cover the bottom of the glass with a small towel. Place the stained area of the fabric on top of the covered glass. Gently dab the stain with perchlorethylene, working from the outside in. Then, using the edge of a clean towel, dab from the center to the outside, blending the wet area with the dry. Repeat twice if necessary. Dry naturally.
Chocolate	Mild Detergent	Mix ¼ tablespoon of detergent with 4 ounces of cool water. Place a towel under the stain. Dampen another towel with the detergent mixture. Gently dab the stain. Using the rounded portion of a spoon, gently rub the stain. Rinse by dabbing with clear water. When the stain is gone, gently dab from the center of the stain, using a clean towel moistened with clear water. This will blend the moist edge of the stain with the dry area. Dry naturally.
Coffee and Tea	Glycerine	Gently dab with glycerine, using the same procedure outlined for chocolate.

STAIN	MATERIALS TO USE	PROCEDURE
Egg	Mild Detergent	If the egg has dried at all, or if there is a buildup, very gently loosen the particles with the edge of a spoon or another non-sharp instrument. Remove loosened particles. Follow the detergent procedure listed under chocolate. Dry naturally.
Grease	Perchlorethylene	Gently sponge, using the procedure listed under butter.

See also ALPACA; ANGORA; and MOHAIR.

WOOL PRODUCTS LABELING ACT

The Wool Products Labeling Act was passed in 1939. The law specified that any article that contains wool must have a label attached to it that specifies the amount and type of wool used. Reused or reprocessed wool must also be specified. If it is a blend with other fibers those fibers must also be called out specifically using their generic names. The act is administered by the FEDERAL TRADE COMMISSION.

WOOLEN SYSTEM

The production of yarn using a multiple carding system. The woolen system differs greatly from the system used for worsted in that after the yarn has been carded it is spun immediately. This process allows shorter and less perfect yarns to be utilized. This system provides for great versatility in the finishing of woolen textiles because of its use of a broad and varied range of fibers.

See also WOOL; WORSTED SYSTEM.

WORSTED

Worsted fabrics are those woven from yarn that has been carded and combed prior to the spinning process. The fibers that are used for worsteds are 3 inches to 6 inches in length and are therefore longer than those used for regular woolen textiles. Worsted fabrics include gabardines, serges, tropical worsteds and other fabrics that are woven tightly and have a more crisp hand. They

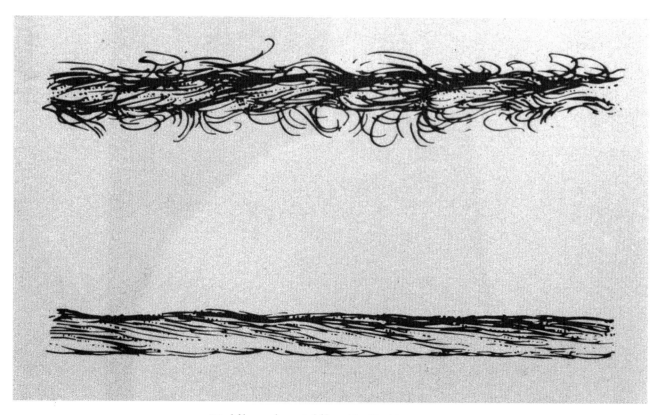

Wool fiber and worsted fiber   The Wool Bureau, Inc.

can be either piece or stock dyed and come in a variety of weaves. The term is derived from the city of Worsted, in the county of Norfolk, England, where the process originated as early as the 14th century.

Worsted flannel is a napped light or medium weight wool fabric in twill or plain weave, made of worsted yarns.

Worsted merino is a gray mixture fabric containing 505 sound, strong wool and 505 long, staple cotton yarns spun on the FRENCH SYSTEM.

See also WOOL.

WORSTED SYSTEM

The worsted system refers to the manufacture of worsted yarns from medium or longer wools, alpaca and mohair. Generally the processes employed are carding, combing, drawing and spinning. There are two basic differences between this system and the woolen system. In worsted yarn making, the short fibers or noils are removed by combing, and the objective is to produce a rather compact yarn by having the fibers parallel. The three basic systems of worsted yarn spinning are the Bradford (or English), French (Alsatian or Continental), and American system.

See also WOOL, WOOLEN SYSTEM.

WORSTED YARNS

See WORSTED

WYATT, JOHN

See PAUL, LEWIS.

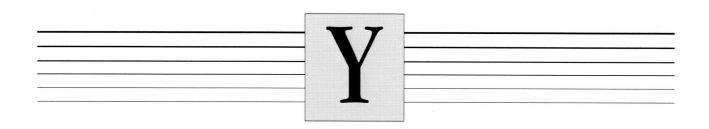

YARN

Yarn is a generic term for the long, continuous threads assembled in the spinning process, and is the first step in the creation of a fabric. There are two types of yarn: those made of MANUFACTURED FIBER that are produced in a continuous strand, and those made from shorter, natural fibers that must be spun to form longer lengths. Although manufactured fibers are formed as continuous filaments, they are often cut into smaller lengths and spun as well so that they resemble natural fibers more closely. Before the industrial revolution, all spinning was done with a spinning wheel. Now most spinning is done by machine as fiber is processed through a series of sophisticated steps, including blending, carding, combing and drawing, prior to spinning. The yarns are then woven to produce textiles.

Today, yarns come in a nearly endless variety. They can be single ply (consisting of a single strand), or double or multi ply (several strands twisted together). The size of all spun yarns is measured in deniers (see DENIER). Various tensions may be applied to the yarns during spinning to create slubbed or other novelty effects. Many specialty yarns, like bouclé and ratine, embody irregularities or are of varying thick- and thinness to lend the woven textile a nubby or tweedy effect.

Some other basic types of yarn include metallic yarns, strips of polyester or metal wrapped around a core of cotton, silk, or linen; high bulk yarns, synthetic yarns with crimped or stretched yarns with air spaces between fibers, increasing volume; stretch yarns, made of manufactured fiber that is twisted at high temperatures to impart elasticity; and pigment yarns, made of manufactured fiber with a dull-finish pigment added before extrusion.

See also SPINNING; WOOL.

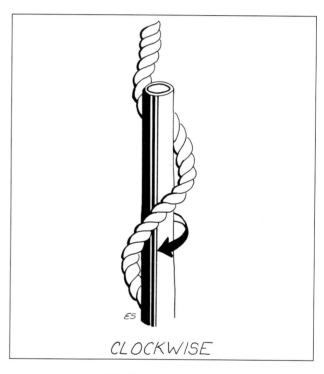

ZEPHYR

Zephyr is a sheer and lightweight textile taking its name from the ancient god of the west wind, Zephrus. Originally created exclusively of wool, today it is found in WOOL, COTTON and MANUFACTURED FIBER, and the term now applies to the airy quality of the textile, not to the fiber that it is made of. Zephyr is executed in a plain weave.

ZIBELINE

Zibeline is a fabric known for its luster and high finish. The surface of zibeline has a raised appearance and a long nap that has been processed so that it lies in one direction. Infrequently, it is given a finish so that it has a very soft hand. The warp of zibeline is usually a worsted yarn and the filling or weft is executed in a specialty fiber, such as CAMEL HAIR or MOHAIR.

Z-TWIST

Z-twist refers to the clockwise direction of the twist in a yarn or thread. It is also called a right twist.

CLOCKWISE

Z-twist Elaine Swenson

BIBLIOGRAPHY

Ahlschwede, George. *Nutrition for Angora Goats*. Research Center, Mohair Council of America. San Angelo, Texas, 1988.

American Fiber Manufacturers Association. *Manufactured Fiber Fact Book*. Washington D.C., 1988.

American Textile Manufacturers Institute. *Made in U.S.A.*, Washington, D.C., 1988.

American Flock Association. *Flocking*. Boston, 1989.

Bendure, Zelma and Gladys Pfeiffer. *America's Fabrics*. New York: Macmillan Co., 1947.

Birrell, Verla. *The Textile Arts*. New York: Schocken Books, 1973.

Brittain, Judy. *Needle Craft*. New York: Bantam Books, 1979.

Brown, Rachel. *The Weaving, Spinning, and Dyeing Book*. New York: Alfred A. Knopf, 1979.

Campbell, Fred R. "Basics of Angora Goats." *Countryside*, Feb. 1980.

Clark, Grahame and Stuart Pigott. *Prehistoric Societies*. New York: Alfred A. Knopf, 1965.

Clarke, Leslie. *The Craftsman in Textiles*. New York: Frederick A. Praeger, 1968.

Denny, Grace. *Fabrics*, 8th ed. Philadelphia: J. B. Lippincott Co., 1962.

Earnshaw, Pat. *The Identification of Lace*. Aylesbury, U. K.: Shire Publications Ltd., 1980.

Embroidery Council of America. *Schiffli Embroidery*. New York, 1987.

Emery, Irene. *The Primary Structures of Fabrics*. New York: The Spiral Press, 1966.

Erickson, Janet. *Block Printing on Textiles*. New York: Watson-Guptill Publications, 1961.

Hall, A. J. *The Standard Handbook of Textiles*, 7th ed. London: Heywood Books, 1969.

Hayes, John. *American Textile Machinery: Its Early History*. Cambridge, England: University Press, 1879.

Held, Shirley E. *Weaving: A Handbook for Fiber Craftsmen*. New York: Holt, Rinehart and Winston, Inc., 1973.

Herbert, V. and A. Bisio. *Synthetic Rubber: A Project that Had to Succeed*. Westport, Connecticut: Greenwood Press, 1985.

International Linen Confederation. *Care of Linen*. New York, 1990.

International Linen Promotion Commission. *Linen*. New York: 1989.

International Linen Promotion Commission (American Branch), *Linen Today*. New York, 1989.

International Mohair Association. *Mohair, A Royal History*. London, 1990.

International Sericultural Commission. *Sericologia*, Vol. 28, Number 4, 1988.

International Silk Association, Office of the Secretary General. *Monthly Newsletter.* "Washable Silk Prints." Jan–Feb 1989.

———. *Monthly Newsletter.* "Silk Standards". March–April 1989.

International Trade Centre. *Silk: A Survey of International Trends in Production and Trade.* London, 1989.

International Wool Secretariat. *Wool Science Review,* Nos. 54–56, 58–65. Ilkley, England.

———. *Carpets.* Ilkley, England.

———. *Lightweight Worsted Woven Fabrics.* Ilkley, England.

———. *Lustrous Yarns for Knitwear.* Ilkley, England.

———. *Printed Knitwear.* Ilkley, England.

———. *Sculptured Wovens.* Ilkley, England.

———. *Sirospun Prints and Wovens.* Ilkley, England.

———. *Sliver Knitting.* Ilkley, England.

———. *Soft Luster Effects,* Nos. 1 and 2. Ilkley, England.

———. *Wool,* FM2. London.

———. *Weaving,* FM1. London.

———. Technical Service Center. *Wool.* Ilkley, England.

———. Textile Technology Group. *Progress in Wool Dyeing, Bleaching, and Printing.* Ilkley, England.

Johnston, Parker, and Kaufman. *Design on Fabrics.* New York: Van Nostrand Reinhold Co., 1967.

Klapper, Marvin. *Fabric Almanac.* New York: Fairchild Publications Inc., 1968.

Knutson, Linda. *Synthetic Dyes for Natural Fibers.* Seattle: Madrona Publishers, 1982.

Krevitsky, Nik. *Batik Art and Craft.* New York: Reinhold Pub. Corp., 1964.

Lesch, Alma. *Vegetable Dyeing.* New York: Watson-Guptill Publications, 1970.

Linton, George E. *Applied Basic Textiles.* New York: Duell, Sloan and Pearce, 1966.

———. *Natural and Manmade Textile Fibers.* New York: Duell, Sloan and Pearce, 1966.

Man-Made Fiber Producers Association, Inc. *Man-made Fibers.* Washington D.C., 1988.

Mincoff, Elizabeth and Margaret Marriage. *Pillow or Bobbin Lace.* New York: Dover Publications, 1987.

Mohair Council of America. *The Story of Mohair.* San Angelo, Texas, 1990.

Munro, Eleanor. *The Encyclopedia of Art.* New York: Golden Press, 1961.

National Geographic. "Silk, The Queen of Textiles." Vol. 165, No. 1, Jan. 1984.

National Geographic. "Wool." Vol. 173, No. 5, May 1988.

Pendleton Woolen Mills. *The Wool Story from Fleece to Fashion,* 6th Ed. Portland, Oregon, 1965.

Peters, R. H. *Textile Chemistry,* Vol. 1. London: Elsevier Pub. Co., 1963.

Potter, David and Bernard Corbman. *Fiber to Fabric,* 3rd Ed. New York: Gregg Publishing Division, McGraw-Hill Book Company, 1959.

Robertson, Seonaid M. *Dyes from Plants.* New York: Van Nostrand Reinhold Co., 1973.

Robinson, Stuart. *A History of Dyed Textiles.* Cambridge: The M.I.T. Press, 1969.

———. *A History of Printed Textiles.* Cambridge: The M.I.T. Press, 1969.

Schwarz, Bruno. *Annual Report of the Swiss Silk Industry and Trade.* International Silk Assoc. Lyons, France, 1988.

Scottish Development Agency, Scottish Tourist Board. *Scotland at Work.* Hawick, Scotland: Buccleuch Printers Ltd., 1989.

Segal, William C. and the Editors of American Fabrics Magazine. *Encyclopedia of Textiles.* Englewood Cliffs, New Jersey: Prentice-Hall, Inc., 1960.

"Silk," translated from "La Soie," European Commission for the Promotion of Silk (France) with the cooperation of Mr. Currie of the Internation Silk Association. Lyons, France, 1990.

Wool Bureau Library. *Wool from Fiber to Fabric.* New York.

———. *Wool, Women's Fashion.* New York.

———. *Knitwear.* New York.

———. *Wool, Purely Professional.* New York.

———. *Wool, Men's Wear.* New York.

Trotman, E. R. *Dyeing and Chemical Technology of Textile Fibers,* 4th Ed. London: Charles Griffin & Co. Ltd., 1970.

United States Department of Agriculture. "China's Cotton Industry." Feb. 1989.

———. "Cotton Sales to China." March 1989.

———. "Pakistan Cotton Production and Consumption, and U.S. Highlights." Feb. 1989.

————. "World Cotton Statistics, 1963–1987." May 1988.

————. "Significant and Emerging Cotton Producers." November 1988.

————. "World Cotton Production." October 1988.

United States Department of Commerce, "Fiber and Fabrics," CIS 1. Washington, D.C.

Weigle, Palmy. *Ancient Dyes for Modern Weavers*. New York: Watson-Guptill Publications, 1974.

Wingate, Isabel B. *Fairchilds Dictionary of Textiles*, 6th Ed. New York: Fairchild Publications, 1979.

Wingate, Isabel B. *Textile Fabrics and their Selection*. New York: Prentice-Hall, 1958.

SUBJECT INDEX